OFF THE ROPES

- '...Ron Lyle exuded a champion's heart throughout his life. He was fearless and stepped into the ring with some of the greatest heavyweights of all time... Ron will be remembered as one of heavyweight boxing's most feared punchers ever. One of the peculiar traits of our sport is that its greatest warriors have often had to fight their greatest battles outside the ring. I admire Ron for the personal victories he has accumulated throughout his tumultuous life... this man is truly a champ in and outside the ring.'

  - former junior welterweight champion and Hall of Fame boxer
  Aaron Pryor in email to author January 2007

- 'Ron Lyle established himself as a great amateur then moved very fast to become a great professional boxer. I respected his ability and I respect the man.'

  - former light heavyweight champion of the world
  Eddie Mustafa Muhammad
  in telephone interview with author December 2006

- 'During Ron Lyle's time in the ring, any of the top ten contenders could have been heavyweight champion. That's never been true before or since. Nowadays, maybe one or two have a chance. Ron was up there with the best... And he is a very gracious, very loveable person.'

  - International Boxing Hall of Fame referee Richard Steele,
  in interview with author November 2005

- '....Ronny's life is complex, interesting, and inspiring. Further, he has an excellent rapport with people of all ages. His communication skill with our youth is phenomenal because he has the ability to reach them; thus enabling them to dare to dream.... his ability to persevere is a story that must be told.'

  - former welterweight contender Harold Weston
  in email message to author December 2006

- 'Nobody ever hit me that hard. No question. I'll remember that punch on my deathbed. A great puncher, a great guy.'
  - heavyweight contender Earnie Shavers in telephone interview with author April 2006

- 'Ron is a gladiator and a gentleman. He's a hero to me.'
  - middleweight boxer Willie Fields in interview with author November 2005

- 'Ron Lyle gave me part of himself - of who he was.'
  - super-middleweight boxer Farid Shahide in interview with author November 2005

- 'The biggest beating I took was from Ron Lyle in 1977... He was one of those tough dudes that just kept coming. It was the only time I thought to myself: 'What am I doing this for?' Going the distance with Ali, Frazier, was not near as bad. I had busted ribs, a sore jaw, you name it. For weeks I was hurting.'
  - heavyweight contender Joe Bugner in interview on Eastside Boxing *February 2004.*

- 'Ron Lyle has shown he has the heart of a lion….Ron was a gentleman then and he's a gentleman now.'
  - PBS Newscaster Peter Boyles in 2000 television interview

- 'A Ron Lyle will always be difficult to come by, and a Clay/Ali will be impossible to duplicate. Students of the Sweet Science need to learn from the past in order for the noble, good stuff to be…. emulated.'
  - Philadelphia broadcaster Roland Riso on his website, 2004

- 'All credit should be given to Ron Lyle. He took some hard punches and gave some - a tremendous fighter.'
  - former heavyweight champion of the world George Foreman in a post-fight interview after 'the greatest slugfest in history.'

OFF THE ROPES

The Ron Lyle Story

Candace Toft

Scratching Shed Publishing Ltd

Copyright © Candace Toft, 2010
All rights reserved
The moral right of the author has been asserted

First published by Scratching Shed Publishing Ltd in 2010
Registered in England & Wales No. 6588772.
Registered office:
47 Street Lane, Leeds, West Yorkshire. LS8 1AP

www.scratchingshedpublishing.co.uk

ISBN 978-0956252623

Unless stated otherwise, all photographs are from the
personal collection of Ron Lyle

Cover photograph: Ron Lyle fights Mohammad Ali on 16 May 1975 in
Las Vegas, Nevada. (Herb Scharfman/Sports Imagery/Getty Images)

A catalogue record for this book is available from the British Library.

Typeset in Warnock Pro Semi Bold and Palatino

Printed and bound in the United Kingdom by
L.P.P.S.Ltd, Wellingborough, Northants, NN8 3PJ

This book is dedicated to the memory of
Nellie Lyle

Acknowledgements

Off the Ropes would never have been written without enthusiastic assistance from a myriad of Ron's family, friends and fans, including:

Bill Lyle, Sharon Dempsey, Kenneth Lyle, Donna Harris, Phillip Lyle, Marilyn Carr, and Karen Lyle, who told wonderful family stories and provided invaluable insights into their brother Ronny;

Friends Russ Perron, Bob Cox, Willy Field, Donny Nelson, Mary and John Kresnik, Walter Gerash, Mary Bransfield, Frank Barron, Richard Steele, Farid Shahide, Jimmy Farrell, David Kilgour, Abby Espinoza, Gary Snyder and Earnie Shavers, who remembered details of key events that tied the Ron Lyle story together from the Curtis Park projects in the early days all the way around to Curtis Park today;

Marjorie Reinhardt, who supplied records from the 1978 murder trial; Barney O'Grady, who collected and presented to Ron five thick scrapbooks of news articles, a resource which saved me hundreds of research hours; and a parade of Denver sportswriters, especially Terry Anderson of the *Denver Post*, who preserved much of Ron's history.

I have greatly appreciated good advice from Michael Grant, Alan Russell, Sue Diaz and Lois Bennett. My work was made so much easier by Judy Eastman, who edited the first draft, Mathew Levine, who participated in all the Denver and Las Vegas interviews, and Bert Sugar, who donated his valuable time and expertise to the final edit.

Finally, I am especially indebted to Dennis Nelson, who not only lent me rare fight tapes and photographs, but also offered memories covering four decades;

Jill Sellers, who shared her heart; Tracy Bowens, who remembered her father so well; and Ron Lyle, who told me the truth.

Contents

*

Foreword

Bert Randolph Sugar

Leaf through that long and winding road of heavyweight challengers, going all the way back to the beginnings of the gloved era - back to Charlie Mitchell challenging John L. Sullivan, down through the alphabetical listing of names to that of Dave Zyglewicz, who challenged Joe Frazier - and you'll find less than a gloveful who acquitted themselves with glory. Of those very few only James J. Corbett (against Jim Jeffries), Billy Conn (against Joe Louis), and Ron Lyle (against Muhammad Ali) can be defined by their losses, remembered as challengers who came this close to winning the title.

But while much has been written about the first two, Corbett and Conn, little is known about Lyle, a name remembered, if at all in the receding echoes of boxing history, for his fight against Ali. Lyle's in-the-ring exploits are accorded no special place of prominence in old *Ring Record* books. Nor in the minds of many boxing fans. But to the *true* boxing fan he is remembered not only for that great

Ali match-up, but also his battle with George Foreman. That bout was called 'The most two-sided fight in boxing history' by the poet laureate of sportswriting, Red Smith.

Now along comes Candace Toft who, in this thoroughly researched and detailed account, relates how Ron Lyle overcame adversity both inside and outside the ring to almost rise to the top of the heavyweight mountain. For this story is not just a boxing story; it is a story of determination and optimism born of hardship and tragedy that became destination-bound, of how Lyle fiercely devoted himself to one goal: the heavyweight championship. And almost made it.

Lyle's story is one told many times before. Of how a fighter used boxing as a way out, as a means of turning his life around and became, in the immortal words of the screenwriter Budd Schulberg: 'a contendah....[a] somebody.'

Take Rocky Graziano, for example, who once said: 'If it hadn't been for boxing, I'd have been electrocuted at Sing-Sing.' Enunciating his 'dese' and 'dose' to sound something that passed for the English language, Graziano explained his transformation from that of a kid who 'never stole nothing' unless it began with an 'A' - 'A car... A truck... A payroll...' - *into* that somebody. For Ron Lyle, it was not quite the same thing, but he too was headed in the wrong direction until he found boxing.

Ultimately, Candace Toft has crafted a story of hardship and triumph. This is a tale that shows how a man is defined not only by his losses, but by his many victories in life, as well as in the ring.

Bert Randolph Sugar
December 27, 2009

'The greatest test of courage on the earth is to bear defeat without losing heart.'
- *Robert G. Ingersoll, The Declaration of Independence*

*

Prologue

Cox-Lyle Youth Center, Denver, Colorado

THE bell sounds for the end of the first round, and José, a wiry sixteen-year-old, walks slowly to his corner. Ron Lyle reaches up through the ropes with a damp rag and nods at the boy to blow his nose. Then blow again. The bell sounds, and the sparring match resumes, both José and his opponent demonstrating the moves they have practiced for months under Lyle's watchful eye. At the end of three rounds, José holds up his arms in a sign of victory, and Lyle, seated against the wall, points to the folding chair beside his own.

Breathing hard, José drops down next to his mentor and Lyle lays his hands on the boy's shoulders. 'You want to get better, right?'

'Yeah.'

'Then you need to keep working, José. I'll set you up with matches, but not if you don't work. Right?'

'Right.'

'Why?'

'Because you don't want to see me get hurt.'

'You got it.'

Ron touches his right fist to José's and waves him away, then turns to a volunteer assistant. 'You gotta be alert to their needs. I know what they need because I was there once. I had the same needs.' He adds with a smile: 'They don't know it yet, but what they need the most is self-discipline.'

Lyle typically wears a wool cap over his shaved head and dark glasses in public, but effectively expresses his sentiments to the kids with big smiles and light touches. He lives his axiom that a trainer has to respond to his fighters' moods, detect any interference with their focus.

How do we reconcile this soft-spoken, gentle man with the 'toughest heavyweight who never won the title'; the guy who served hard time for second-degree murder before he even started his amateur boxing career; the third-ranked fighter who had Muhammad Ali beat for ten rounds in a title bout; the guy who fought George Foreman in a brawl with four knockdowns, known in boxing lore as 'The One For the Ages'; the guy who was arrested for murder a second time?

Ron Lyle is one of those names you almost remember, but not quite - until you see him. The 67-year-old former heavyweight carries his weight upright on his 6ft 3½-inch frame and looks two decades younger than his age. He still runs regularly, and even though he can no longer do his famous thousand push-ups an hour, he easily manages sets of one hundred. But when he takes off his glasses, it is the intensity in those black eyes that brings it all back. He has always looked his interviewers straight in the eye.

Lyle is a philosopher. He talks about being true to the game and about life being a test and about not blaming anybody else for your troubles. He says you can't straighten out until you make a commitment. He says you have to always prepare for the unexpected and never look back. He says he would live his life over just the same - that he had to learn from his mistakes. He says he is a God-fearing man.

It's time to go and the kids line up along the side of the ring. Ron moves along the line and touches each of them - a clap on the shoulder, a fist-to-fist or a high five. They seem reluctant to leave and linger for a few minutes until first one boy, then the others begin filing out of the gym. Another Saturday morning.

Ron teaches his kids to think smart, to believe in themselves and to practice self-discipline, characteristics he epitomised in his 1975 World Heavyweight Championship fight with Muhammad Ali.

The Convention Center, Las Vegas, Nevada. May 16, 1975

GOING into the tenth round, Ron Lyle had Ali beat. Most observers and at least two of the three judges had him way ahead on points. The champion had tried to use Ron up with the 'rope-a-dope' strategy that worked so well on George Foreman in Zaire, but as his own physician said after the second round, 'Lyle is too smart to go for it,' and Ali has since found himself alone on the ropes or covering up in the centre of the ring. Even Howard Cosell, broadcasting the fight, commented: 'Lyle has no fear of this man.'

In the seventh round, roared on by screaming fans in the background, Lyle had dominated from bell to bell, Cosell noting that: 'Ali must be concerned.' Round eight, which the champion had called for his win, came and went.

In the ninth, Ron's greater commitment to intense physical conditioning had showed as a weary Ali headed directly for the ropes, moving out only after Ron gestured to him, before returning to his corner after a few desultory hits and covering up. He stayed there for most of the round.

Now, seconds before the bell for round ten, Ron's trainer Chickie Ferrara is sponging down his fighter's brow when he glances up to see Muhammad Ali's glazed stare from across the ring. The trainer tells Lyle that Ali is desperate and that all he has to do is stay with it through the remainder of the fifteen-round bout and he will be the next heavyweight champion of the world. Ron nods, certain his long-held dream is about to be fulfilled.

The bell rings and both fighters travel slowly to the centre of the ring.

Then Ali backs off and raises his gloves to his face. Lyle goes in low with a hard shot to the middle and pulls back, circling the champion until both push off and Ali grazes Lyle's shoulder with an ineffective left. Ron pushes him back and Ali bends down with his gloves once again flat against his face.

Ron swings a hard right to Ali's left side and the fighters exchange light thumps until Ali covers up for the third time, backing up until he is once again leaning on the ropes. Ron gets in some punches to the head, forcing Ali to break free and step across the ring only to fall against the ropes on the other side and resume his covered-up position.

Lyle goes to the body, pummelling with a right, then a left, then right again. Ali's gloves are tight against his face, but Ron manages a left uppercut, then a punishing right slam to the side of Ali's head. He thrusts his own face against Ali's gloves, then leans back to land another left uppercut. Ali remains, covered up, on the ropes.

Ron pushes off and backs into the centre of the ring, waiting for Ali to follow. Cosell tells viewers: 'I must say that although Ali continues to talk to Lyle... he's talking right now... he is doing nothing... Lyle is paying no attention.... Lyle has not lost his composure.'

In the final few seconds, Ali starts to swing, but with

every harmless punch, Lyle answers. The bell rings to end the round and both fighters move slowly to their corners.

Ron knew he had Ali on the ropes. And he knew exactly what it had taken to get him there.

1

*

Beginnings

ONE early morning in May, Ronny Lyle sat on the curb in front of his house, with his best friends Roy Tyler and Russ Perron. They were folding their delivery copies of the *Rocky Mountain News*, preparing for their daily door-to-door delivery in the Curtis Park projects, Denver, a routine that included not only dropping papers on their customers' porches, but grabbing rival copies of the *Denver Post* off other porches to sell on the street in the Five Points area, a couple miles north of the neighbourhood. They figured that was okay because the kids that delivered the *Post* did the same thing with the *News* when they got there first.

Ronny packed the papers in his bag and stood up just as Joe Willie White went flying by on his bike.

'Hey, Joe Willie,' he called.

The other boys piped in. 'Where ya goin'?' 'Where's the fire?'

Every few days Joe Willie brought by chocolate and orange milk after the other boys had finished their deliveries and returned with their *Denver Post* profits. Some days he even had doughnuts. Funny thing, they never asked where he got the food, just took it for granted as part of the weekly routine. But that morning all came clear as the milk truck, followed closely by the Dolly Madison pastry truck, came racing down the street headed in the same direction as Joe Willie. The driver of the milk truck stopped in the middle of the street, the pastry truck pulling up behind, and called out: 'You see a kid come by here on a bike?'

Ronny pointed up a side street. 'That way,' and the other boys pointed in the same direction.

The driver leaned out his window and gestured to the driver of the Dolly Madison truck to follow, then hit the gas and headed up the street where Joe Willie had disappeared. Russ said: 'He knew you would lie. That's why he asked.' Ronny laughed. 'Next time we tell the truth.'

Fifty years later, the men who were there still laugh about that day and Joe Willie White. Ron's older brother Bill roars with laughter as he learns for the first time where all those doughnuts came from. Somebody mentions the old Easter Sundays, another memory that amuses the old 'group of brothers.' Ron tells how they used to dress up in the best clothes they had and proceed to make the rounds at as many sunrise services as they could jam in.

'We were after the free breakfasts,' Russ chimes. The only time he could remember getting caught was when Reverend W.T. Liggins from the Zion Baptist Church shooed them away, shouting: 'You boys ate up all the sausage last year. That isn't going to happen this morning.'

EVER since his family moved to the Curtis Park projects, Ronny Lyle had hung around with seven other boys in the neighbourhood, three of them black and four who called themselves *Chicano* back then. Through the years, the boys moved so gradually from innocent childhood play to mischievous acts like raiding the sunrise service breakfasts that it didn't seem to them like they were doing much of anything wrong. And they always stood up for each other.

Ronny learned early about the importance of protecting his companions. When he was eight years old, a bigger kid had walked up to his big brother Bill and threatened him with a stick. Heeding his mother's admonition always to walk away from fighting, Ronny turned and ran, not walked, for blocks before looking back at his brother, who was being thrashed vigorously with that stick. When he got home that afternoon, his mother gave him a severe whuppin' for not protecting his brother.

'Your brother's fight is your fight,' she told him. 'Don't start no fights, but don't run from one, neither.'

Ron laughs now, 'I couldn't win. If I fought, I got whupped; when I ran, I got whupped.' But the lesson had been learned. And it was reinforced a few months later when family friend Pastor Roland Martin took the three oldest Lyle boys aside and gave them preliminary lessons on how to handle themselves with bullies - how to keep from running away. As it turned out, Pastor Martin's lessons carried the brothers through many a scuffle.

Roy Tyler and Ronny did their best to protect each other, from the time they were in fourth grade when a couple of older boys had jumped Ronny and Roy had charged in, arms waving. The 'code' was born that day, the promise to fight when attacked and to always defend each other. Gradually other boys came into the fold - Connor Hill, Beau Peat, Phillip Dawson, Russell Perron, Gerald Wade and, finally, Roy's younger brother Sonny Boy - but the code never changed. Ron's most vivid memories of those elementary school years are of his friends honouring themselves by taking care of each other.

By the time the boys reached early adolescence, it seemed a natural progression from fighting to committing misdemeanors, such as selling newspapers they lifted from porches. But it was only a couple of years later, when Ronny and Roy moved into petty theft, resulting eventually in their incarceration at the Buena Vista Correctional Facility, that his friends got scared.

Ron doesn't make excuses for his behaviour back in those days. 'I had good parents. My Dad had three jobs to try and make it better for us. I didn't understand how important that was, and I got caught up in stuff I shouldn't have. I wasn't thinking.'

An even more difficult question is how the kids from Curtis Park proceeded from what was labelled 'juvenile delinquency' to serious trouble. Even today, Russ and Ronny deny ever being in a gang as defined by current standards. They talk about how they represented different races and ethnicities, that they never had colours and never named themselves. They were just friends. But when Ronny was indicted for first-degree murder at age 19, some of his old friends were at the scene and the crime was reported as gang related. Nobody could believe that the Lyle family was involved in the worst thing that had ever happened in their neighbourhood.

WILLIAM HENLY and Nellie Louise Lyle were both born in Dayton, Ohio to families that were steeped in a traditional African-American culture, even though William's mother was white and his father claimed Native American blood. Work was hard to find after the Depression, and both families struggled, even after William and Nellie were married in the late-thirties.

By the time Ronny was the third child born on February 12, 1941, they were living with Nellie's parents, and William was helping the family make ends meet by working in what their children now call a 'brothel/casino.' Nellie's father was a preacher who had, years before, set about building his own church, 'literally brick by brick, layer by layer.' But both of her parents, far from disapproving of William's job, welcomed the extra income.

William and Nellie already had six children in 1946, when everything changed. Their oldest child Barbara died of rheumatic fever, the catalyst for William joining the rest of the family in being 'saved.' He left his job and began his ministry in Holiness Church, a Pentecostal denomination that followed even stricter rules than the church of Nellie's family, demanding behaviour that was the antithesis of everything William had seen in the 'brothel/casino.' He became the strongest voice for reform in the community, and his success as a minister was confirmed when in only two years, he was appointed one of 25 ministers to the Ohio District State Council.

A few months later, William had a dream that began a family tradition. He told Nellie about the vision that came to him, of coming to a city near a mountain and building a church there. He believed that God wanted him to '....find them, teach them, guide them, and save them.' Within a few months the message in the dream was confirmed by two church leaders, Bishop Davis from Kansas and Bishop Bass from Ohio, who met and agreed that Pastor Lyle was chosen by God to pioneer a church in Denver, Colorado. He was directed to start his church from scratch.

Both William and Nellie were certain that the move had been determined by God because it came out of a dream, and they never had any doubts as to their purpose. In 1949, with seven children in tow, including eight-year-old Ronny, the Lyles left Dayton behind, took a bus to Denver and never looked back.

With Nellie's help, William established a church in Denver, though it would be four more years before that church had a physical home. The Lyles never lost their faith in Biblical tenets, one of which was to 'be fruitful and multiply and replenish the earth,' and they would eventually have eleven more children. Nellie always said that they were blessed to have such a large family, and she made sure that each of the brothers and sisters, as soon as they could talk, learned to recite the first and middle names of those who eventually became the nineteen Lyle children in order, an accomplishment they never lost:

Barbara Joanne - died of rheumatic fever, 1946
William Alfred
Ronald David
Kenneth Henry
Edward Thomas
Michael Anthony - died in Vietnam, 1966
Donna Louise
Sharon Dolores
Joyce Elaine
Raymond Alvin
Phillip Paul
Robert D.
Marilyn Anne
Mark Anthony
James Marvin
Norman Daniel
John John - died of cerebral palsy, 1981
Gerald Matthew - died of AIDS, 2004
Karen Elizabeth.

It is difficult to imagine how William and Nellie cared for their family in a four-bedroom brick house in the projects with all the attending laundry and cleaning, not to mention feeding. The oldest brother Bill suggests that to understand what it was like, the outsider should think of the children in 'sets,' with the older group caring for the younger all the way down the line.

ON a Saturday afternoon in September 1955, the Lyles gathered as they did every week in the small living room - William, Nellie and Bill on the couch, thirteen-year-old Ronny holding baby Phillip on the rocker, and all the other children sitting cross-legged on the floor.

Nellie called on each child in turn, beginning with Bill: 'Tell us about your week.' Every one of the Lyle kids looked forward to this weekly review of their lives, and most prepared in advance the best news they could remember. Bill probably reported on his grades in school, almost always good. Ronny was more likely to tell about neighbourhood sports in which he excelled, often a pick-up basketball game. And Nellie always encouraged the appointed speaker before she moved on.

'Good for you. Kenny?' And on through Eddy and Michael and Donna and Sharon and Joyce and Raymond as each related highlights - passing a math test, showing a drawing, even singing a hymn. At the end, Ron tossed baby Phillip a few inches in the air and got a happy squeal in return. The whole family laughed, and William let the sound die down before he announced the scripture for the week, maybe even the passage upon which his Denver church was founded:

> *Acts 2:38.* Peter replied, "Repent and be baptised, every one of you, in the name of Jesus Christ for the forgiveness of your sins. And you will receive the gift of the Holy Spirit."

And with that, the family dispersed, each to his and her assigned chores for the week.

Nellie was a stickler for hygiene. Her horror when Joyce as a baby had been bitten on the cheek by a rat shortly after the family first moved to Denver never entirely left her, and the cleaning regimen she established when they moved to the projects continued until the day she died.

Ronny's task that afternoon was to continue washing down the walls he had begun the Saturday before. With little Phillip in the carrier accompanying him on every step, he emptied the trash can in the bathroom, poured in a cup of bleach and a squirt of dish detergent, and filled the can with hot water from the kitchen sink. He then proceeded to the girls' bedroom and easily moved the bed and dresser to the middle of the room. With the help of a small stool, he managed to reach all the way to the top of the walls, ending up on his knees as he followed the floorboard around the room. He talked to Phillip the whole time, rewarded by the baby babbling back.

At 5:15 he handed Phillip over to his mother, poured the dirty water down the toilet, and wiped out the trash can. The following week he would wash down the walls in his and Raymond's room. But in the meantime, he was free to head outside for an hour with Roy and Russ before supper.

'Family and friends. I had it good, you know?' Ron Lyle, like his brothers and sisters, remembers those days as sometimes chaotic, even stressful, but always loving. 'I know it's hard for other people to imagine having that many kids, but we were together. We always had each other.' He adds: 'And we still do.'

They didn't always get along, of course. The whole family remembers how Bill and Ronny used to fight. Bill had the longer reach for many years and Ron remembers his brother's hand on his forehead, holding him back while he swung wildly in the air. Sharon says that the only thing that made Nellie mad was any of her children fighting. 'You should want to be together,' she would tell them.

Bill recalls that when he went to college, he felt alone. Even surrounded by other students in the dorm, he missed his family. 'Even now, when my brothers and sisters are not around, it feels like something is lost.'

Donna, who lives near San Diego these days, thinks of her family every single day. 'We're still together in our hearts, though, even when we haven't seen each other for a long time.' She remembers those Saturday meetings, sitting on the floor listening to everybody tell about their week, as the happiest time in her life.

Whether it was William's raw energy, Nellie's loving patience, the example they set as a close family or a combination of all three, by all accounts the Lyles were not only the spiritual, but the social heart of the community. And what a community it was.

2

*

TO many who lived in the outlying suburbs of Denver, the Curtis Park and Five Points districts evoked dangerous territory, a place where you wouldn't want to be after dark. But to the inhabitants, the neighbourhoods north east of downtown were places of refuge, rich in history and a sanctuary for the African American community.

Most residents of Five Points recall the story of how the area was named in the early 1900's; the city's tramway company used the nickname because the street car signs were not big enough to list all the street names at the end-of-the-line stop.

The history of the area is centred on Benny Hooper, the first African-American drafted in Denver for World War One. He opened up a hotel and club for black servicemen in 1920 and managed to attract the greatest jazz musicians of the time on their circuits, including Duke Ellington and Charlie Parker. Later, he was responsible for getting the city of Denver to allow black soldiers to be a part of the Veterans

Day parade. 'Coloureds' were not allowed to march with weapons, so he had wooden guns carved and painted, made sure every man's shoes were spit-polished and led the men downtown. They were told to go last in the parade, but they did march, and Benny always maintained they were the best-dressed unit. The pride Benny Hooper engendered in Five Points residents and omnipresent through the decades, continues to this day.

While Five Points was beginning to be known as a cultural landmark in the 1950s, Curtis Park was labelled the so-called ghetto area of Denver, even though the small Victorian Queen Anne houses built in the 1870s and 1880s were already starting to be recognised as architectural treasures. Built around Denver's oldest park, developed in 1868 with donated land from Postmaster Samuel S. Curtis, the area has managed to retain its charm for well over a century. But during the time the Lyles lived there, the mere presence of a large African-American population somehow reflected danger to a significant portion of the population still mired in racial prejudice.

The Curtis Park district may be considered a microcosm of Denver's ethnic history. Settled mostly by Germans in the nineteenth century, the area saw a great influx of Latinos, Blacks and Japanese after the first war, continuing into the fifties. Today the area is about half Latino, a quarter African-American and another quarter white. Finally celebrating the cultural diversity of the community, the park itself was recently renamed Mestizo-Curtis Park. Just a few blocks from Ron's gym, with an outdoor pool, tennis and basketball courts, horseshoe pits, a soccer field and a new playground, the park is the focal point of the community.

The area may have been perceived in the fifties as a slum by outsiders, but Russell Perron and Ron Lyle remember something else about Curtis Park. They remember that people there, whatever their race, had a chance to do what they wanted to do with their lives.

The Lyles settled in at 34th and Arapahoe, in the core of the district right across the street from Curtis Park. All the units in the projects were red brick duplexes of varying size and depth. No fences broke the continuity of the neighbourhood, just as no racial barriers existed in that part of Denver. And the people who grew up there remember how difficult it was to get away with anything.

'You couldn't so much as throw a rock that somebody in the neighbourhood wouldn't call your folks about. And if they weren't home, the neighbour would do the whuppin',' Kenneth Lyle remembers.

Keeping an eye on their kids might have been the neighbours' way of paying the Lyles back for their many kindnesses. Almost from the very beginning, the families in the Curtis Park projects knew they could call on William and Nellie to help out. Whether a family was short of food, in trouble with the law or in need of spiritual guidance, they counted on the Lyles for support.

By the time Ronny had started his paper route, Nellie Lyle was known in Curtis Park as a missionary, not only for her tireless efforts at collecting money and goods for foreign missions, but for her charity. Donna recalls: 'Mom was a jewel. She loved everybody in the neighbourhood and would feed anybody who was hungry.' If the recipients of her altruistic efforts found God in the process, so much the better, but she didn't discriminate in her many acts of kindness.

Pastor Sharon Lyle Dempsey, who inherited her mother's missionary mantle, remembers her family as the centre of the neighbourhood. 'It didn't matter if they belonged to the Church. My mom and dad were there to help. Anybody who was sick or hungry or in trouble came to my parents and they would figure out a way to make things better for everybody.' Later, she added: 'Another thing you should know about mom and daddy. Their best friends were Jews, Latinos, whoever they cared about. Race didn't matter to our family.'

If Nellie was the missionary, William Lyle was the undisputed head of the family, the neighbourhood and the church he founded in Curtis Park. He was not only a minister, he held three other jobs the entire time his children were at home. One of his jobs was always custodial, though employers varied through the years. The best paying was as a vulcaniser at Gates Rubber, a skilled position in which he made 'space on the tyres for the tread.' And he always had a maintenance job at Burt Chevrolet, the dealership that evolved into the Burt Automotive Group where Bill, the oldest, was employed for decades, before he retired as Burt Lincoln-Mercury sales manager.

However many hours William put in at his jobs, he sprang into action when anyone in the neighbourhood was in trouble. The family looks back and wonders when their father had time to sleep, let alone spend time with them.

Sharon: 'People we didn't even know would come to the house because they were in some kind of trouble - with the law or maybe they owed money. Dad and mom would do what they could to help. And dad was always running to the Church day or night, sometimes praying all night long.'

Bill remembers, though, that even with his dad's extra three jobs, the money was never quite enough. Nellie did manage to buy and cook enough food for all her children, but meals were mostly pinto beans, pig's feet and pig's tails with chicken sometimes on Sundays. Kenneth remembers hauling huge bags of sugar and other bulk items from the store, and they all remember the administration of cod liver oil twice a day, every day, every kid. They couldn't afford to get sick.

The Lyles lived within their means, but there was barely enough left over for extras. Clothes were always from 'Goodwill' and those went to the older children; the younger almost always got hand-me-downs.

They did have a number of vehicles through the years. Bill remembers an old Ford that they had to stop every six blocks to put water in the radiator. He and Ronny had to get out and push the thing uphill, then jump in as it caught speed. Kenneth recalls a beat-up old truck they bought in 1957 and Karen says she will never forget 'an ugly green '54 station wagon.' Sharon remembers a big old Hudson and says there were more vehicles, too, because none of them lasted long. She adds: 'But with all that came the lessons that got us through.'

The Lyle children learned early on that everything was 'God's will.' Before he was married, William had wanted to join the Navy, but was rejected because an X-ray revealed a spot on his lung. He never in his life experienced any health problem with his lungs and always believed God had put the spot on that X-ray to save him for the Church.

Nellie was saved when she was eight years old. While William had a working experience with the secular world, Nellie never saw a movie or danced or went to a party. Under her influence, the Lyle kids were all taught that every word in the Bible was the literal truth. If they questioned or argued with any directive from their parents, they were told simply: 'Don't talk back.' They adhered to a strict dress code, which included no jewellery, and the older boys were enlisted in enforcing the no-dating rules for the girls.

'If a boy even looked at me,' Marilyn remembers, 'Ronny would get all over him to back off.'

Sharon still talks about an evening with Donna and Raymond and Joyce when everyone else in the family was away. They had borrowed a turntable and some records and with Joyce leading the way, they sang and played rock and roll songs for hours, until one of their neighbours called William at Church. Their father rushed home and broke every record, one at a time, and returned the turntable that night. None of the children ever brought outside music back into the house again.

All of the brothers and sisters speak of trying to do what the Bible and their parents told them to do, and mostly they succeeded. But sometimes those teachings conflicted with the reality of life in the projects.

3

*

AT age thirteen, Ronny had already grown to 5 feet 11 inches and was acknowledged by everybody in the Lyle orbit as not only the tallest kid in the neighbourhood, but also the strongest and most energetic. Springing into adolescence, he began to fill every one of his days with activity, from the time he woke up in the morning until he dropped into bed at night. He and his buddies attended Cole Junior High, but school became more and more difficult for him, and he found much greater success, not to mention entertainment, in the neighbourhood.

Russ Perron remembers the 'group of brothers' continuing to hang out together during junior high school. 'We would go to the Epworth Recreation Center on 31st between Arapahoe and Lawrence, just a short walk from the projects. We played basketball and messed around and talked to girls. Ron was the best at all three.'

Most of Ronny's friends represented the unique multi-ethnic culture of the district. Long before mixed marriages became a controversial issue among Denver activists, the boys took for granted each other's diverse parentage. Black mother, white father. *Chicano* mother, black father. None of that mattered to the 'brothers.' What did matter was that Ronny's mom expected good behaviour from all of them.

Family continued to be the major influence in Ronny's life. As the two oldest boys, he and big brother Bill were expected to care for the younger children. They both felt responsible for their siblings' welfare and took their obligations seriously. Tears in her eyes, Donna remembers, 'Bill and Ronny. They were the best. They took such good care of us.'

The older brothers also assumed major responsibility for organising the housekeeping chores. Ron remembers the first time he could assign the wall-washing task to his younger brother Kenneth. 'I told him we had to keep germs away from the kids,' he says.

Nobody remembers oldest brother Bill ever getting into trouble, and today, he laughs about it. 'I didn't have time. I was too busying keeping track of the others, especially Ronny.'

When Bill was 14, he managed to get a job caddying at the Denver Country Club golf course, a prestigious club then and now, a meeting place for many of Denver's movers and shakers. He would get up early Saturday and Sunday mornings, signing into the caddy shack around 7:00, hoping to get in two rounds both days. Golfers started arriving about 8:00, but the caddies had to 'go by the numbers,' that is, the lowest numbers assigned to the kids who had been working the longest. Bill still remembers he started at C149, but some of the caddies dropped out and, after he had been there a while, he worked his way into the A's and was getting two rounds in regularly. Bill might get as much as $36 a day including tips; good money for the time, especially for an adolescent, but 'every nickel' went back to the family. After a few months, Bill thought Ronny was old enough to caddy with him, and he managed to get his brother on at the club. He figured, not only that the extra money would help out at home, but that caddying on weekends might keep Ronny out of trouble.

It worked for a while. Bill Connelly, the caddy master, took an interest in the Lyle brothers, and steered some important members their way. Bill went out with then Governor Dan Thornton a few times, and was soon picked to be his special caddy, sometimes even carrying double bags for double pay. Ronny caddied for C.L. Patterson and R.W. Gordon, both wealthy businessmen, and later he picked up Gerald Phipps, who ended up owning the Denver Broncos. Connelly also worked out a deal for the boys to play for free up to 36 holes on Mondays.

Prodded by Phillip, Ron tells of the day he lost that caddying job. One morning on the front nine C.L. Patterson knocked his ball into the creek, a natural water hazard that also served to irrigate the golf course. Patterson told Ronny to retrieve the ball from the creek, but Ron shook his head. The businessman then repeated the order to his caddy. He was to wade into the creek, reach down, find his ball and bring it back to him.

Ronny said: 'No, I won't. I don't want to get wet.'

Patterson directed him a third time, 'You will get my ball,' whereupon Ronny grabbed the man's golf bag and hurled it 20 feet into the creek. His only regret at the time was that his act of defiance ended the opportunity to bring all that good money home. Years later, remembering the loss of the country club wages and tips, he and Bill set up his boxing revenues as Lyle Enterprises with a portion of every purse going directly to the family.

SHARON remembers that the summer Ronny was 13, like most other summers, both sides of the family from Ohio visited for a week or so. 'Aunts and uncles and cousins always took our beds, just like the visiting ministers did. We ended up sleeping on floors all over the house. If we were lucky, we'd get a pallet to lie on. Almost every day, we'd pile in cars and take day trips, sometimes to the mountains - Pike's Peak or Lookout Mountain - sometimes to Lakeside or City Park. It was always dad's idea, but mom would fix greens, peach cobbler and fried apples.'

Ronny's friends and family continued to fill his life, but the year he turned 14, somehow, almost imperceptibly, things started to go wrong.

Maybe because he was an all-around athlete and bigger than the other boys his age, Ronny became a kind of guardian for his buddies. 'I wasn't tougher, though,' he insists. 'We were all tough.' When the brothers started going into neighbourhood houses to swipe 'nickel and dime stuff,' Ronny was almost always there. A memorable take from that time was a whole batch of cupcakes, consumed a few blocks away. They didn't consider what they were doing as break-ins, until the cops called it that the first time they were caught and released to their parents.

Ronny continued to struggle in school, especially with reading. Most of his grades freshman year at Manual High School were failing, and in the spring, he finally made the fateful decision to drop out, along with Roy and Sonny Boy Tyler. The delinquency continued, break-ins turned into burglaries and before the summer was over, Ronny had been arrested for stealing a pocketful of bubble gum and held for a couple of months in Juvenile Hall.

Ron's own eyes fill with tears when he remembers his mother crying in court and again when he was released. 'She always told us that she had to '....raise up the child in the way he should go, and when he's older, he won't depart.' For a long time it didn't work out that way with me, and I've always been sorry at what I put her through. But in the end, she knows I won't depart.'

It has been reported that Ron Lyle rebelled against his strict religious upbringing, but he doesn't remember it that way. 'I always respected my parents and I feared God. I was just like a lot of other kids, caught up in the excitement.' He adds: 'Sometimes you have to stray to find your way.'

Asked in 2001 by newscaster Peter Boyle to name his greatest opponent, Ron responded without pausing: 'The toughest guy I ever fought was my father, and I never got to throw a punch.'

Later, he describes his mixed feelings about his father. 'Kids always resent their parents, but for me, the resentment was with respect. You know what I mean? My father had all the power, and I wanted to take control of my own life. But both my parents knew me. They always knew me. They knew I didn't want to hurt anyone.'

That fall Ronny and Roy, along with Connor Hill and Phillip Dawson, learned how to 'hop a freight' and took the first of three trips to parts unknown. The next year they went to Gary, Indiana, and the following year to Chicago, where they were rescued by Ronny's Aunt Bertie. That first time, though, the train happened to be headed toward Great Falls, Montana.

'A hobo down by the train yards' had taught them the basics. Ron remembers: 'He showed us how to spike the doors of the freight cars. He said we should always set up more than one car, in case we saw some bad guys already settled in when the train started to move.'

By the time they arrived in Great Falls two days later, they were not only hungry, having devoured their bag of sandwiches the day before, they had started to feel the cold of the spitting wet snow outside. Ronny had lost a shoe jumping onto the moving car back in Denver, and the second he stepped on the ground he felt the cold all the way into his teeth. The boys barely lasted two days before the police picked them up and called their parents in Denver. William told the cop who called to hold Ronny overnight, just to teach him a lesson, but the message backfired when he reacted with a 'Thank you, Jesus' for the warm cell and hot food.

Back in Denver, Bill was spending more time out 'evangelising' with his father, and when Ronny returned, Nellie began to lean more heavily on him, not only with housekeeping chores, but as the primary care-giver in the family. Whether or not this new arrangement was part of the effort to get him back on track, Ronny and his mother grew closer, and he tried hard to instill the same sense of responsibility and love of God into his siblings that his mother had encouraged in him.

But the misdemeanours continued. The boys started 'going jackin' - one distracting a store clerk while the others snatched all the small items they could stuff in their jeans. Twice more Ronny was brought before a judge and twice more sentenced to juvenile hall. Shortly after he was released the last time, he was caught red-handed, along with Roy Tyler, snatching a purse.

Finally, William and Nellie threw in the towel. When the judge told them he needed to get Ronny's attention, and didn't know how to do that without incarceration, they agreed. William said: 'I can't keep my foot on his neck all the time,' and Nellie nodded her affirmation. The judge expressed regret at sending sixteen-year-old Ronny Lyle away from 'a good home,' but sentenced both Roy Tyler and him to 18 months in the Buena Vista Correctional Facility.

As the only Colorado state reform school, Buena Vista

had a reputation in those days for 'punishment, not coddling,' and Ron got his first taste of incarceration. He still remembers his prisoner number was 14948 and Roy's was 14949. The two friends had watched each other's backs since they were eight years old, and in 1957, they were doing it behind bars.

William and Nellie had tried to keep Ron on the right path, along with all their other children, and not one of his brothers or sisters was ever arrested. Only Ron. His parents were confounded by his behaviour, but neither ever gave up on him. Nellie, especially, continued to express her confidence in her second oldest and did everything she could to support him, visiting constantly and bringing him little gifts, but mostly praying.

Ron still idolises his mother and regrets causing her so much pain. He can only explain his behaviour as: 'The problem was I got out of the backyard and into the alley. Once I'd seen the alley, they couldn't get me back into the yard.'

4

*

IN Buena Vista, Ronny learned some basic, unofficial rules of confinement. 'Mind your own business' especially served him well later when he did 'hard time.' Even in reform school, he had a daunting reputation as a tough guy, probably because of his size and stature. But he also began to apply a personal code of defence, later confirmed and solidified in the ring: 'If you get hit, it's your own fault.'

Buena Vista operated like most juvenile correctional facilities in those days, as a toned-down model of adult prisons. The boys were locked in at night, and activities were tightly controlled and guarded. Teachers were available, but classes were not designed to accommodate students with learning disabilities, a fairly new educational concept in the late-sixties. Ronny probably had some form of dyslexia, as reading has been difficult for him throughout his life, though he has always demonstrated the ability to comprehend and explore complex ideas. At Buena Vista, he had the choice of going to school or working, and most of the time he worked - as the fireman in the boiler house shoveling coal into the furnace whenever the fire was low.

Most of the kids in reform school were black or *Chicano*, just like his neighbourhood, and Ronny treated his fellow prisoners with respect, '....as long as they deserved it.' He doesn't remember his time there as too bad, probably because for the first time an adult recognised his athletic ability.

Mr. Kelly was the Athletic Director at Buena Vista, and unlike high school coaches who had to turn Ronny away from teams because of his failing grades, Mr. Kelly recognised his prowess, especially on the basketball court. For the first time, Ronny felt he could be an outstanding athlete. He felt it in his speed and quickness and, most of all, in his dedication to practice.

Looking back, Ron knows that in reform school he accomplished more than just doing his time. 'In Buena Vista, I started to learn self-discipline,' he says.

RELEASED in 1959 at age 17, he went back to his life at home and on the streets. His brother Bill had already graduated and was headed to college. Two more brothers had come along, with the youngest Karen yet to be born. Life was moving on, but Ronny didn't know how to move with it. He loved and admired Bill, but couldn't begin to live up to his brother's accomplishments and 'sterling reputation.' And Bill consistently refused Ron's invitations to join what he called Ron's 'Zulu Tribe' and what their Dad called 'that bunch' in stirring up trouble.

As a result of Mr. Kelly's encouragement, Ronny spent more time playing pick-up games as he could in the neighbourhood and at the Epworth Recreation Center. He loved all sports, including baseball, football and boxing, but he remembers basketball as his best game. Shortly after he left reform school, he tried out for a semi-pro basketball team called the Boston All-Stars. He made the team and in early winter began travelling to small towns, making little more than expenses but earning a reputation for enthusiasm and the ability to focus on the game.

By the end of the season the eighteen-year old had earned the starting forward position. It's tempting to wonder what kind of opportunities he might have had to play and excel at organised sports if he had been a better student at Manual High School, but Ron refuses to spend any time in that kind of regret. He is grateful to Epworth Center, where he practiced the self-discipline he had learned from Mr. Kelly in reform school.

Self-discipline was mostly set aside when Ronny was on the streets. Even as he was enjoying success with the Boston All-Stars, he continued running with his friends. He picked up pretty much where he left off, and in the next two years committed a long series of petty crimes. He and Roy had learned some tricks at Buena Vista and they managed to avoid getting caught.

The time Ronny had served at Buena Vista, along with his physical ability and his quick reaction to unexpected situations, made it seem inevitable that he would evolve into the generally accepted leader of the 'group of brothers.'

Ron looks back on those years as crucial to his evolution as a boxer, not only for the self-discipline he achieved on the basketball court, but also for his risk-taking in the streets. He doesn't try to make excuses for his behaviour, although his friends and family frequently do - 'It was hard for Ronny to say no to his friends,' or 'He was so big, they wouldn't leave him alone.'

When asked if he has any regrets, Ron comments on his street experiences and every other detour he made in his life by saying: '*If* is a crooked word that will never be straightened.' And if the listener doesn't quite get it, he will add: 'If a frog had wings, he wouldn't bump his ass when he hops.' The only regret Ron Lyle ever expresses about those days is for the hurt he caused his mother.

The kids in the 'group of brothers' naturally looked to Ronny for protection, but some remember him as reluctant to initiate trouble. He would try diplomacy first, quoting his mother: 'What's wrong with people in the world today is they don't know how to show respect.' If that didn't work, he would do all he could to inspire so much fear in his adversaries that they wouldn't fight. Today he describes that strategy as: 'I tried to scare their disrespect out of them.'

By 1960 a rivalry between the 'group of brothers' and a bunch of older guys that did fit all the criteria of a gang became full-blown and acknowledged throughout the neighbourhood. Russ Perron remembers the gang as 'very tough and very mean.' One guy in particular, Douglas 'Flash' Byrd, was known for beating other kids with whatever blunt object was available.

Ronny set about staving off Byrd's gang through intimidation and, as with other bullies, that strategy seemed to work; for months, the gang did not openly attack his friends. In the end, though, Ronny failed to keep them at bay, and the results were disastrous.

5

*

SHORTLY after lunch On May 16, 1961, Mr. Wilhoit glanced out the window of his Manual High School science classroom toward the park across the street. He stopped in the middle of a sentence and continued to stare outside. One of the two original members of the 'group of brothers' still in high school, Russ Perron, was seated two rows in, and he followed his teacher's gaze. He could clearly see six of his friends chasing the gang of neighbourhood tough guys across the grass.

'Pretty soon the whole class was standing up and watching what was going on in the park. They must have had ten or 12 guys, older guys, running around down there, and I kept thinking we were outnumbered. I wanted to go out and help, but then we all started to see what was happening. Ronny was out in front, and our guys were beating up their guys. It was something.'

After all the guys had left the park, a police car arrived, and Russ got a bad feeling that something more was going to happen. A couple of hours later he boarded a bus with his team-mates, headed to a track meet at South High School. 'Just then two car-loads of our guys drove up to the bus, and somebody yelled out: 'We gotta rumble.' Gil Kruter, our coach, wouldn't let me off the bus, so we took off for the meet. When I got home after 5:30, I walked back to the projects, and my mother's boyfriend met me at the door.

'"Where were you this afternoon?" he hollered at me. I looked up at the television screen, and there it was, the whole thing, the park and an alley behind Roy Tyler's house, and they were talking about a shooting. Somebody had shot 'Flash' Byrd. This was a guy who was known for knocking people around with lead pipes and tyre irons and even a jack hammer. I knew something really bad had happened.

'Just about all our guys had guns by then. You could buy a .22 pistol on the street for $15 in those days. Later on, when I found out the police were holding all of them and wouldn't let them go until somebody confessed, I knew Ronny would take the fall. I just knew it.'

Ron Lyle still remembers everything about that day, and he tells his story, but only up to a point. He says the friends in the park with him were Connor Hill, Beau Peat, Phillip Dawson, Roy Tyler, Gerald Wade and Sonny Boy Tyler. He shakes his head: 'The whole thing was about a girl.'

Leaning forward, Ron lowers his voice. 'We were minding our own business, just hanging around like we usually did in that park across from Manual High School. This dude named Poncho thought Connor had taken his girlfriend, and he brought a bunch of friends to help beat him up. It wasn't about drugs or money and we weren't a gang. It was about a girl.

'Well, naturally, we had to help Connor out when a bunch of guys jumped him. We did a pretty good job, too. We were just there to help. You know what I mean? Pretty soon, they started running out of the park, and we grabbed a couple cars and chased 'em for a few minutes, then headed back to Roy's place. When we got to Roy's, we found out his sister Sue was there, and that made a big difference, because after these guys picked up 'Flash' Byrd, they came back in cars and had guns. I once saw this guy beat a kid almost to death for refusing to give up his lunch money. 'Flash' was one mean guy. They drove through the alley and started shooting into Roy's house. They could have hit Sue, you know?'

As Ron moves to the end of his story, his voice is barely above a whisper, and he speaks in short, choppy sentences. 'So we followed them. 'Flash' was driving. He stopped in the alley. I went over to the driver's side. I told him: "Get out of the car." He opened the door. He was swinging a big lead pipe. The shooting started. 'Flash' ran down the alley. I chased him, but he got away. We saw the police coming. We went back to Roy's. The cops came and took us all in.'

He adds: 'Don't ask who did the shooting. Ever since the trial, I have never talked about it and I never will.'

Excerpts from the *Denver Post*:

> May 19, 1961
> 'Youth Tells of Shooting Two Men'
> A 20-year-old youth Thursday admitted firing at least three shots at almost point-blank range at the two victims of an East Denver shooting, Detective Capt. Roy Tangye said.
>
> Tangye identified the youth as Ronald D. Lyle, who, along with seven other young men, was jailed after the shooting Tuesday afternoon.
>
> After giving Detectives Ron Hammonds and Charles Roden a written statement, Tangye said, Lyle took them to look for the weapon which he said he hid

in the Five Points area. Killed in the fray was Douglas Byrd, 22. An autopsy showed he died of .22-calliber bullet wounds, rather than shotgun wounds, as police first believed.

A companion, Larry Williams, 23 suffered a minor head wound. He was treated at Denver General Hospital, jailed overnight for investigation and then released.

January 23, 1962
'Jury of 14 to Hear Trial for Murder'
One of the first 14 member juries in state history was authorized Tuesday in Denver District Court for the murder trial of a basketball star facing a possible death penalty.

Judge Gerald E. McAuliffe suggested the expanded panel and it was quickly approved by defence and prosecution attorneys as trial began for Ronny Lyle.

Lyle, a 6 foot $3^1/_2$ inch forward for a Denver semi-pro team called the Boston All- Stars, is accused of killing one man and shooting another near Five Points May 16, 1961.

Ordinarily 12 jurors, with possibly one alternate, sit in criminal cases. New court rules, however, permit 14, which includes two alternates.

The trial for the second shooting, in which case he is accused of assault with a deadly weapon, is scheduled for next month.

Edward Carelli and Gil Alexander, deputy district attorneys, said they are seeking the death penalty in the current trial....

January 25, 1962
'Slay Charge Filed After Gang Fight'
Murder charges and a separate charge of assault with a deadly weapon were filed Wednesday in District Court

against Ronald D. Lyle, the outgrowth of a gang fight and shooting on May 16.

Lyle admitted to police that he was the gunman who shot and killed Douglas Byrd, 22 and wounded Larry Williams, 23 during the fight in the Five Points area.

Judge Saul Pinchick ordered that Lyle be held without bail on the murder charge. As a formality, the judge set bond on the assault charge at $3000.

Under the separate filings by Dist. Atty. Bert Keating, Lyle may be tried both for murder and for assault with a deadly weapon. Maximum punishment on the murder charge could be death in the gas chamber. Maximum punishment on the assault charge could be 14 years in prison.

Police said a total of seven men were jailed after the shootings which killed Byrd and wounded Williams. The officers said the fight apparently was over a girl.

January 27, 1962
'Saturday Judge Fines, Jails Murder Case Juror'
A Denver man chosen as a juror to decide the life-or-death fate of an accused murderer was himself jailed for 30 days and fined $500 late Friday for discussing the case.

District Judge Gerald E. McAuliffe imposed the sentence on Carl McClung, 46, a transportation company dock worker.

The judge convicted McClung of contempt of court after a dramatic day-long probe in court chambers during which two other jurors and City Councilman Kenneth MacIntosh testified.

Mistrial Declared
After the contempt conviction, the judge went to the bench in the courtroom, announced what had

happened and declared a mistrial in the murder case of Ronny Lyle 20, Denver basketball player accused of killing one man and shooting a second....

....A high point of the court's investigation came at 2p.m. Friday when one juror, Mrs. Aliene E. Mitchell was called into chambers to confront McClung. She identified him as the man who spoke to her Wednesday morning in a court hallway and who 'inferred he knew a great deal about the case and that the defendant was guilty.'

'Don't you remember, Mr. McClung?' the woman said.

'I didn't refer directly to this case, McClung replied, 'I don't recall what I said.

'The only thing I said was that I didn't care what the color of a person's skin was and that what was in his heart and mind was the important thing.'

McClung denied he was prejudiced against the defendant or that he had made any prejudicial remarks.

Judge McAuliffe, commenting that the woman would have no purpose to lie about the matter, found McClung guilty. He pointed out that in the questioning of jurors, McClung had denied any knowledge of the case or of having any opinion on it.

'Because of your action,' the judge told McClung, 'I must declare a mistrial after four days of work in this case at great expense. The defendant is on trial for his life. We can't risk a miscarriage of justice.'

Wednesday, May 2, 1962
'Jury of 14 picked in the Slay Trial of Denver
Basketball Player'
....The panel of eight men, four women and two male alternates was sworn in by District Judge Gerald E. McAuliffe after only two days of jury interrogation.

In January, jury selection in the case consumed four

days before a mistrial was declared because a juror was found guilty of discussing the case contrary to court order.

Edward Carelli and Gil Alexander, deputy district attorneys, told the jury in an opening statement that the evidence would show that Lyle killed Byrd without provocation....

John Mueller and Dan Diamond, defence attorneys, are seeking acquittal on grounds that Lyle shot Byrd in self defence. Lyle has been jailed with no bail permitted since the slaying.

May 4, 1962
'Dying Man Took to Heels, Relates Slay Trial Witness'
Ronny Lyle shot Douglas Byrd three times and then chased him down the alley, a witness testified Friday in Denver District Count.

Benjamin Hall, 21, said he was sitting next to Byrd in the front seat of a pickup truck when Lyle pumped the bullets through the window.

Hall said he was not struck during the shooting May 16, 1961 in an alley between Franklin and Gilpin Sts. off E. 31st Ave.

Ironically, Hall was hit by a bullet a few months later in a fight with another man, unidentified. That wound caused amputation of his left leg and Hall hobbled to the witness stand Friday on crutches. Hall testified the shooting climaxed a continuing dispute that started with a fight at noon near Manual High School, over a girl he knew only as Lynn.

On cross-examination by Dan Diamond and John Mueller, defence attorneys, Hall admitted the pickup truck driven by Byrd attempted several times that day to 'curb' a Mercury sedan driven by Lyle. The cars finally met head-on in the alley.

Hall said there was no conversation before Lyle

came up to the truck and fired at Byrd. Although fatally wounded, Byrd got out of the truck and ran down the alley, with Lyle, a 6 foot 4 inch basketball player, in pursuit.

The stricken Byrd apparently outran the forward for the Boston All-Stars, because Lyle came back and said: 'You tell Flash (Byrd) that if I ever see him again I will kill him,' the witness testified. About 90 minutes after the shooting Byrd died of his wounds.

Larry Williams, 20 testified he was seated on the right of Hall in the truck's front seat and was struck in the back of the head by a bullet fired by someone. He identified Lyle as the man who shot Byrd, but he couldn't say if Lyle's gun inflicted his own wound.

Williams himself has been charged with assault to murder last fall in another case and is expected to receive a trial date next week.

Defence attorneys contend that Lyle fired in self defence and should be acquitted. Gill Alexander and Edward Carelli, deputy district attorneys, qualified the jury to return a possible death penalty.

May 6, 1962
'Murder Case Jurors Get Glimpse of Alley
Where Slaying Occurred'
Fourteen Denver District Court jurors Saturday went to an alley in northeast Denver to see where Douglas Byrd, 22, was shot three times on May 16, 1961.

The jury was transported by sheriff's officers to the scene where Ronny Lyle, 21, is charged with inflicting the fatal gunshot wounds as the climax to a bizarre gang fight.

Judge Gerald E. McAuliffe recessed the murder trial until Monday but authorized the jury trip to the alley between Franklin and Gilpin Sts. off E. 31st Ave.

Edward Carelli and Gil Alexander, deputy district

attorneys, are expected to conclude their case Monday with submission of a signed statement in which Lyle admitted shooting Byrd but claimed he did so as the victim was going to hit him.

John Mueller and Dan Diamond, defence counsel, are seeking acquittal on grounds of self defence.

The trial began last Monday and jurors were qualified to return a possible death penalty. Lyle, a 6 foot 4 basketball player, has been jailed with no bail permitted since the killing.

June 3, 1961
'One of Fifteen Children Is Guilty'
A 21-year-old Denver man described as 'an outstanding athlete who believes in fair play' was sentenced to the State Penitentiary Friday for 15 to 25 years for a killing he claimed was in self-defence.

Ronny Lyle, second oldest in a family of 15 children, received the penalty on a Denver District Court jury conviction for second degree murder.

A 6 foot 4 inch semi-pro basketball player, Lyle admitted pumping three bullets into Douglas Byrd, 22, to climax an afternoon-long gang fight in east Denver May 16, 1961.

Dan Diamond and John Mueller, defence attorneys, urged leniency on grounds that Lyle became involved in the fatal dispute only to protect a friend who was being abused.

They claimed Lyle obtained a gun only after Byrd threatened to kill him. The actual shooting occurred when Lyle thought Byrd was coming at him with a dangerous weapon, the lawyers said.

Report Made
Probation officers, in a report to Judge Gerald E. McAuliffee, described Byrd as a 'belligerent individual

who was quite prone to hit with any weapon available and could be counted upon to really bruise an opponent.' Lyle, on the other hand, normally had good habits and came from a family in which the father was a part-time minister, the report said.

Lyle was forward for a Denver basketball team called the Boston All-Stars and was planning a career in professional sports when arrested.

Judge McAuliffe said there were several factors working against Lyle as shown by the trial evidence.

Lyle failed to avoid a showdown with Byrd, refused to call police although allegedly 'in fear of his life,' and made a specific trip to borrow a gun over an uncle's objection just before the slaying, the judge said.

'The jury rejected your claim of self-defence,' McAulife said. 'You took the law into your own hands.'

The background report to the court showed that Lyle's mother expressed sorrow over the killing but accepted the trial result philosophically.

'Mrs. Lyle remarked that she hopes that some good will come out of all this - namely, that her other children will learn by the mistake Ronny made and will disassociate themselves from evil companions from now on,' the report said.

Defence counsel said there will be no appeal of the conviction. They said they would not risk a possible death penalty or life sentence in another trial.

RON says his vivid memory of May 16, 1961 begins to fade after the police arrive. He knows he and his friends spent many hours in the police station, but he doesn't remember exactly how long. He remembers being told they would all stay in jail until somebody confessed, but he doesn't remember when he decided to tell them he shot 'Flash' Byrd. He remembers being locked up, but he doesn't remember how long it was before a public defender showed up.

Ron seems surprised when reminded he spent more than a year in jail, first awaiting trial, then starting over when a mistrial was declared and finally waiting for the verdict, followed by the sentencing. It hardly registered that he would spend 15 to 25 years in prison. Mostly, he remembers his mother crying.

Dennis Nelson, who didn't know Ron back then, but who would eventually become a lifelong friend, says with conviction: 'I know Ron didn't pull the trigger, and I know that he would never roll over on a friend - never.'

Members of the family react to the sentence today the same way they did then. Kenny still can't believe it happened. His big brother, '....always loved, respected, admired, going to prison. How could that be?'

Sharon remembers her fear first of all - that her protection was gone. Sister Marilyn felt the same way. 'Without Ron, we knew we would now be meat to eat.'

Bill was most concerned about their mother. 'She was devastated. Ronny was close to her in a way none of the rest of us were.'

Donna was '...angry, hurt, disappointed, even disgusted, but mostly hurt. How could he do that to us?'

His family would eventually learn to cope with the loss of their favourite son, but the life Ronny Lyle had known was finished. He would leave his family and his friends to enter an environment worse than anything he could have imagined, but one which would also lead to his triumph.

6

*

Canon City

II

R ON tried to apply the lessons he had learned in Buena Vista to life in the State Penitentiary, but he lost his way almost immediately. Reform school rules are woefully inadequate for doing hard time. And Canon City was harder time than most.

Conditions in 'Old Max' were so appalling that as late as 1977 prisoner Fidel Ramos sued the state, charging that the Department of Corrections was inflicting cruel and unusual punishment on its inmates. A federal judge agreed, but too late for Ron Lyle and the hundreds of prisoners that served with him.

'*Ramos* was, without a doubt, the case that led to the modernisation of Colorado prisons,' says David Miller, former legal director of the Colorado ACLU. 'People forget that Old Max was a hellhole. Cells were 28 square feet, and people were locked down in them for long periods of time. Sewage came up the pipes. The food was often inedible. Violence was rampant. The stronger inmates really ran the prison.'[1]

During the time Ron was incarcerated, murders were so frequent as to seem commonplace to the inmates. The most gruesome method was fashioning a gas bomb and throwing it into a cell, burning the adversary alive.

Probably because of his size, Ron found himself constantly being challenged by inmates who bore no resemblance to the kids he knew in reform school. The majority of the prisoners were still black and *Chicano*, but the brotherhood between the races that had strengthened the friendships there did not exist in Canon City. He was as likely to be tripped or pushed by a black or *Chicano* guy as by a white. And he pushed back.

Within weeks of his arrival, Ron found himself locked up in solitary confinement for fighting. On subsequent occasions, he found himself in lock-down with all the other inmates for no other reason than as an 'administrative' measure. Prisoners were often kept in their cells between 22 and 23 hours a day without congregate dining, exercise, work opportunities or religious services, let alone reading material.

Nellie Lyle travelled to Canon City almost every week to visit her son, sometimes driven by Bill, other times taking the four-hour bus trip. On several occasions that first year, she arrived at the prison only to find that she couldn't see him because he was in solitary confinement or lock-down. She would wait for the return bus, hoping to see him when she took the trip again the next week.

Ron trusted no one, keeping to himself as much as he could. But when threatened, he always gave at least as much as he got. At one point, after a fight, he'd been stripped, thrown in quarantine and left there for 23 hours. Finally released to the yard, he wandered dazed, wondering if he was going crazy.

One of the old-timers walked right up to him and told

him he needed to follow three rules and he'd be okay: 'First, mind your own business.' So far, so good; Ron knew that rule from Buena Vista.

'Second, don't go into another man's cell, and third, don't steal anything from anybody.'

He followed those three rules all the time he stayed in Canon, but he got into trouble, anyway, because he wouldn't take guff from anybody. 'Don't stick a stake in a lion's den,' was Russ Perron's explanation of Ronny fighting other prisoners. 'Remember, he was pretty disillusioned.'

Disillusioned and bitter. Ron had no reason to believe he would spend less than 15 years in Canon, maybe up to 25. Life seemed over before it could begin. 'I was a troublemaker. For a long time I didn't know how to live there. In prison. It was the start of what lasted most of my life - trying to reconcile my Christian background with the code I learned in prison.'

That code was to fight back whenever he was threatened and never to squeal on anybody. Even though it got him in more and more trouble as the months wore on, the code was all he had to fall back on. Then Lt. Clifford Maddox entered his life.

Maddox served as part-time guard, part-time recreation director at Canon City. Physically unimposing, barely 5 feet 9 inches with glasses and a receding hairline, he nevertheless commanded respect from everyone in the prison, convicts and fellow guards alike. He had worked at Canon for 27 years, earning some leeway in his dealings with prisoners. One day he approached Ron Lyle in the yard and asked if he'd ever played on athletic teams.

'I told Maddox I had always been interested in sports, but could never make the teams in high school because of my grades. I told him I had played on a semi-pro basketball team, and he said that's where I should start then. He let me know that in prison, everything was up to me. I had to take the first step. So, after a while, I did.'

The relationship between convict and guard didn't go smoothly at first. Ron remembers Maddox trying to get him to open up and his own response, in effect: 'Man, you're a screw and I'm a convict. I came here by myself and I'll leave the same way.'

But the guard kept prodding and Ron kept going to practice, and before long, he was the mainstay of all three Canon City teams - basketball, football and baseball. His performance from the winter of 1962 through the fall of 1963 is part of the record. The first basketball season, he averaged 23 points a game. When baseball came around, he batted .400. And in the fall he routinely kicked 50-yard field-goals for the prison football team, the Rock Busters, while throwing touchdown passes, one for 70 yards. And it was the football team that brought Ron his first real friend in prison.

Ron had heard the name 'Doobie' Vigil ever since he had been in reform school, when some guys there said that when Vigil was in Buena Vista, he was the toughest guy there. Ron heard the same thing when he arrived at Canon, but he didn't meet 'Doobie' until he started playing football. Both 6 foot 3 inches and over 200 pounds, Ron and 'Doobie' were the most physically daunting members of the team, and the hard-hitting Latino reminded Ron of some of the guys back in the projects. Maybe it was a natural that the two started immediately to build a team alliance and a friendship that managed to survive not only incarceration but release many years later.

The Rock Busters with Ron Lyle and 'Doobie' Vigil did so well, they were invited to play an exhibition game against a semi-pro football team called the Colorado Colts. Former Colts player Gary Snyder remembers Ron Lyle on the field that day: 'We kidded around about playing the prison team at first, saying the referees should wear checks instead of stripes and that the police wouldn't let the wide receivers go long, but after the game started and we saw Ronny Lyle play, it was a different story. We won the game, but just barely, and afterward, everybody, including our team, voted him MVP.'

EVEN as athletics relieved the generally unrelenting pressure of prison life for Ron, the high point of each week continued to be his mother's visit. She never failed to tell him how much she believed in him and would always end their half-hour with a prayer.

When Bill took word of Ronny's prowess in the prison athletic programme back to the family, they started to hope things would get better for him, but Nellie never needed to hope - she had faith in her second oldest son.

Ron says he never has been 'saved,' at least not like Bill, who 'spoke in tongues' as he emerged from the holy water. 'But it didn't matter, you know? My mom had enough faith for both of us.' He adds: 'She made sure I believed, too. God knows I have never completely lost faith, not even in prison.' Athletics helped.

Nobody in Canon City, not even any of his team-mates, doubted that Ron Lyle was the best athlete among the 1400 convicts. And for the first time in his life, Ron started to believe that he was blessed with an exceptional physical ability. But he was still angry.

'Maddox constantly got on my back, even during a game. He used to sit behind the baseball backstop and tell everyone how lousy I was. It got to me at first. I mean, here I am, the best player on the field and he's making me look like a fool.'

But slowly, if reluctantly, Ron grew closer to Maddox, or at least more dependent on his programme. He remembers that the guard was 'not the kind who'll pat you on the back. Instead, he'll stay on you and try to get you to do that little bit extra. It worked for me, but only after he hassled me to death.'

During football season, Clifford Maddox would hold team meetings and Ron started to get the feeling the coach was talking directly to him as he urged the players to put out a little more. He threw out indirect messages and taunts during the games and Ron started to get it.

'One day Maddox had been on my back, and I told him he needed to respect me as a convict and I would respect him as an officer. I told him about my code and how I lived by it. I told him I could have brought six buddies with me, but I didn't squeal on anyone.'

Maddox mostly just listened, but Ron remembers that conversation as the first time they connected as two people, setting aside for just a little while their respective roles of player and coach, inmate and guard.

As the seasons wore on and basketball returned, there were other such moments. Ron knows now that they were beginning to understand each other and that Maddox was not only making him a better player but a better person. Whether influenced by the guard or his mother or a little of both, Ron started lending a helping hand to other inmates on occasion.

He remembers the day he noticed a young convict hiding in a corner of the gym, watching him shoot at the basket. He had seen the kid before, mostly hanging around alone, a couple of times taking guff from some of the inmates, probably because he looked so young. Ron had guessed he was still in his teens and had even thought about talking to the kid because he knew how tough it was to spend so much time alone but had decided against it. First rule, mind your own business.

But that morning, the kid looked so meek, standing back

in the shadows, that Ron nodded at him and got a shy smile in return. He went back to shooting lay-ups with what had become an exceptional ability to focus on the athletic task at hand, and he forgot the kid was there.

The next day the young convict was back in the gym when Ron arrived, sitting on the floor closer to the court this time. He gave a half wave when Ron walked over to the ball rack.

What the hell. 'Wanna learn how to play?'

'Sure.' The kid jumped to his feet with a big smile, and Ron lobbed the ball to him. The second real friendship Ron formed in prison began that day. He worked out with the kid every day they both had recreation privileges, and before long they were playing on the same team, even though the kid was on the bench as a back-up guard most of the time.

'He got out of the joint long before I did,' Ron remembers. 'But I'll never forget the letter I got one day while I was still in prison. It was from him. He said he had married, found a job and was going straight, and that I was his idol. Nobody ever told me that before. I had such a great feeling that I had helped somebody and he appreciated it.'

Ron never forgot that feeling. For the rest of his life, he has sought opportunities to help kids that need something from him. But he doesn't see himself or want others to see him as some kind do-gooder. 'I just never got tired of feeling appreciated, of being somebody's idol.'

RON had seen his first prison boxing match a few months after he arrived at Canon City, and Lt. Maddox had asked him if he wanted to be a part of the boxing programme, but he was just starting to get into the rhythm of playing on teams and wasn't particularly interested in the rigours of boxing - not then. Not until something happened that once again turned his world wrong-side-out.

7

*

A little over a year after Ron entered prison, he still found it difficult to confide in anyone. He had begun to appreciate Maddox in the same way the kid he mentored in basketball appreciated him, but he couldn't bring himself to trust the men at Canon. Except for 'Doobie,' even his team-mates were suspect, because anybody could be bribed or paid off by anybody else in prison, inmate or guard. After practice, he kept to himself as much as possible. It was worse after he had gained some success during athletic contests, as several of the inmates took to pestering him, sometimes during meals and sometimes in the yard.

'Some days it seemed that everybody in prison was mean,' Ron said years later. 'At least in the beginning, it felt that way.'

One guy in particular was on his back almost every day, and Ron kept shoving him away. He didn't want fighting to get him back in the hole. Finally, one morning at breakfast, the guy challenged him to meet in the laundry room, and Ron, sick of the confrontations and knowing his own superior strength, took him up on the dare.

They had barely squared off when the guy pulled a homemade shiv out of his pants and shoved it to the hilt into Ron's abdomen. The tip of the knife pierced an artery near his spine, and by the time the guards got him into the hospital wing, he had bled out a dangerous quantity of blood.

The doctors took him into surgery just before ten o'clock, labouring to find the artery and stop the bleeding. When they rolled him out seven-and-a-half hours later, Ron Lyle had received 35 pints of blood in transfusions and had twice been declared clinically dead. His death certificate had been signed.

Years later, asked if he survived the stabbing in prison because of his physical strength and 'hard-nosed attitude,' Ron smiled and shook his head. 'I survived because my mother saved me.' He said that when he woke up after surgery, the first thing he remembered was '....sliding down a long tube. Then my mother reached down and pulled me back. That's why I'm alive. She wanted me to live.'

The devastating prison assault turned out to be the defining moment in Ron Lyle's life, not only because he learned to believe in his mother's power to save him. Two other extraordinary events pointed him in the direction the rest of his life would take. It started with his first visitors.

When he fully awakened the next morning, he opened his eyes to his mother holding his left hand and on his right, Lt. Clifford Maddox, bending over him and asking how he felt. It wasn't until Maddox began to cry that Ron knew the old guard cared about him. 'He didn't have to come to the hospital and see me. After all, Maddox had been depending on me for the baseball team, and I knew I had let him down again, just like other times before.'

Ron finds it difficult to describe how that visit made such a change in his outlook on life. 'They were both there together, my mother and Clifford Maddox, both caring about me. I knew then that Maddox was a good man, and I figured there had to be other good people out there, too. I started to believe that day, not only in my mother's faith, but in the decency of others.'

And then there was the dream.

Vivid dreams in the Lyle family were often seen as visions, messages from God, and beginning with William dreaming of building a church near the mountains, life decisions were sometimes made based on those dreams.

Ron's vision happened while he was still in the hospital. He had barely closed his eyes one night before he found himself in a vivid dream, fighting for the heavyweight boxing championship of the world. When he woke up he remembered every round, every punch.

For years after his boxing career was over, Ron would tell about that dream - how he fought for the title, how he didn't know his opponent, but how the fight he eventually had with Muhammad Ali was exactly the fight he had dreamed about. In the dream he knew he had all the punches and could put them together in a series. He remembered a hard jab to the head, a right uppercut and a left hook to the body. He just didn't know how the fight ended.

With that vision Ron Lyle began to dream of becoming the heavyweight champion of the world. Every day he lay in the hospital, he became more and more convinced that boxing was the path chosen for him, the way to redeem himself in the eyes of his mother. Then he remembered the white prison guard who was wearing a badge when he bent over the hospital bed, his face filled with concern, the second thing Ron saw when he awakened in the hospital. And he knew how he was going to live his dream.

When Maddox had talked to him a couple of times before about joining the boxing team, Ron had been far more interested in improving his team skills, especially in basketball. But after the stabbing and the dream, he knew what he wanted, not only in athletics, but in life.

'I had a lot of time to think and I wanted something out of life better than I had up to this time.....I wanted a way to beat the system that society puts on you when a con gets out of the pen.'

That way would be professional boxing. But he had a very long way to go.

8

*

Pastor Sharon sums up her brother Ron's experiences by quoting *Proverbs 24:16*, 'A good man will fall seven times and get back up,' then adds her own wisdom: 'Each time he gets back up, he'll be stronger.' And so it seemed in the fall of 1963.

First he had to achieve full recovery from a near fatal injury. Then, after weeks of hospitalisation, unbelievably, he was placed back in solitary confinement as punishment for the fight that could have killed him. After 90 days in the hole, he was sent to the rock gang on the hill above the prison for another 90 days because an officer thought he had instigated the fight by going to the laundry room. But Ron doesn't make much of all that. He remembers spending his time in the hole with the exercise regimen Clifford Maddox had assigned, doubling, tripling and quadrupling the numbers until he was doing 1000 push-ups an hour, one every 3.6 seconds. Long after his professional boxing years were behind him, he would continue to demonstrate that incredible feat.

Off the Ropes

Maddox had told him that boxers have to be in better shape than any other athlete, and that in order to get there, he had to work harder than he'd ever worked in his life. And so he did; most of his waking time during the locked-in 23-hour days was spent in gaining strength and stamina. But because he could do little more than stretch out his body the length of the cell, he limited his initial workouts to mostly push-ups, sit-ups and running on the spot.

Ron Lyle learned more lessons and passed more tests during the rest of his prison years, but it was in that last term of solitary confinement that he developed both the desire to reach a maximum level of physical fitness and the self-discipline it takes to get there.

When Ron entered Canon City, Sonny Liston was World Boxing Association heavyweight champion, but by the time he got out of solitary confinement in 1964, a young Cassius Clay, remembered vaguely by Lyle as the Rome Olympics light heavyweight champ, had won the title. It was time to get to work - to go after the dream.

Lyle started, not by sparring, but by getting into the best shape of his life. He invented his regimen from a variety of sources, mainly from Maddox and from a couple of inmates who had boxed pro for a time. He also did his own research.

'I would read *Ring* magazine from cover to cover every month and try to pick up ideas by reading about the top-ranked fighters. I never tried to copy their styles because I fight my own way, but I did pick up some good training tips.'

Whenever Maddox could get him permission, he watched bouts on television, always thinking he could do better than what he saw on the screen. And when he knew he was ready, he started working out in the ring. Before long he had mastered the basic skills, and Maddox set him up in his first fight.

Lyle did not make a very auspicious debut behind prison walls, losing to a fellow inmate by the name of 'Texas' Johnson, but as he continued to do for the rest of his life, he learned by his mistakes. He beat Johnson soundly in a rematch and didn't lose to another inmate again.

Maddox had never seen anyone work as hard as Lyle. The ever-more promising fighter worked out on bags in the gym when Maddox could get him in, ran whenever he was in the prison yard, and continued his daily 1000 push-ups an hour, discovering in the process his own rhythm, which he would later describe to newscaster Peter Boyles as 'budda boom, budda bing.'

Before long Ronny Lyle was considered the scourge of Canon City, and it got so that nobody within the walls would take him on. Maddox had to bring in boxers from the outside, mainly from Fort Carson Army Base, 30 miles way.

Jimmy Farrell fought middleweight on that Army team and remembers the first time they travelled to Canyon City. 'Our heavyweight was a highly regarded boxer named Howard Smith who went on to become ranked professionally. We were surprised this convict could beat him so easily. That was the first time I ever saw Ronny Lyle.' Ron won every one of the frequently scheduled bouts against the Ft. Carson team, and his reputation, along with that of the Canon City Rock Busters team grew, reaching Denver and the notable boxing supporters in that city.

By the summer of 1966 Ron had used up almost every conceivable opponent, and Maddox was looking to Denver and the Rocks, an amateur boxing team that had just become a charter member of the now-defunct International Boxing League. He contacted the club's owner Bill Daniels, a prophetic move as it turned out.

Daniels was a cable television magnate, enormously wealthy and an avid sports fan. He had been the undefeated

Golden Gloves champion of New Mexico, but he had also invested in automobile racing and an American Basketball team, the Los Angeles Stars, which he later moved to Utah. He served as president of the A.B.A. and was a founder of the United States Football League. Daniels was one of the first cable owners to focus on sports programming, a pioneer in what is now a highly popular medium.

Beyond all that, Daniels was a war hero and a humanitarian. In World War II and the Korean War he was a naval fighter pilot, serving for a time as the Commander of the Blue Angels. Later he helped found Cenikor, a non-profit rehabilitation centre for drug addicts, alcoholics and people with criminal behaviour problems. He donated his $7 million mansion, Cableland, to Denver so the city would have an official mayoral residence.

In 1966, Ron could barely hope to be released from prison in time to develop a professional career, and was dependent on whatever good boxers Maddox could scare up. That year, it wasn't to be the Denver Rocks top heavyweight.

Dennis Nelson, who was training his brother, the Rocks light heavyweight Donny Nelson, remembers that Barnell Stidham, their best heavyweight, refused to box the formidable Lyle. 'Ronny scared the you-know-what out of him,' Dennis says. 'He was that good. In fact, the first time my dad and I saw him box, he told me we had just seen the next heavyweight champion of the world, but neither of us could figure out how a 25-year-old guy with at least 11 more years to serve in prison could even get a chance to try.' The answer was Bill Daniels.

As an expression of his belief in Cenikor and its dedication to the rehabilitation of convicts, Daniels frequently visited the Colorado State Penitentiary. It was on one of those visits that he first heard of Ron Lyle, and he arranged for his next Canon City trip to coincide with one of his bouts.

From the first time he saw Ron Lyle box, Daniels wanted to help the young convict. He began almost at once to exert his considerable political influence throughout the state in hopes of winning Lyle parole. But even for Bill Daniels, it wasn't going to be easy.

He managed to obtain a parole hearing in 1967, but Ron's devotion to his dream of a professional boxing career was a major stumbling block. In spite of positive testimony from Maddox and others, the parole board turned him down; members were not accustomed to releasing prisoners to become professional boxers.

'I went to the parole board, and they sent me back for a year, two years,' Ron says. 'They said boxing's not a parole plan. The head of the parole board said he didn't think I could fight my way out of a wet bag. They didn't think I'd make it. I told them that this is what I'm going to do when I get out. They said: "Prove it to us."'

Ron didn't get angry. And he didn't give up. He just kept working, sparring and getting fights when he could. Maddox kept after him, prodding him to work harder, squeezing the best out of him. And they both kept learning - the art of defence, the combination punches, the rhythm. Ron got better and better. And because Bill Daniels and Clifford Maddox believed in him, he started to believe in himself - that boxing would give him a second chance at life.

Ron grapples with the difference between street-fighting and boxing. 'In high school, boxing didn't interest me much, mainly because I was always having to fight my way out of a lot of after-school scraps. When I had to fight, I didn't enjoy it,' Lyle said in an interview. And the fights he had behind bars, 'personal squabbles,' he called them, had been a continuation of his life on the streets, only more meaningless and disheartening. Boxing was different. It not only became the controlling force of his life in prison, it continued to guide his life long after he was released.

After he had entered the professional arena years later, he told a reporter: 'Fighting is something that I need, an individual competitiveness, the supreme battle of man against man. Whatever it is, I need boxing, because in prison it gave me the will and determination to constantly better myself during the times when it was rough.'

Ron also remembers 1967 and 1968 as a time for focusing on what he had learned was most important: 'My father tried to teach me things I couldn't understand at the time. In prison I started to know what he was trying to do. I learned how important self-discipline is. And my mother taught me how to believe God was there with me in prison. I had to have faith. You lose faith; you lose hope.'

The hardest lesson for Ron Lyle was learning respect: 'Respect was something that took me a long time to get used to. In fact, I think the first person I ever respected outside of my family was Lt. Maddox. He changed my entire outlook. And he didn't do it by conning me - he did it by respecting me as a person. To him, I wasn't another prison number. I didn't always keep my nose clean, even then. But all the time I was in the joint, he never once asked me about another convict. He kept me out of trouble a lot of times that he could have just as easily put me in the hole. He treated me fairly.'

Some years later, Clifford Maddox was quoted as saying: 'I don't like to take any credit for what happened, but Ron turned into a real gentleman.'

9

*

ife moves on, even for families with a loved one in prison. While his mother did all she could to lift Ron's spirits during her weekly visits, and his sister Joyce wrote letters of encouragement, he found it more and more difficult to be away from the Lyle home during the years of so much change.

He had missed Bill going off to college at the University of Denver in 1961 to study accounting and business administration, Michael joining the Army in 1963 and being assigned to Bravo Company, Kenneth being hospitalised in 1964 with what is now recognised as bipolar disorder. The worst was in 1966 when Michael was killed in Vietnam.

Maybe because Michael Lyle was considered a war hero, or maybe because his brother Ron was starting to gain the respect of the prison powers-that-be, Deputy Warden Fred Wyse made it possible for Ron to go to his younger brother's funeral, an unusual privilege in those days.

Ron remembers being driven by the Fremont County

Sheriff himself from Canon City straight to the Denver City jail, where he was kept overnight. He was driven to the funeral the next day, and his handcuffs were removed before he stepped into the temporary company of his family and Michael's friends, but he wasn't allowed to socialise. Right after the service, he was delivered straight back to Canon City and incarceration.

WEDDINGS and new babies, trade schools and jobs kept happening to the Lyle family, faster than Ron could keep track. Sharon was married in 1967, and Raymond earned a scholarship to Colorado State University while their beloved big brother Ronny continued to be locked up every night.

Boxing kept him going. But even as he trained, sparred, knocked out the opponents Maddox could muster, that world, too, was changing.

After Cassius Clay beat Liston in early 1964, an immediate rematch was set, a violation of W.B.A. rules, and in June that organisation withdrew its recognition of Clay, who had changed his name to Muhammad Ali as part of his conversion to Islam. The World Boxing Council continued to recognise Ali as champion until he refused to go into the United States Army subsequent to being drafted for Vietnam in early 1967, at which point all sanctioning bodies withdrew recognition. So, in 1968, Joe Frazier, champion of the WBC, and Jimmy Ellis, recognised by WBA, became the guys to beat.

Ron read articles about Angelo Dundee, Ali's trainer, in *Ring* magazine and decided to write him a letter. To his amazement, Dundee not only wrote back, but encouraged Ron not to lose hope. He answered some of Ron's basic questions about training and offered to meet with him whenever he was released. Dundee's letter was just one more reason to keep going - another person to trust. The trainer did, in fact, have a number of conversations with Ron in the years following that letter - another promise fulfilled. Ron remembers Dundee this way: 'He really held the door open for me on the professional end. He's a very special person. I love him. He's a good man.'

By late 1968, Ron began to believe that he would be released. The faith Nellie had instilled in him took hold, and he told Lt. Maddox that he knew that he was meant to go to prison, to pass the tests, to learn the lessons, but that the time had come to live the dream.

Ron is quoted by Stephen Brunt in his book, *Facing Ali*, thus:

> Having the misfortune to be incarcerated, it taught me patience, but it also taught me how to look ahead, to plan ahead and to be able to see the dream when it appears. If I don't pursue it, I miss the boat. That's the way I approached it.... I think that's the route that God intended me to travel. He's the one that gave me the dream, so obviously that was the route. I had to follow the route. And I did.[2]

All his life, Ron Lyle has tried not to express regrets. Even today, when asked what would be one thing he could go back and do differently, he says: 'Nothing. I live it as it comes. Whatever the reason I was in prison, I accepted it as God's way of making me prove myself.' He adds with a smile: 'The situation didn't allow for a lot of control. If you want to live, you learn to accept.'

Ron probably could have been paroled earlier if he had told the parole board he would take one of the low-paying jobs offered to him by some members of his growing fan base in Denver, but as he later described it to a reporter: 'I was firmly convinced that I could succeed as a pro boxer and I wasn't going to lie to them.'

Finally, in November 1969, Bill Daniels provided the parole board with the assurance they required. He testified that he would guarantee Ron Lyle a regular job as a welder with a firm he owned while the parolee worked on his boxing career.

On Saturday, November 22, 1969 Ron Lyle was paroled from Colorado State Penitentiary in Canon City. The day he left prison, he followed the advice of an old bank robber named Tom Johnson, who told him to never look back. 'Even on the bus, I never turned around to look at the place where I had been for so long.' He never dreamed he would return to Canon City again and again in the years to come.

Ron Lyle had served seven-and-a-half years behind bars. He was two months away from his 29th birthday, the peak age for most professional boxers, and he had yet to pay his dues as an amateur.

10

*

Denver Rocks

III

SHORTLY before Ron was released from prison, his parents purchased a six-bedroom house on Hudson Street in Park Hill, about three miles east of the Curtis Park projects. Everybody in the family had contributed to the down payment, including Ron, who put in all the money he had inherited from being named a beneficiary, along with his mother, on his brother Michael's Army life insurance policy.

After a separation of seven-and-a-half years, Ron gratefully moved back in with his family. The house was one of the largest in the neighbourhood and provided plenty of room for the Lyles, comparatively speaking. Only ten children were left at home, including toddler Karen, the last of Nellie and William's nineteen children. A step up from the projects, Park Hill had wide, tree-lined streets with an assortment of mostly wooden bungalows topped off by gently pitched gable roofs.

The year before, Denver had experienced its own version of the race riots consuming larger cities. Skirmishes between black youths and police in Five Points had spread to Park Hill, where an 18-year-old was shot by police in a shopping centre. Within a few months both black and white activists in the predominantly black neighbourhood agreed to join forces to fight segregation, and the white membership of the Park Hill Action Committee merged with the black dominated Northeast Park Hill Civic Association to form the Greater Park Hill Community, Inc. Again the Lyles found themselves living in a mixed, generally harmonious community.

The volatile sixties had appeared and reached their peak while Ron was locked away. John F. Kennedy had been assassinated; the Vietnam War had begun and was still raging, as were war protesters on the streets and college campuses. Malcolm X had become the national minister of the Nation of Islam and a champion of African American black separatism and pride. In 1963, more than 200,000 people had marched on Washington D.C., the largest civil rights demonstration ever and had heard Martin Luther King, Jr. give his 'I Have a Dream' speech, but the brutality continued as four African American girls were killed in the bombing of the Sixteenth Street Baptist Church in Birmingham, Alabama. In 1964, President Lyndon Johnson had signed the Civil Rights Act, and Dr. King had been awarded the Nobel Peace Prize.

Ron didn't fully realise his frustration at being left out of the greatest civil rights movement in history until he heard how the family had reacted to events - the march led by Dr. King from Selma to Montgomery, the assassination of Malcolm X, the passage of the Voting Rights Act in 1965, the race riots in Watts, Stokely Carmichael, Hewy Newton, Bobby Seales. Black power. But the Lyles' involvement in the struggle followed their own tradition, paralleling that of the Reverend Martin Luther King. Nellie led the way, reminding family and neighbours that God wants us to show love and respect for people of all colour.

The assassination of Dr. King in 1968 had somehow stoked the fire that raged within Ron Lyle to live his own dream. Still in prison, but convinced he would soon be paroled, he vowed to represent not only his family but his race with honour. When asked not long ago what he remembered as the high point of his professional life, he answered without hesitation: 'The highest point of my life boxing was when I was an amateur. I was representing the United States Boxing Team on the amateur tour in Yugoslavia - Belgrade. They played the National Anthem and I was standing proud in the ring. I was representing my race and my country and all the convicts left alone in prison.' He added: 'That's when I knew I belonged there.'

Dr. King also influenced Ron in his vow to stay clean. The 'juvenile delinquent,' the young man convicted of murder, has never, for the rest of his life, taken a drink ('not even a beer'), has never done drugs, has never smoked a cigarette. When asked how he managed to avoid all those temptations, he answers: 'I needed my body to carry me where I wanted to go.' Then he adds with a smile: 'And, besides, my mother didn't want me to.'

The afternoon Ron was paroled from prison, he appeared at the Denver Elks Gymnasium and made it official; he told Bill Daniels he wanted a spot as heavyweight on the Denver Rocks boxing team. Donny Nelson, the Rocks' light heavyweight, was training that day with his father Albert and brother Dennis in attendance. Dennis remembers his father predicting not only that Ron would bring greatness upon himself, but that in the process, he would elevate the Rocks to prominence in the U.S. boxing world.

Featherweight Abby Espinoza was at the Elks that first

day, too. Eight years younger, Abby considered himself in good shape, but he had never seen anybody as 'chiselled' as Ron Lyle. 'My dad Joe Espinoza was a good friend of our coach Joe Garcia,' Abby says. 'We all watched Ronny work out every day, and I told my Dad he would be the next champion of the world. I believed that.'

It only took a week for Ron Lyle to replace Barnell Stidham, the team heavyweight who had refused to fight him in Canon City. As the Nelsons and the Espinozas watched Ron unequivocally knock out Stidham in an early round, Donny remembers: 'My Dad asked me how I would like to fight Ronny and I told him "not at all."'

Less than a month after being paroled, on December 19, Ron made his amateur debut in Denver against Fred Houpe of the Chicago Clippers, knocking him out in the third round. That match was only the third league fight for the Rocks, who had met the Clippers in Chicago two weeks before when Houpe had knocked out Stidham. Ron was elated. His boxing career had begun with a powerful punch, and the Rocks were on the map, a force to be reckoned with.

A month later he was in Louisville, Kentucky, his first trip out of Colorado since his freight-hopping days. He lost a decision to Tommie Garrett on a split decision, and his coaches Joe Garcia and Art Irlando put him through even harder paces when he returned to Denver. By now he was running through the streets at five every morning, followed by sit-ups and push-ups before he reported to his welding job. In the afternoon he punched bags, did footwork and sparred with whatever boxers his coaches could nail down; more often than not, those sparring matches were with Donny Nelson.

Donny remembers Lyle as incredibly focused, unlikely to participate in the small talk and kidding that floated around the gym. 'In a way, he was kind of hard to get to know,'

Donny remembers. 'He had his work to do and he just did it.'

Jimmy Farrell, released from the Army about the same time Ron had been paroled, had also joined the Denver Rocks. He remembers how hard Ron worked: 'He was more driven than the rest of us. In fact, I've never seen anyone train so hard.'

Ron says: 'I was a loner in those days. I stayed away from old friends in the neighbourhood, because I knew I had to keep my parole. Meeting the Nelsons was good for me. Alfred kind of reminded me of Lt. Maddox, another white guy who seemed to just accept who I was. And gradually, I came to trust Dennis and Donny, too, then some of the other guys, like Abby Espinoza and Jimmy Farrell.'

Ron was always conscious of the time he had to make up, and he took every fight that came along, partly to build his reputation, partly to fill in the gaps - to learn what he didn't know.

On January 21 and February 7 he knocked out his next two opponents in rounds two and three respectively, then travelled to St. Louis, where he met one Joe Brown. The Rocks had been losing ground, in spite of Ron's wins, and the St. Louis match was seen as a 'must win' in order to retake the IBL Western Division second-place spot. Donny Nelson had unleashed a furious last-ditch effort in the third round of a tough fight, winning by points and bringing the team to within two points of victory.

Ron climbed into the ring, knowing he had to score at least a unanimous decision if the Rocks were to win. As recorded by Mike Hayes, *Denver Post* sportswriter:

> Fifty-five seconds later, a crowd of 1,622 roared as the Denver anchor man caught Joe Brown with a stunning short right which sent him sprawling to the

mat for the ten count, and the Rocks had a come-from-behind 39-31 International Boxing League victory.

Not only had he kept his winning streaking going, he had consciously contributed to the team he had started to love. From that point on, Ron became a real team member and the soul of the Denver boxing community.

Barney O'Grady, a Colorado State University student, symbolised the devotion of hometown fans early in Ron's amateur career by beginning a series of Ron Lyle scrapbooks he would update for the next 35 years. Barney even went back into *Rocky Mountain News* and *Denver Post* archives to complete the record.

Ron's reputation was also beginning to expand beyond die-hard fight fans. The story of how he had started boxing in prison had been written a couple of times in the *Denver Post* and *Rocky Mountain News*, and after the Joe Brown fight, his name started to become a familiar item on local sports radio and television. Somehow this hometown boy making good after doing hard time began to capture the imagination and the hearts of the Denver public. That year marked the beginning of the lifelong affection between Ron Lyle and his hometown.

DANIELS paid his boxer above minimum wage for what was essentially part-time work as a welder, and Ron gave most of his earnings to his family. The girls, especially, remember how he slipped right back into the role of their protector and provider, which lasted for the next decade.

'I didn't get off the hook, just because I was so much younger,' Karen remembers. 'Years later, Ronny wouldn't let any boy near me, either.' She laughs. 'Even when I was only 12 years old. But he was also big-hearted.'

She remembers one late summer when he took her for

the first of a series of back-to-school shopping trips and bought her a leather jacket. 'I still remember that jacket. It was the nicest thing I had ever owned.'

Ron shrugs off his generosity. 'I was just doing what all my brothers and sisters did, giving back to my family. Everybody gave what they could.'

Mark remembers how his big brother Ronny taught him to fight. 'It wasn't fun,' he says. 'I was about 13 and our brother Gerry was 15. Ron made us stand up and fight - so we could learn to protect ourselves. I was the quiet one and Gerry was pretty aggressive. One day he beat the pants off me. I had a bloody nose, but I learned how to fight.' Ron chimes in, laughing: 'He sure did.'

On some days Ron missed his old friends, but even then knew it was a good thing that his family had moved from the projects and taken him away from temptation. Roy Tyler was off to parts unknown, and the Curtis Park neighbourhood was just far enough away that he didn't run into the other guys. It was easier to stick with his family and the guys from the gym.

He did stop in to see Russell Perron one day in early winter. Ron was proud of the friend who had accomplished so much, finishing college, teaching P.E. part-time at two local community colleges and running two karate schools in East Denver. He had won the U.S. Open Karate Championship in 1969 and had even taught a few moves to Sonny Liston, which especially impressed Ron. The two vowed to stay in touch.

Ron also met and start dating a girl named Sarah early in 1970, but didn't get serious. In fact, today he can't even remember her last name, only that she was a nice girl, but that he had too much work to do in the ring. His intense relationships with women would be put off until later. First he had to make good in the amateur ring, and he was a long way from where he wanted to be.

Off the Ropes

Dennis Nelson says that Ron has always been a boxer-puncher whose greatest strength was defence, but in early 1970, he depended on his ability to move in fast, catch his opponent off-guard and hit him hard enough to keep him down for the count. That strategy worked through February with three first-round knockouts, one to capture the Colorado Golden Gloves championship, the other two against Charles Schollmeyer and Charles Bank in Salt Lake City to win the Regional Golden Gloves. From there, it was a short jump to Las Vegas and the National Golden Gloves Championship tournament.

The *Denver Post* reported that: 'Lyle set up his first opponent with three quick jabs and finished [Lerdy] Sargent with a right and left hook combination.' With that fight, Denver boxing fans, along with the local press, moved from sitting up and taking notice to becoming an informal travelling booster club.

After watching their local guy perform his fourth consecutive first-round knockout in the opening round of the tournament, sportswriters now called him the favourite for the national heavyweight title, and a contingent of Denver fans arrived in time to watch him run his string of successive knockouts to seven straight with his next opponent in the tournament, Kit Boursse of Las Vegas.

He won his third bout by a decision, taking him to the semi-finals, where the bubble finally burst when he lost a split decision to Billy Thompson of Chicago. The National Golden Gloves would turn out to be the only major amateur title that would elude Ron Lyle, but the Denver fans didn't miss a beat. From that point on, steadily gaining in number, they followed Ron Lyle's boxing career through to the end.

11

*

IT generally takes a long time to train a boxer - some say four years, others ten. And any fighter who wants to be a serious contender needs to be ranked by his late twenties or he doesn't have a chance. That was the conventional wisdom in 1970 and it continues to prevail today.

Ron Lyle trained himself inside prison walls from 1964 to 1969, and many of his moves crossed over into the real world, but others had to be discarded, replaced by more effective combinations. As for his age, his Denver Rocks coach Joe Garcia, himself a former professional boxer in the bantamweight division, called Lyle: '....the greatest I've ever seen at this stage and he's proving it. Ron's got the stuff to be a pro champion and I don't think his age [29] will be a handicap to him at all.'

And so he moved on, winning three of his next four bouts, the first of which caught the attention of Denver sportswriter Jim Graham. In his regular column 'Keeping Posted,' Graham admitted to being slow at recognising the excitement of the Rocks led by Ron Lyle. 'You know that old saw about you don't know what you're missing. I found out Friday night - the Denver Rocks.' He went on to call Lyle a 'sensational heavyweight... awfully crude, but his punch has the kick of a triple vodka.'

Two days after his loss to Billy Thompson in Las Vegas, Lyle arrived in New York to face Louis Jimenez in his fourth I.B.L. bout, and Graham had gone along for the ride: 'Lyle rocked Louis Jimenez of the New York Jolts to dreamland with a thundering left hook-right cross combination to score his fourth International Boxing League victory of the season.' Graham suggested that even though 'Ronny is a little old to be getting started as a pro ....punchers can begin later.....Rocky Marciano was 25 before he started pro fighting in earnest.' He neglected to mention that Ron was 29 at the time and at least a year away from professional status. Nevertheless, Graham invited his mainstream sports audience to get on the bandwagon. 'There's no doubt about it. Denver likes what it sees at the Rocks' bouts. Home attendance this season for four shows totals about 25,000.' And that column brought in even more fans.

Ron attributes his years in prison as the factor which allowed him to reach his peak so much later than other boxers. 'I had to stay clean there - no bad habits, including women. It kept me younger.' Whatever the reason, Ron Lyle stayed in magnificent condition throughout the next ten years and way beyond.

The elder Lyles were never among the spectators at his bouts. A newspaper article quoted Ron at the time: '"Dad is a minister, so naturally he doesn't believe in boxing. But he knows I'm happy, so he's happy for me. Mothers are all alike and mom worries about me. She keeps warning me about getting hit on the nose," he said, laughing.'

But Ron getting hit was not a laughing matter for Bill

Daniels. While appreciative of the fact that his star fighter had turned into a tremendous defensive boxer who could 'roll with the punches,' he was concerned that Lyle had yet to be 'clipped,' and that nobody yet knew if he could take a punch. And nobody *would* know, at least during his amateur career.

It was about that time that two professional sports franchises put out feelers - the Denver Broncos invited Ron to a walk-on try-out for any number of positions, and the Astros encouraged him to try out for catcher in Houston. But Ron had already made his decision; for better or worse, his destiny lay with boxing.

His personal life was beginning to settle down, too. He had met a good-looking young woman at his parent's church a few months before, and within a few weeks, they had moved together to a small apartment not far from the house on Hudson Street. For the first time in his life, Ron had a place of his own and a woman he cared about. Nadine Spencer was younger than Ron and relatively inexperienced, but she seemed to adapt to the singular world of boxing. For a while, at least.

In the meantime, the pace continued to pick up. In four months Ron had fought 15 times, winning 12, eight by knockouts, and in April, it was time to prove himself at the National Amateur Athletic Union Championships in Trenton, New Jersey. Breezing through, he blistered three fighters in three days, two by knockouts, before capturing the national crown with a decision over Joe Frazier's sparring partner, previously unbeaten Mike Montgomery of Philadelphia. Ronny Lyle had reached the zenith of American amateur boxing in less than five months, and it was time to go international.

In May the National A.A.U. Executive Director Donald Hull announced that Ron Lyle of the Denver Rocks had been selected to represent the United States in the North

American Boxing Championships in Vancouver on the 27th and would also represent the U.S. team in Italy a month later and in subsequent matches in Yugoslavia and Romania. Ron started training at the U.S. Military Academy at West Point, New York, for the first of his international matches. The guy from the projects, fresh out of prison, was beginning to attract serious national attention.

During the five months leading up to his international debut, Ronny managed to spend almost all of his spare time with both his families. Nadine was already pregnant, and it was understood that Nellie expected Ron to marry her. He promptly did, in a quiet ceremony, after which he fell into the same pattern as most expectant fathers did in those days - he became exceedingly solicitous. He discouraged Nadine from any physical activity, picking up most of the household chores.

Marilyn also remembers his continuing commitment to the dream that year. 'He was incredibly focused on that goal, winning the heavyweight title, and he worked so hard. Ronny was a motivator. He was always talking about how you have to work for anything you want. He would say, "If something comes easy, the goal isn't high enough."

'Later on, it was Ronny's encouragement that led me to try out for the track team in my junior year at Manual High School. And I made it, too. I was really good at the 100-yard hurdles. That was because of Ronny.'

Ron always attributes his work ethic to his parents' influence, but Marilyn says he went way beyond their example. 'He worked even harder than dad, and he was so focused,' she repeats. 'He motivated all of us.' She cites the athletic success of her son Phillip, who won third in the National Junior Olympics 100m dash when he was 12 years old as an example of his uncle Ron's tradition and motivation.

At the gym, he had the Nelsons. Albert, who was a tile

setter for Coors Brewery, managed to get to the Elks after work every day to encourage his son Donny, and he began to watch out for Ronny Lyle as well. Early on, he had started what would turn out to be the regular routine of taking his 'boys,' Donny and Ronny, out to a steak dinner at the Frontier before every bout.

Ron grew ever closer to Albert, who had begun to stand in for Clifford Maddox as another white guy who could be trusted without reservation. The elder Nelson had a significant impact on the young man who had already begun to change - the world Ronny Lyle had long perceived as treacherous was starting to feel safe.

But it was his friendship with Dennis Nelson that would prove to be the most enduring. Dennis had boxed two years before, but was forced to quit the ring after a devastating head injury from a lead pipe in a street fight with three boot camp Marines. After he recovered, he had immediately begun helping his brother Donny, who held on in the ring for years, eventually winning the WAA heavyweight title in 1973.

After Ron Lyle showed up at the Elks 'Punchbowl' in December of '69, Dennis started spending even more time with his dad at the gym, picking up training tips and supporting not only his brother, but also Ronny during workouts and sparring. He became what a Denver sportscaster called, '...one hell of a trainer,' and continued to serve in Ron Lyle's corner during all the ensuing good years and bad. In 1970, Dennis was still learning while Ron continued to advance.

Abby Espinoza still thinks of Dennis Nelson and Ronny Lyle as the two nicest people he has ever known. 'I don't really get close to people,' he says, 'but those two felt like friends from the beginning and still do.'

On June 4, boxing for the United States, Ron Lyle of the Denver Rocks won the North American Heavyweight

Championship in a unanimous decision over Canadian Jack Meda in Vancouver, British Columbia. It was after that fight, Ron remembers, that he knew without a doubt he would reach the summit - he would fight for the heavyweight championship.

Ron's friendship with the Nelsons continued to deepen, even when Donny moved into the heavyweight class and found himself unable to compete with Ron for the upcoming International Boxing League championships. He failed to shed enough weight to qualify in the light heavyweight class and so joined his dad and Dennis in Ron's corner.

The bouts were held in Denver in recognition of the enormous strides the Rocks, led by Ron Lyle, had made over the preceding few months. The IBL provided an opportunity for Ron to make up for his loss of the Golden Gloves championship in March, and he was anxious to prove himself. No problem. He beat Billy Freeman of Kentucky in the semi-finals, then completely dominated Jasper Evans of New York for the championship.

It is a measure of Ron's friendship with the Nelsons that he also remembers watching Donny that night beat St. Louis' Ronny Miller, an 8-2 decision in a thrilling, if brutal, exhibition match. Both Denver fighters received standing ovations and both took pride in each other's performance.

In just six months, Ron Lyle had fought 22 times, losing only three bouts, and he now held the International Boxing League heavyweight championship, the USA national heavyweight championship and the North American heavyweight championship. Not only had Ronny found his stride, he felt himself moving closer and closer to fulfilling the dream, the reason he had started boxing in the first place.

He continued to depend on his family, Nadine and the Nelsons to help him stay grounded. Some reporters wanted to hear about his prison experiences, which were still too vivid for him to shake off, and he found himself retreating from contacts outside the ring. He was starting to come to terms with his life experiences as part of a plan; necessary stepping stones to his goal of heavyweight champion of the world, but he wasn't yet ready to talk about his growing conviction with outsiders. So he just worked harder.

As the official heavyweight representative on the U.S. Boxing Team, Ron had only one week after the IBL Championship before he faced his first European opponents on the Continent. Still making up for lost time, his daily routine continued to include the runs, the push-ups, sparring and reporting for his welding job, but the overwhelming number and weight of his experiences inside the ring - he had fought an average of one bout a week since February - took its toll. He discovered that even Ron Lyle could get tired.

Focus. He found he could renew his energy whenever he focused on his ultimate goal, so he consciously willed himself to view the European tour as a jumping off place for that goal. He slept on the overseas flight, and on June 22, he faced off with Amadeo Laurentic, the Italian champion, in Rome. With only two minutes, 21 seconds gone in the first round, he knocked out his first European opponent. Once again, no problem.

The epiphany came four days later. He entered the ring in Belgrade to face Yugoslavian champion Anton Vukusiz. The American flag was raised, the 'Star Spangled Banner' played, and Ron looked out at the sea of white faces. He knew he was where he belonged, the representative of his country and his race. And he would fight for convicts who deserved a second chance in life. Even though winning the bout wasn't as important as being there, Ron Lyle knocked out the highly-rated Yugoslavian in the third round. Budda boom, budda bing.

12

*

RON lost his scheduled bout with Romanian Ivan Alexi in a split-decision, but it hardly mattered. His driving force was to prepare for his next fight, and his next, and his next. In August, when the Rocks met the Mexican All Stars, he polished off champion Pete Chiano with a knockout in the first round.

His last great challenges as an amateur were yet to come, and he had a few months to prepare. Maybe because he never forgot the feeling of being appreciated by the young convict at Canon City, of being somebody's idol, it was during this hiatus in late 1970 that he first sought serious opportunities to work with kids. Once he got the word out to Denver writer Carl Skiff and others, invitations poured in. Ron visited dozens of schools and camps, and to his own amazement, he turned out to be a dynamic speaker, especially when he talked about how self-discipline could work for anybody, how any kid could make good.

Marilyn remembers her pride when her big brother

spoke at her junior high school assembly. 'I was in the eighth grade at Kunsmiller Junior High,' she said. 'He told the kids to never give up, but he did it in a way that got through to them. Everybody loved him.'

He joined and became a major spokesperson for Partners, an organisation formed to match adult volunteers with kids who had been in trouble with the law, and he spent more and more time at Lookout Mountain School for Boys, the State Industrial School a few miles west of Denver, near Golden. The residential facility was established in 1881 for boys considered 'misfits,' a term Ron abhors. 'They're just kids,' he says.

He liked rapping with the kids, mostly listening. He asked them about sports, girls, even sex, in what he called 'their own language,' and they inevitably answered, communicating with the ex-con in a way they couldn't with other adults at the facility. Inevitably Ron would think of Clifford Maddox and he thought he knew how the old guard felt helping others. 'I didn't preach, but they knew I was telling them to go straight, even though I didn't say it in so many words.'

It was also during the weeks following his European tour that Ron started noticing that whenever he was fusing machinery at work, his eyes would burn and water, a common complaint of welders. One day he had his safety hood up when the welder next to him lit his torch, and he felt a searing in his right eye. It was only a temporary injury, but Bill Daniels told him to lay off the job for a few weeks. Great news. Welding would turn out to be the only job Ron ever had that he really disliked. And time away from the shop gave him even more time to see kids in schools, reformatories and detention centres.

Whether Daniels was impressed by Ron's work with kids, worried about the welding affecting his eyesight, or just believed he had discovered a rare talent, it was about this time that the influential entrepreneur started trying to persuade his friend Governor John Love to pardon Lyle. Initially turned down by the Governor, Daniels did convince the Parole Board that a stipend for training expenses could be considered a legitimate livelihood and got Ron released from the welding job, an enormous relief for the fighter.

ON October 3, 1970, Albert Nelson died suddenly in his sleep. Barely in his fifties, Al had never demonstrated any illness that his sons could discern. For years after his divorce, he had been the primary care-giver for Dennis and Donny, but just a few months before, the Nelsons had reconciled, remarrying in March.

Even in his sorrow, Dennis remembers anticipating the effect that his father's death would have on Ron, and he made sure that his friend, along with others of the Denver Rocks, served as a pallbearer for Albert Nelson's funeral.

Ron remembers feeling that he had lost a great friend and somebody he had learned to trust. But he also recognised how hard it was for Donny and Dennis, and he grew even closer to the Nelson sons. Dennis had always been there for him, at every boxing match, and it was time to give back to his friend. For the first time since he had been with his 'band of brothers,' Ron Lyle felt friends as an extension of his family.

Al's brother Robert Nelson, 'Uncle Buck' to the family, remembers Ron at the funeral. 'Al thought the world of Ronny,' he says. 'After he died, I tried to keep track of him.' Robert Nelson was a career F.B.I. officer who would turn out to be there for Ron at a critical point in his life. Like all the people surrounding Ron, 'Uncle Buck' would play what almost seemed like an assigned role in his life.

Watching Ron fight was clearly not his parents' role, and

he didn't blame them. 'Mom and dad still don't attend my fights,' he told a reporter that fall. 'My mother is worried I'll get hurt, I guess. Dad always asks me before a fight, "Are you ready? How do you feel?" and then he'll listen to the fight on the radio.'

Sharon offers some insight into her father's reason for not attending Ronny's bouts. Quoting scripture, she says: '"Come out from among them and be separated." Our father was *in* the world but not *of* the world, so he couldn't go to any of his children's athletic events.' She smiles and adds: 'But somehow, God allowed him to listen to Ron's fights on radio and later watch his professional bouts on television.'

It all worked - Nellie and William listening at home, the Nelsons working Ron in his corner, his brothers and sisters expressing their pride in him. As he waited with Nadine for the birth of their child, he had all the emotional support he needed, at least for the moment.

THE next time Ron fought was in January at Ft. Carson, Colorado to secure a 1971 spot on the USA team. Denver excitement was high since the United States team was poised to meet the Russian All Star team a week later in an international event in Las Vegas, and whoever beat the Russians at any weight would be undisputed world amateur champions. It was at that point that the Ron Lyle story came to the attention of Mike Wallace and the producers of *60 Minutes*.

In those days the popular television show generally featured exposés with Wallace, camera crew in tow, confronting reluctant 'suspects,' but periodically, Wallace would seek out a human interest story to balance his image. He was convinced that a man who served prison time for murder before becoming what many considered the greatest heavyweight amateur boxer in the world would generate wide viewer interest, and CBS camera crews started following Lyle around.

Ron's opponent for the USA team heavyweight spot was the formidable Duane Bobick, the Armed Forces heavyweight champ, a slugging Navy veteran. Even though he had kept his strict training regimen, Ron had had a long lay-off, and Denver fans were concerned that he might have become rusty. Not to worry. He achieved his most spectacular win yet over Bobick with a second-round combination punch knockout that put the serviceman to sleep for five minutes. *60 Minutes* had it on tape. And when Nadine gave birth to their son Monte the same month, Ron thought life was as good as it could get.

When the USA team landed in Las Vegas for the showdown between the United States and the Soviet Union, Ronny Lyle found himself the centre of American hopes. Interest was especially high since no American heavyweight had ever beaten his Russian opponent. Patriotic pride was at stake. His bout with the top Russian heavyweight Kamo Saroyan was set to be televised from Caesars Palace on ABC's *Wide World of Sport*, along with supplementary film coverage of the human interest side to be aired by *60 Minutes*.

From *Denver Post* sportswriter, Terry Anderson:

> Lyle played it cautious in the first round, feeling out the Russian ....and consequently lost [it] on points. But he came on quickly at the start of the second.
>
> Finding an opening, Lyle used a left hook to the midsection and a right to the head that sent Saroyan reeling onto the ropes. With Saroyan groggy and holding onto the ropes, Russian referee Vasily Romanov halted the bout but didn't begin to count.
>
> Lyles's aides in his corner began shouting that the Russian fighter was being given too much time to recover. All the while, Lyle pranced in a neutral corner,

eager to continue the fight, and finally charged back at Saroyan. It was then that Romanov stopped the bout.

But with both fighters standing in their corners, interpreters surrounding the officials at ringside exchanged heated words for five minutes and rumors spread that Lyle was being disqualified for interrupting the temporary halt of the fight by the referee.

'After much discussion,' said the ring announcer minutes later, 'the fight has been awarded to Ron Lyle after 20 seconds of the second round on a technical knockout.'

EVEN though the USA team lost the dual meet that night in Las Vegas, Ron Lyle became the only American heavyweight ever to knock out his Russian opponent. But Saroyan wasn't finished. Fighting mad, he demanded an immediate rematch. Bill Daniels had already arranged for an exhibition bout with members of the Russian team in Denver the following week, so interest in a rematch between the heavyweights was high. But Ron remembers an even more important event that week.

'I'll never forget the day Bill Daniels called and told me he had somebody in his office he wanted me to meet. When I got there, I saw the man most people in the world recognised back then - Joe Louis.' Daniels had managed to secure Louis as a co-sponsor for the rematch with Saroyan, even though the former heavyweight champ had fallen on hard times, hospitalised for mental illness earlier that year. 'Yeah, he'd been sick, but he was still Joe Louis and he encouraged me. I'll never forget it as long as I live. I wanted to show him what I could do.'

But when the time came for the Lyle-Saroyan rematch, the Russians sprang a surprise. Citing international boxing rules that state an amateur fighter cannot box for 30 days once he is knocked out in a fight, Soviet boxing officials declined the bout. The USA team had taken for granted that the rule didn't apply as Lyle scored a technical, not an actual knockout. Denver fans reacted angrily, as reported by the *Denver Post*: 'One is led to believe that the real reason for the cancellation is that the Russians don't want Saroyan back in the ring with Denver's national AAU and North American heavyweight champion.' That was confirmed when Saroyan fought and gained a technical knockout over Al Braxton in St. Louis the following week Even the Russians did not relish facing an ever-improving Ron Lyle.

In order to keep Lyle on the Denver fight ticket, Bill Daniels brought in Jim Waltenburg, the Pacific Northwest Golden Gloves heavyweight champion from Seattle. Politics played a role that night as picket lines formed in front of the Auditorium Arena with members of the American Jewish Conference on Soviet Jewry protesting the appearance of the Russian boxers in Denver. But even with a large contingent of fans sympathetic to the Jewish protest, Rocks fever had reached such a high pitch that the stadium was filled.

Terry Anderson described the fight:

> Waltenburg, labelled the fighting farmer from Seattle, should have stayed down on the farm after watching Lyle beat Saroyan in Las Vegas.
>
> Lyle used a strong left hand to down Waltenburg with four seconds to go in the opening round. The bell saved Waltenburg momentarily, but he came out still dazed by the blow at the start of the second, and he was down for the count with just 28 seconds gone in the round.

In 14 months, Ron had won 25 of 29 fights, 17 by knockouts. And still nobody knew if he could take a punch. Stephen Brunt summarised the impact Ron Lyle had on the amateur scene in one short year: 'He was a man fighting boys.'

13

*

R ON turned 30 in February, and the Olympics were
still over a year away. As much as he wanted the gold
medal for his country, Ron couldn't wait that long;
the decision to go professional had to be made. As it turned
out, Duane Bobick went to Munich as the U.S. heavyweight,
and was knocked out by Cuba's Teofilo Stevenson, an event
that saddened Lyle. He knew he could have won.

But Ron knows he made the right decision: 'I felt that I
was at my peak as an athlete. An athlete knows when he's at
his peak. He knows when he's gone as far as he can go at the
level that he's at. I felt like I had gone as far as I could go as
an amateur. And to wait around another year-and-a-half,
that's not a guarantee. Because as an amateur, you don't
know who you fight. As a pro, you know who you fight, how
to prepare for him, what he can do and what he can't do.'

It was time, with Bill Daniels' backing, to map out a plan
for his professional career. But first he had to finish filming
the *60 Minutes* feature. To help dramatise his journey from

prison to professional boxer, the producers of the programme arranged for Ron to visit the camps of both Muhammad Ali and Joe Frazier, then in the final stages of preparation for their first heavyweight championship bout, billed as 'The Fight of the Century.'

The fight would be unique. For the first time in history, it would match an unbeaten former heavyweight champion against the unbeaten current champ, and Ron considered it a privilege to visit both camps just weeks before their historic clash. The experience of meeting both boxers was almost overshadowed, however, by the presence of two heroes in the Ali camp. For the second time in just a few weeks, he had a chance to talk to Joe Louis, who, on that occasion, formally endorsed Ron Lyle as a professional boxer. He also met Angelo Dundee, Ali's trainer who had written to him in prison. Dundee had followed Ron's amateur career and was optimistic about his chances of winning a title.

'Talking to Joe Louis and Angelo Dundee gave me more confidence that day than anything else ever did. If both those guys thought I could make it, then I knew could, too. It was that simple.'

On the eve of the March 1971 historic bout between Ali and Frazier, *Empire* magazine published Ron's account of his experiences with both fighters:

> I met Muhammad Ali in the Fifth Street Gym at Miami Beach, Florida on Saturday, Jan. 30. There were about 20 fighters working out when I got there at 12:30 p.m. I warmed up for a half-hour before Ali arrived. There was quite a crowd - kids, middle-aged people, elderly and all gathered around to watch him punch the bag.
>
> I watched Ali carefully as he went four rounds with one of his sparring mates, and I could tell that he wasn't yet in shape. His skin hung on him, not all of his

muscles had hardened yet as they will be tomorrow night. He weighed about 225 pounds at that time, and I expect he'll be down to around 210 for the Frazier fight. [He was.]

Ali's trainer, Angelo Dundee, then introduced me and Ali told Dundee to tell the crowd about me and my achievements. Then I sparred two rounds with him, at three minutes each.

Nervous? Sure. After all, I was in the ring with the world's greatest. I had read a lot about him, and then all of a sudden there I was, fighting him. It was an honour to be in the ring with him - I wasn't out to get any reputation by trying to put him away.

I wasn't trying anything special; I simply went out and sparred with him. I landed a few, and he hit me some, too, but I don't recall any of his punches hurting.

I had heard that Ali's left jab is fast, and believe me, it's true. He's a polished fighter, he's got class. Basically he's like most fighters I've competed against. The moves are the same - there's a right, then a left, the footwork, etc. But Ali has all of them polished, and that's what makes a champion.

Once during our match I threw a right at him, missed and threw another right. Right away he said: 'When you miss with one like that, retreat. If you throw a right hand behind a right hand, you're in trouble.'

As we boxed, he told me to relax. He could tell I was a little tight. After we were through, we talked a while. He turned to the audience and asked them what they thought of me, and they said I'd be all right.

Ali didn't clown around with me at all, but he did tell me that Joe Frazier was a little clumsy and that if I would fight Frazier I would make him look bad. Ali also told Mike Wallace….that Frazier was flatfooted.

That night I left for Frazier's camp, located at the Concord Hotel, a fancy resort in the Catskill Mountains of New York. This would be a great place to train for a fight, the wilderness is so peaceful and quiet.

It was after noon that Sunday when I suited up in my room and went to Frazier's training area, one of the hotel's convention halls. I worked out a bit and observed Frazier spar two rounds each with three fighters.

I would have liked to spar with Frazier, but his handlers felt I hadn't had enough experience. All of Frazier's sparring mates are experienced professionals and Frazier fights for keeps, even in training. In the ring he's punching all the time, keeping constant pressure on his opponent.

When Frazier was finished I went a round with one of his sparring mates, Ken Norton. After that Frazier came over and we talked. He told me I had a good defence and moved around well, but that I should throw more punches.

Frazier weighed about 215 then, and looked a little sluggish. But, once again, this was more than a month before the fight. I didn't hear either Ali or Frazier predict a certain round would end tomorrow night's fight, though both appeared highly confident. I did hear Frazier's handlers say they thought Joe would put Ali away within seven rounds.

Another reason why it's impossible to predict a winner is the difficulty in knowing what the mental attitude of each fighter is. Before my fights I have to get in top mental shape, too. I like to walk alone at night, working out in my mind how I will fight my opponent.

To be the best you have to know you're the best, and that's what I want to be.

Frazier went on to win the historic bout with Ali, going the distance for a unanimous decision, and in the meantime, Ron Lyle left the camps confident that he, too, would someday fight for the championship. He was quoted in *Empire* magazine: 'Being at those camps was a tremendous experience, just tremendous. They and their training camps are top-notch. This is the way it is when you're at the top. I'll be there someday. It may take me two or three years, but I'll be there.'

It would take him four.

After the *60 Minutes* episode aired, Ron was overwhelmed with the outpouring of love and support from the Denver community that ranged way beyond the tight-knit band of boxing enthusiasts. Somehow he had become a symbol for coming out of the worst circumstances into a world of hope.

He responded to every request for interviews and speaking opportunities, and a number of reports highlighted his being 'a tough guy with a gentle nature.' He tried to correct the impression he was a ghetto kid who didn't have any chances growing up, and almost always talked about how his parents had supported him. True to form, he always took responsibility for everything. No excuses; no regrets. But somehow the stereotype of a tough kid making it on his own hung around for many years.

Whatever the community perception of his background, opinion on his skill in the ring was unanimous. Art Irlando's assessment of Ron Lyle reflected what the boxing community knew in 1971. 'Ron has a lot of speed, strength and stamina, but most of all it's his punching ability that makes him so good. And he's a good in-fighter, too. A lot of amateur fighters, and even some professionals, will tie you up and grab when in close, but not Ron. He'll stay in and jab at you....Once he gets inside, he's hard to beat.'

Ron had started to train with the idea of likening his boxing style to a chess match. 'You have to be ready for any move with a move of your own,' he said.

Bill Daniels put Ron on a small salary while he trained for his first professional bout, the prevailing system at the time. The trade-off for Daniels would be a higher percentage of the purse when the big matches started coming. Ron considered the arrangement both fair and effective. 'The way Bill Daniels saw it was, "Keep 'em hungry and you'll keep 'em working," and I did work, harder than ever in my life.'

The salary was enough for Ron to put a small payment down on a house in Green Mountain, a middle-class suburb west of Denver, where he felt Nadine and Monte would be safe and comfortable. In the meantime, though, he had his first professional fight to think about.

IN her classic book, *On Boxing*, Joyce Carol Oates writes that there is '....no evident relationship between the man outside the ring and inside the ring.'[3] By all accounts, Ron Lyle was a case in point. A man devoted to his family and friends, he also continued to allocate hours every week to visiting detention centres and schools, but in the ring, he perfected his technique for knocking out most of his opponents - a combination left jab, right cross, left hook to the side and right uppercut. The boxing style was frequently described as brutal, but the man was something else.

During his amateur year and thereafter, it seemed Denver reporters found it difficult not to gush when they described that city's greatest athlete. They praised his personal and professional self-discipline, his devotion to young people, his affability, not to mention his sheer strength.

But In 1971 the time had come for this remarkable man to discover whether or not he had what it took to live out his dream.

14

✳

Gaining Momentum

IV

'THE best advice I ever got was from an old pro, Arthur Mack, who came to fight with me in prison. He said: "Be true to the game. Never disrespect the game." And I was true to the game through my whole professional career,' Ron Lyle declares.

He concedes that in boxing, the fix is sometimes in. With big money flowing among managers, fighters and gamblers, the temptation to get in on the pay-off presents itself to everybody in the game. But Bill Daniels and Ron Lyle played it straight. And they found a like-minded trainer in Bobby Lewis. Sometimes described as diminutive or wiry, the 5 foot 6 inch African American trainer was highly respected in both amateur and professional circles. Lewis would go on to coach the 1972 Olympics team after guiding Lyle through the first year of his professional career.

In the late winter of '71, days after the Denver Rocks had announced that Ron Lyle was moving into the professional ranks, Daniels moved him to a New York hotel near the gym where Bobby Lewis had set up a rigorous training programme for the talented amateur.

Sportswriter Terry Anderson quoted Lewis for a *Denver Post* piece: 'An amateur fighter can make four or five mistakes and still win. A pro can lose if he makes just one mistake.' Acutely aware of Lyle's late start, Lewis had put him in the ring with an experienced professional, Pedro Agosto, who had an 18-2 record, 16 of those wins by knockouts. Lewis went on to say: 'I may be criticised by some people for throwing Lyle in with an experienced pro like Agosto, but I figure that's the way he'll develop the fastest.' Lyle did just fine, giving back as good as he got, as the sparring match turned into a slugfest.

Ron viewed his first professional training experience as very precise. He told Anderson: 'Every part of your body and mind must function with split-second timing. The rigours of training are comparable to honing a knife. The more you hone, the sharper that knife is going to cut. I'm no different, and my trainer is making sure I'm well honed.'

Lyle made extraordinary progress in training camp. Bobby Lewis again spoke with Terry Anderson: 'Ron's determined, he's dedicated, but what's more important, he takes instructions and absorbs.' Lewis and Daniels decided their fighter would be ready to take on a highly-rated boxer as early as April. No fooling around with mere build-up bouts for the Lyle camp - not enough time.

If training was going well in those early weeks of Ron's professional career, his personal life was not. Leaving Nadine at home just weeks after baby Monte was born and heading for New York did not go over well with his young bride.

Ron admits that he was so focused on training, he had not tried to reassure Nadine. 'I knew they'd be all right,' he says, 'and I could hardly think of anything else but just getting ready for my first professional fight.' He promised himself he would make it up to her when he got back home and continued training rigorously.

Then, after just seven weeks of preparation, Ron had the opportunity to fight his first professional bout in Madison Square Garden. Surprising even Bobby Lewis, he declined. The official word out of the Lyle camp was that even though the Garden was the most prestigious location for a debut, Ron Lyle wanted to reciprocate the loyalty of Colorado fans and had requested his first fight to be in Denver.

ON April 23, Ron Lyle made his professional debut in Denver against A.J. Staples of St. Louis, Missouri. After the decision to fight in Denver had been made, Bill Daniels and Lewis had carefully selected Staples as a worthy first opponent for Ron. The southpaw had started his pro career in 1968 and had a 10-4 record with eight knockouts, all four losses by decision.

Interest by Denver fans reached a new level with Ron turning pro, and they weren't disappointed in his first fight. The *Denver Post* reported:

> Lyle came out in the first round and spent most of the time chasing Staples from corner to corner. It wasn't until two minutes were gone in the round that he landed his first professional punch.
>
> With 18 seconds left in the opening round, Lyle sent Staples into the lower ropes with a right to the body and a left hook.
>
> Then he put Staples down in the 2:31 mark of the second when he grazed Staples' temple with a right. Thirty seconds later, Staples was down again and went down for good with 1:10 seconds left in the second round. Those knockdowns represented the first time that Staples has even been sent to the floor in 15 professional fights.

Ron Lyle had made a spectacular professional debut, and in the following weeks, the momentum continued with headlines reading:

May 23: 'Ron Lyle Wins by Knockout in Fifth Round'
June 20: 'Former Rock Lyle Knocks Out Bates for Third Victory'

And so it went. In his second bout with solid fighter Art Miller in Boston, Lyle delighted Bobby Lewis with the length of the fight, of all things. Instead of knocking out Miller early on as he had done throughout his amateur career and in his fight with Staples, Ron consciously tried to apply everything he had learned from Lewis, knocking Miller down twice on his way to a fifth-round knockout.

The third bout with Gary Bates, a seasoned pro with 20 fights under his belt, was televised from Lake Tahoe and lasted only three rounds. Bates was the hardest to hit because he kept withdrawing into a shell; Ron had to keep using an uppercut to pull him out. Early in the third round he caught Bates with a left hook, followed with a right uppercut and another left hook to finish him off, a combination Lewis had him working on in the gym.

Back in New York after each bout, Ron tried to make it up to Nadine by calling almost every day, and his mother looked in on the Green Mountain house whenever she could. The young mother found caring for a young baby all on her own difficult and lonely, but Ron wouldn't even consider the option of giving up training in New York and coming home. He had a great trainer in a great boxing city and was headed in the direction of fulfilling his dream. His wife would just have to understand.

By this time, Ron's gruelling training schedule took 13 hours a day. He began each day at 6:00 a.m. with a four-mile run around New York's Central Park, followed by three rounds of loosening up, three more of shadow boxing, six more rounds on the heavy punching bag, another three on the speed bag and two more rounds of rope-skipping, then taking on a sparring partner. He generally went to Bobby Lewis' New York home for dinner, then back to his hotel room for 150-200 half-squats with a New York phone book perched on each knee. He was losing as much as five pounds during an average daily workout.

Terry Anderson quoted Bobby Lewis as saying: 'I've had him so tired that it's been hard for him to walk a flight of stairs. Then he gets into a fight and he's ready to go.' But he was learning. Lewis went on to say: 'The amazing thing about Ron right now is his will to learn. That makes it easier to teach him. And I don't worry about him doing something I tell him to.'

RON seldom got back to Denver that first year, and it would have done little good for Nadine and Monte to join him in New York with his non-stop training regimen. He began to feel a kind of loneliness akin to his separation from his family during the Canon City years. But he never entertained the notion of quitting or even lightening his training load. He would do whatever it took to be a contender, and he trusted Bobby Lewis to know what that was.

The women who hung around boxers in New York back then were never a temptation for Ron. Years later, he told Jill Sellers: 'They started coming on to me, so I took to not brushing my teeth. I figured that would turn them off and I wouldn't have to tell them no.' And so the beat went on.

Three weeks after the Bates fight, Ron met Jamaican heavyweight champion Edmund Stewart in New York. After stalking his opponent for the first minute of round one, he managed to utilise combination punches, backing Stewart into a corner and throwing a flurry of punches until the Jamaican was dazed at the bell. Then 56 seconds into the second round, he trapped Steward on the ropes, and the referee stopped the fight. The only down side was Ron not getting seriously hit, and it was still not known if he could take it.

Eight days later, on July 24, Ron beat Leroy Caldwell in a unanimous decision at the Playboy Club in Lake Geneva, Wisconsin. That fight marked the first time he failed to knock out his opponent. Caldwell was considered 'ordinary,' but he had recently run a streak of six straight wins and had developed a kind of canny defence albeit to no avail against the formidable Lyle.

Ron's next two fights were in Las Vegas, a necessary venue for up-and-coming pros, especially heavyweights. With a 23-pound advantage, he won his sixth bout with Frankie 'Snakebite' Niblett, staggering the tough but smaller boxer several times before the referee called a halt at 2:12 for a technical knockout in the ninth round. Ron got a hit a few times, but it didn't seem to faze him, pleasing Bobby Lewis and Bill Daniels.

A month later, on September 11, he again scored a technical knockout in Las Vegas, this time in the seventh round against the experienced Stoney Land. Land had held his own through the early rounds with hard rights and lefts to Lyle's head and body, but Ron began to pinpoint short rights to his rival's face in the fourth and finally drove him through the ropes in the sixth.

In the seventh, Land again fell through the ropes after a series of short rights to the head and took a mandatory eight count from the referee. Seconds later, Lyle drove his opponent through the ropes a third time with hard rights to the face, causing the referee to stop the bout. Relentlessness had been added to his fighting profile. It was time to fight a challenging opponent - and Bobby Lewis landed him a big one.

15

*

October found Ron Lyle back in Colorado preparing for his toughest opponent yet - Manuel Ramos, the heavyweight champion of Mexico. Persuading Bobby Lewis that he needed to spend the week before the fight training in the mile-high city of Denver to get himself acclimatised to the altitude, Ron revelled in the tiny bits of time he could spend with both of his families, but he had mixed feelings about leaving New York.

He remembers Bobby Lewis as '....the guy I never argued with. Whatever he said, I did. We were together a lot, at the gym and at night. I was at his home more than my hotel room. His wife was kind of like a second mother. Bobby and I always thought alike, almost with the same soul. In the ring, after a while, he wouldn't have to tell me what to do. I would know what he wanted.'

The flip side of leaving Bobby Lewis in New York was finally having time to get acquainted with his son, and Ron belatedly fell in love. He eased up on the training for a few days, hauling Monte around wherever he went. Nadine seemed pacified at having her husband home and devoting time to their son, and he thought she was beginning to understand the importance of his dream. At home, contentment momentarily reigned. He also revelled in the time he had to spend with his family, especially his mother.

Another event occurred that month, beginning a lifelong practice. Ron responded to a request from Clifford Maddox to return to Canon City - to boost the morale of the inmates. He travelled to the prison just before the Ramos bout and spent the day talking to some of the convicts he had known, even working out with 'Doobie' Vigil and the Rock Busters football squad. Once again, he felt appreciated, even idolised.

The fight with Ramos would also reunite Ron with the Nelsons. Donny was scheduled to appear in a preliminary amateur bout as the Rocks' new heavyweight - a fight he would win - and the two boxers, along with Dennis, managed some time together, pumping up and catching up. Everything in his life that week felt like home, but he finally had to turn his attention to Manuel Ramos. Bobby Lewis and others had told Ron that his October 9 fight would be his toughest yet. Ramos had been the heavyweight champion of Mexico for an age, and Ron knew that he couldn't have held on that long unless he was very good.

The 'Tale of the Tape' showed almost identical stats - both 6 feet 3½ inches, Lyle 215, Ramos 214, Lyle 76-inch reach, Ramos, 76½. They were the same age, too, but Ron only had seven pro fights under his belt while Ramos had 46, beating such talented opponents as Ernie Terrell and Tony Doyle.

Interest in the fight was the highest ever for Denver fans. Articles previewing both fighters appeared almost every day, including quotes from Ramos: 'I've fought many other boxers with better punching credentials than Lyle's....I'm not predicting any knockouts, just that I'll win. I've come to fight and I've got too much at stake to lose.' Both fighters had much at stake. The victor would be considered a serious contender and assured of a chance to box in the next two months at Madison Square Garden. Officials in New York were well aware of Ramos's reputation as a tremendous puncher who could knock out an opponent with either hand, but they also knew Lyle had never been knocked out, knocked down, or even cut in his amateur and pro careers. Harry Markson, Director of Boxing at the Garden, would watch the fight with great interest.

Local columnist Jim Graham got back on the Lyle bandwagon, too, thinking this would be the fight where his long-standing question - 'Can Ron Lyle take a good punch?' - would finally be answered. He echoed the Denver point of view regarding their local boy making good: 'Bill Daniels....gave him another chance in society and Lyle has responded by staying clean, reflecting nothing but credit on his sponsor, and more importantly, himself.'

The fight was carried live by KHOW radio, and Ron had asked that special arrangements be made for piping the broadcast into the state penitentiary in Canon City, so inmates could hear the fight first-hand. The crowd at the Auditorium Arena was standing-room only.

Ron started the first round in his slugger mode, and Bobby Lewis admitted: 'I had to get mad at him [Lyle]. Ramos is a fighter, not a boxer. Ron started fighting him. I wanted Ron to box because I knew he could out-box Ramos.'

Starting in the second round, but getting his full stride in the fourth, Ron boxed, and ended up scoring a unanimous ten-round decision. The referee scored the fight nine rounds for Lyle and one round even. One judge gave Lyle six rounds, three to Ramos and one even, and the other judge credited Lyle with seven rounds while giving two to Ramos and calling one round even. It wasn't even close.

The *Denver Post* reported that:

> Neither fighter was hurt, although Lyle managed to sting Ramos several times in the fight. Lyle bloodied Ramos' nose in the third round with a right-hand punch. And in the tenth, Lyle closed in with a flurry of punches that momentarily stunned Ramos on the ropes with just under a minute left in the fight.

In one of his rare interviews days afterwards, Bill Daniels showed his feelings for Ron Lyle and his determination to obtain a pardon for his protégé. 'Getting a full pardon is almost as important to Ron as winning the heavyweight title. Ron doesn't smoke, drink or swear, and he's not a playboy, either....But he's bugged that he's the only one in his family that ever got into any kind of trouble. That bothers him.'

Ron agrees that he was bothered by his prison record, but he found that by focusing on his professional career and his family, he could forget the past for longer stretches of time. And somehow, his visit to Canon City had not served to remind him of the bad days, but to look ahead to the good. 'I just had to keep playing by the rules,' he says.

Led by Nellie, the Lyle family was also beginning to get past the sadness of Ronny's hard years. Both Sharon and Bill remember their mother likening their brother to the Biblical David. 'Mother would tell us that some become warriors and others priests,' Sharon says, 'and that Ronny was like a warrior, fighting bears and lions.'

Ron continued to train for most of his fights in New York and was eager to appear again at Madison Square Garden, but in spite of official assurances, it would be a year-and-a-half before he got another fight in the New York venue. It hardly mattered. A month after the Ramos bout, he easily overcame his next opponent, another young, promising boxer named Joey Lewis.

After knocking Lewis down early in the third round, he floored the young boxer with a left to the body with only four seconds left in the round. Another knockout, this time in front of a huge audience in Las Vegas. More importantly, he had earned a shot at Jack 'The Giant' O'Hallaron, a highly ranked heavyweight named as a potential opponent to world champion Joe Frazier - if he beat Ron Lyle.

O'Hallaron could be a daunting opponent. Most often identified years later as 'the guy with the metal teeth in the James Bond and Superman movies,' he had a huge advantage, statistically, over Lyle. Six feet six inches tall and outweighing Ron by 35 pounds, the heavyweight had 15-inch fists and a $7^{1}/_{2}$-inch reach advantage. And he was brimming with confidence.

Referring to Lyle, O'Halloran told *Denver Post* sportswriter Terry Anderson: 'He's not really a test for me. What it boils down to is that I'm a test for him. I'm not worried about our fight. I feel good, I'm in shape and I don't think our fight will be much trouble for me.' He should have worried. The *Post* headlines the day after the November 26 fight were big and bold: 'Lyle Fells O'Halloran in Four Rounds'.

The sell-out Denver crowd roared from the opening bell, confident that it was just a matter of time before their hometown hero would knock out this guy everybody else thought would win. And they were right. That night was only the second time in 36 professional fights that O'Halloran had been counted out. Terry Anderson described each round and concluded:

> Ranked just 48th in the world heavyweight ranks, Lyle looked as if he belonged in the top ten in a fight

in which he did everything a solid contender should do. He stood his ground in the first and slugged it out with his opponent, then became so elusive in the remainder of the fight, bobbing this way, weaving that way and ducking under O'Halloran's glancing blows, that the bewildered O'Halloran failed to land a solid punch in the fight.

When O'Halloran came into Denver early in the week, he had told a gathering of newsmen that he would give Lyle a 'quick shave and a haircut' in a brief pit-stop before meeting Frazier for the title in February. Lyle not only shut O'Halloran's mouth, he shut out his chances of fighting Frazier any time soon.

16

*

AS Ron trained for his next bout with Bill Drover, ranked number two in Canada behind George Chuvalo, a Canadian documentary film crew followed him around to capture a touching portrait of the aspiring heavyweight. The film opens with the last few seconds of the O'Halloran fight as Ron fells 'The Giant,' who crashes to the floor and stays put.

The next scene features Ron running around the park before dawn, talking in voice-over of how he likes to be by himself so he can 'think things out'. The camera then moves to the gym where Bobby Lewis leans into the ring, offering soothing advice, ending with: 'I know what you're thinking. My mind is following yours.'

The documentary follows Ron to Canon City and records what had already become his ritual before every fight. This visit is especially poignant, since the prisoners had been shut down because of a riot before the O'Halloran bout and because Lyle was to stay overnight. In the film, inmates gather around Ron in the yard and in the dining hall as he laughs and jokes with old friends along the way.

Ron Lyle voice-over: 'Some of these guys will never get out. Coming to see them is the least I can do. I know what they're going through - I've been in the same hold, the same solitary confinement....I know what it feels like to go into the cell at 5:30, and they slam the door shut on you. And you're there, the rest of the night in your cell. That's when the reality comes. "Here I am. One more day gone." You watch guys being killed for cigarettes or for no reason at all....I don't preach to them or try to tell them what to do. I go back because they're a part of me.'

Somebody mentions Sam and Ron says: 'Sam? What's Sam doing back here? Life? He got life?' He is momentarily wordless, then goes on to greet 'Kemo,' a small, older black man who hugs the fighter like he'll never let go. He works his way to the prison gym and spars with one of the prisoners, surrounded by every inmate they can jam into the place, cheering and clapping.

A Denver newspaper carried the story about the Canon City visit. 'Deputy Warden Fred Wyse views the two-day session as a great morale booster for the inmates. "Every time Ron comes down here, the spirit of the guys picks up greatly," he said. "Ron is an inspiration to them, someone who has made it after leaving here."' The documentary films Ron leaving Canon, his voice quieter, more intense. 'Some of these guys get institutionalised. They're okay because they get three meals a day, a place to sleep at night. But for me, during the whole seven-and-a-half years, I didn't like no part of it.'

In the next scene Ron Lyle is lying motionless on the bench in an empty locker room. The camera holds for long seconds, then cuts to Ron entering the ring, generating a huge roar from a full house of Denver fans. In the first round of the Ron Lyle-Bill Drover fight, the boxers dance around and poke at each other until we can hear Bobby Lewis from the corner: 'You're waiting too long.' In round two, Ron comes out boxing and within seconds has slammed Drover with a right cross, followed immediately by a right uppercut. The knockout took only 45 seconds into the second round. A dozen kids flock into the ring and surround Lyle, who gives them a big smile.

Afterwards, back in the locker room, Ron is greeted by Nadine and baby Monte. He holds them on the bench before the traditional lay-on of hands by Lyle, Lewis and his other cornermen is completed with Mrs. Bill Daniels standing in for her husband. The camera then moves to the home of Nellie and William Lyle, filled with Lyle children and grandchildren and captures laughing, hugging and excited talking, highlighted by Ron hugging his mother: 'This is my love, right here; my number one girl.'

In the final scene of the film, Ron is once again running all alone, long before the sun comes up.

THE headlines the morning after the Drover fight again dominated the sports page, this time announcing only: 'Bang…Bang'.

Another fight on that night's card also held much interest for Denver fans. Donny Nelson had been given the chance of taking on Duane Bobick. Described as 'garnering more amateur heavyweight titles, national and international, than any other amateur boxer since Ron Lyle's amateur days,' Bobick was favoured for a knockout. But Donny held on, only to lose by a split decision, practically guaranteeing Bobick being named in the U.S. Olympic team.

Once Ron was home in Denver, he settled into his Green Mountain home with an ease that reassured Nadine, even though the long weeks when he was away in New York or

Las Vegas were starting to wear more and more on the young mother. Monte took after his father, in constant motion even before he started to walk. Because Ron managed the baby so well at home, it was doubly difficult for Nadine when he went away again. The Lyle family provided back-up support, but couldn't make up for all the time lost to the couple's first married year.

The money helped - Ron was starting to make between $5000 and $10,000 as his 50 per cent on each bout. Most standard fighter contracts split $66^{2/3}$ - $33^{1/3}$ between boxer and manager, after training salaries and other expenses were taken off the top. But because Bill Daniels had subsidised Ron during amateur years, not to mention helping obtain his parole, the 50/50 split seemed fair.

Ron continued to give a portion of every cheque to his parents and spent some of what remained on his siblings and friends, even on strangers. A small piece in the *Rocky Mountain News* a couple of weeks after the Drover fight was headlined 'Lyle Rewards Four Boys Who Found $29,741': 'Boxer Ron Lyle dug into his own pocket to come up with rewards for young fans of his who turned in $29,741 to police after finding the money in a box on a bank of the South Platte River. Learning that the four boys were fight fans of his, Lyle gave each of them $100 and tickets for his Saturday bout against Chuck Leslie at the Auditorium Arena.'

The fight was supposed to have been with José Orbillo of Los Angeles, a former Army boxer who had compiled an impressive 18-4-1 record as a professional. But in what would soon become a pattern, Orbillo backed out, reportedly because he felt he didn't have enough time to properly train for his bout with Lyle. As it turned out, Lyle gained a stronger opponent in Chuck Leslie.

A veteran with 45 fights under his belt, Leslie was ranked 31st among heavyweight contenders, three notches higher than Lyle. He obviously had the experience advantage and he exuded confidence on the eve of the bout, saying he was in peak condition and making sure everybody who was listening knew he had fought good opponents and wasn't scared of the Denver guy with the knockout punch. He claimed to have built his reputation as a 'giant killer' by beating guys who were picked as favourites.

But Bobby Lewis and Ron Lyle were ready for Chuck Leslie, in spite of the last- minute substitution. Having come into professional boxing primarily as a slugger, Ron had been turned into a boxer who could also stand and slug it out. That was the way Bobby planned it, and that's the way it worked out on January 22, 1972.

The now routine headline 'Lyle Scores TKO' appeared over *Denver Post* sportswriter Terry Anderson's piece, subtitled: '12th Straight Win Comes in Third Round.' After reporting the hard-fought first two rounds, Anderson described Lyle's combinations and lefts to Leslie's chin that knocked him through the ropes in the third round. The sportswriter suggested that Ron Lyle had successfully entered phase two of his march through the ranks by quoting Bobby Lewis:

> The plan and schedule now is to fight the runners. You can't fight guys who stand in front and slug all the time. You have to eventually fight the boxers who know how to fight and move. The dancers, like Muhammad Ali. Tonight Ron got his first dancer. One down.
>
> Ron and I play a chess game out there. We think alike. I was going to say just one thing to him out there when he took a right uppercut, but Lyle reacted the way he was supposed to. He remembered when Manuel Ramos hit him in the same way and he reacted like he should.

Lewis went on to say that the day would come when he wouldn't even have to think about telling Lyle anything in the ring. When that day came, Lyle would be ready for a title fight.

Bang…bang…bang… *Rocky Mountain News* sportswriter Roy Holman's article on January 25 focused on Lyle's future. Ron had been a guest speaker at the Colorado Springs Quarterback Club and had responded to questions ranging from the chances of boxing in Mile High Stadium to his early-round knockouts, such as the third round of the Leslie bout.

'I'd like to go on a little longer….maybe eight rounds or so,' Ron said. 'But in the heat of the fight, you get sort of excited and when the chance comes, you just react to it.'

Holman added that Ron Lyle seemed to be building a knockout reputation and that some boxers were shying away from a contract with him. He suggested that Lyle was climbing the ranking ladder fairly quickly. Had the sports reporter waited a few days, he might have used the term 'meteoric' to describe Lyle's rise, when the World Boxing Association ranked him in the top ten among world contenders. He had gone from 34th to 10th in one fight.

Lyle himself showed more interest in his coming bouts than in his rank. From an interview with Terry Anderson:

> 'All I want to do is to continue my progress toward the world heavyweight title,' he said. 'If the ratings will help me, fine. But the only thing that's going to help me inside the ring is experience. Until I get enough experience, I'm not going to worry about how high I'm ranked. Besides, I don't think I should be ranked number ten until all the rating services have me there.'[4]

Other sportswriters complained about his handlers not

giving him opportunities against more skilled opponents. *Rocky Mountain News* sports columnist Chet Nelson interpreted the third-round knockout in the Leslie fight as evidence of 'an obvious mismatch' and urged a higher level of competition, even as he acknowledged that: 'cash customers have been adoringly satisfied while projecting the Denver heavyweight onto a popularity plane unmatched in the history of modern boxing hereabouts.'

Ron's opponents had been carefully picked for style in accordance with the educational plan devised by Bobby Lewis, and Leslie had been his first 'boxer.' But the time had come to up the ante.

17

*

CONTENDERS, major and minor, were hard to come by. They had little to gain and much to lose in facing Lyle, and the word was getting out that the green heavyweight was damned hard to hit - maybe impossible to knock out. Case in point: Tony Doyle.

Ranked ninth the year before, Doyle had agreed to fight Ron in Denver on February 26. The bout was put off a month to March 25 after Tony's manager/father Nugent reported the heavyweight had developed a case of tendonitis in his left shoulder. Then on March 5, Nugent Doyle made a request for a bigger ring as part of the contract negations for the fight. The ring at the Auditorium Arena was 16 feet, but Doyle, presumably because of his style and speed, preferred a 20-foot ring.

From the *Denver Post*: '"That 16-foot ring is just too small for me," Doyle said Saturday from his Salt Lake City home. "My style is to move in and out, feint my opponent out of position and counterpunch. To do that I need room. I don't

126

want to fight Ron's fight if I don't have to."' In the same story, Bobby Lewis responded: 'Ron can fight in a phone booth or on a field; it doesn't matter, just as long as his opponent is there.' The promoter Action Sports ordered the bigger ring for the fight scheduled in the Coliseum, a much larger venue than the Auditorium Arena and announced it would be ready for the Lyle-Doyle fight, expected to be an 11,000 capacity sell-out.

A few days later, it was announced that Tony Doyle would have to cancel the March appearance because of a 'severe ankle sprain...', epitomising the frustration for the Lyle camp as they constantly scrambled to fill cards left vacant by opponents cancelling at the last minute. On March 25, that filler turned out to be George 'Scrap Iron' Johnson, a seasoned veteran who had the distinction of being just one of three boxers to go the distance against heavyweight champion Joe Frazier. Johnson, known for his durability, had yet to be knocked out after eleven professional years.

So, in the brand new ring ordered by the absent Tony Doyle, the durable Johnson met the boxer/slugger Lyle. The fighters spent most of the first round leaning against each other, head to head, feeling each other out. Then Lyle opened up in the second round with a flurry of combination punches. Terry Anderson reported that: 'When Johnson momentarily got Lyle against the ropes, the Denver heavyweight reacted like an angry bear trying to stave off bee stings, knocking Johnson's ineffective punches aside.'

In the third round, Lyle came out and immediately started throwing right crosses to Johnson's head and, at 31 seconds in the third round, 'Scrap Iron' ended up in a heap on the floor.

THE Commissioner of the Colorado State Athletic Commission, Eddie Bohn, announced at a press conference that it appeared definite that a Lyle bout would be held in

Mile high Stadium, likely to draw at least 35,000 fans. Bohn hoped they could lure Floyd Patterson to draw the largest boxing crowd in Denver history. His opinion was that the only other top contenders who could make a real fight of it for Lyle would be Joe Frazier, Muhammad Ali, George Foreman, Jerry Quarry and Oscar Bonavena. He added that Lyle 'could be another Joe Louis, if he'd just smile a little bit, but maybe he's a little shy.' The Commissioner obviously hadn't seen Lyle surrounded by kids.

It wasn't until May that Ron managed to get another fight, this time in Las Vegas. The *Post* reported: 'Denver heavyweight Ron Lyle went through a light workout Wednesday night at the Silver Slipper here to win his 14th consecutive fight, knocking out Mel Turnbow in the seventh round.' The only notable feature of the Turnbow bout was when Lyle got hit with a right to the side of his face, a rare occurrence, midway through the fifth round.

The Turnbow fight had been postponed three times from April 19 (Turnbow bruised shoulder) to May 3 (Turnbow bruised elbow) to May 10 (Turnbow didn't feel he was in shape yet). In between Turnbow cancellations, Ron went to Seattle to fight Rufus Brassell. After he arrived all he got was a phone call from Brassell's manager informing him that Brassell had just had his front teeth knocked out in a sparring session against Canadian champion George Chuvalo. Ron had been forced to either postpone or cancel six fights since the first of the year, and the frustration in the Lyle camp grew.

Finally, an opportunity arose to meet a 'worthy opponent,' contender Mike Boswell, on a card that would include the heavyweight title fight between Joe Frazier and Ron Stander in Omaha, Nebraska. Bill Daniels was ecstatic, seeing the fight as a great chance for Ron to receive some well-deserved recognition, since the boxing world would be watching the Frazier-Stander title fight and presumably the lead-in bout.

It turned out that many fans, including all of Denver, were less impressed by Frazier knocking out Stander in the fifth round than the performance of the amazing new contender earlier in the evening. As had become his tradition, Ron had a slow first round, sizing up his opponent. He opened fast in the second round and pinned Boswell against the ropes several times. In the third, he picked his spots carefully and at 2:10 in the round, disposed of Boswell's mouthpiece with a left head shot. Then, 30 seconds later, Ron hit his opponent with a right uppercut that left him groggy on the floor. Boswell got up and went into a shell when Lyle scored another left with four seconds remaining in the round. Boswell walked to the wrong corner and when the bell rang for the fourth round, he failed to answer giving Ron the fight on a technical knockout.

Terry Anderson wrote about that fight: 'Trainer Bobby Lewis has had Ron Lyle singing George Gershwin songs lately, including *I've Got Rhythm*, in his bid to keep the Denver heavyweight boxer unbeaten.' Today Ron laughs when he reads that article. He says he got his rhythm down early in that fight, but adds that he couldn't then, and can't now, carry a tune. He says: 'When I sing in the shower, the water goes back up into the spout to get away from me.'

What sportswriters called Ron's first 'Big Name Test' came two months later when he got a crack at Vincente Rondon, the 1971 World Boxing Association light heavyweight champion of the world, in Mile High Stadium. Rondon had never suffered defeat to any light heavyweight in his career until Bob Foster took the championship away from him the previous April.

Reporting for *The Sports Desk* in an exclusive interview with Ron Lyle, Chuck Roach quoted Ron: 'I'm hoping this fight will open doors for me. I try not to be impressed with the guys I'm going to fight, but I realise Rondon has held the championship.' Described as 'nattily attired in a seersucker suit,' Lyle told Roach he had never seen Rondon in person or on film, but 'Bobby Lewis has seen Rondon and thinks I can whip him.'

For their part, the Rondon camp was brimming with confidence. The difficulties Rondon had had in the past keeping his weight down to the 175 pound limit for light heavyweights was over. Manager Felix Zabala told Roach: 'Right now, Vincente is at 194 pounds, a weight that he feels very, very comfortable at. At that weight, he keeps all of his fast moves and his punches are stronger.'

Ron wasn't worried. He remembers telling Roach that he had a lot of confidence in his left hand and that he was used to fighting outdoors because of all the fights he had at Canon City. He even talked about his plan to be in a championship match within a year.

Rondon arrived in Denver a week early, and his trainer told reporters: 'Don't worry about Vicente not being in shape. Your man Lyle has never fought a fighter who has been so superbly conditioned as Vicente.' Both fighters engaged in pre-bout braggadocio, typical for the time. Rondon: '....I see mistakes that Lyle makes and I will take advantage of them....Once he makes a mistake, I'll hurt him.' Lyle: 'He has to fight when he gets into that ring. He'll be hurting when I get through with him.'

Rondon was a veteran of 45 professional fights, losing only six, compared to Lyle's record of 15-0. On the other hand, Ron had 20 pounds on his opponent, two inches height and an inch longer reach. It promised to be a terrific fight - it wasn't. Ron knocked out the former champion in the second round.

18

*

WHILE Ron was fighting to make his mark, life in the Lyle family continued to move on. Marriages, babies, career - the pace picked up in 1972. That was the year sister Donna had a dream about a long blue bridge that turned out to be the Coronado in San Diego, and she persuaded her trailer mechanic husband Jimmy Harris to turn down a transfer to Omaha and move to San Diego instead. Her little sister Joyce was already modelling in L.A., and although Donna hated to leave her parents, Nellie reminded her that even Abraham had to leave his tribe. Her only prayer for her daughter was to seek God's help in finding a Church in California.

Donna and Jimmy boarded a Greyhound bus in downtown Denver with their three boys and all of their belongings. Two days later they got off the bus in National City, just south of San Diego, and within blocks found not only a church, but an apartment complex looking for a manager. They lived, managed and maintained that complex for the next 14 years. 'Ronny and I both followed our dreams, and it worked out for both of us,' she says today.

Twenty-nine-year-old Kenneth had overcome physical and mental problems to begin working on his high school diploma, and he continued to choose his own destiny, eventually joining the Mormon Church, an incongruity for a black man in those days, not to mention a Lyle. 'Ron didn't just teach me about life; he showed me,' Kenneth says softly in the presence of his beloved brother.

When in Denver, Ron paid as much attention to both his families as he thought he could afford, but sometimes he felt there wasn't enough of him to go around. Given his new *Ring* magazine number-eight ranking and the upcoming fight with Mac Foster, the press kicked it up a notch, calling or dropping in at the gym almost every day. Word had gotten out that the prize for the winner of the Lyle-Foster bout would be a fight in Madison Square Garden on the September 20 card, which would feature the nationally televised Muhammad Ali-Floyd Patterson match-up. The big time.

Foster had a near spotless record, 28 knockouts in 30 fights. His only losses were in a 15-rounder with Ali and an early bout with Jerry Quarry. Terry Anderson quoted Foster: '....Lyle needs a lesson, and I'm going to be the teacher...I'm not taking anything away from Lyle, but he's just not the same calibre fighter as me. I'm a seasoned fighter and that will be the difference. Both of us are strong, but I've beaten other boxers just as strong. The thing you need is skill and finesse.'

Ron was chomping at the bit to show Foster *his* skill and finesse, but all predictions were for an early knockout by one fighter or the other, since both had made a practice of ending fights early. The Lyle fans didn't seem to mind that their tickets for full round bouts were usually over within four rounds. Seeing the Denver hero knock an opponent out was always worth it.

With Bobby Lewis in Munich coaching the Olympic team headed by Duane Bobick, a part-time steamfitter from New York by the name of Frank Smith took over Ron's training the week before the Foster fight. The 62-year-old former boxer had been assisting Lewis for nine years, but found his greatest pleasure in working with Lyle. Ron liked Smith, too, saying he was the one man who was able to get him relaxed before a fight. In spite of New York odds-makers picking Foster as a 9-5 favourite, Smith was convinced his fighter would win. As for Ron, his statement to Anderson was unequivocal: 'My goal in life is to be the heavyweight champion of the world. In my heart I know I'm going to win the title and Foster is a roadblock in my plans. So he's got to go and he will.'

Then, two days before the fight scheduled for Saturday, it happened again. Foster said he had been injured sparring and complained of a possible broken nose and a spur in his left shoulder. He had been examined by a physician representing the Colorado Boxing Commission, but Foster wasn't satisfied with the conclusion and called his doctor in California who had performed surgery on the elbow before. Then the incident morphed into high drama.

Foster and his manager Richard Shaw were on their way to make a 7:15 flight to Los Angeles to make a Friday appointment with Foster's doctor when they were stopped by Mike Hayes, vice president of the Denver Boxing Club, who told them they needed to meet with the Colorado Boxing Commission. The meeting, which took place at Eddie Bohn's restaurant on West Colfax turned into an ugly confrontation. Attended by the three members of the Commission, two attorneys representing the Denver Boxing Club and a court reporter, the meeting concluded with one of the attorneys presenting Foster with a court summons. Verbal threats included having Foster suspended and a $50,000 suit for breach of contract. Clearly, the Denver boxing community was fed up with cancellations of Ron Lyle fights.

Shaw granted an interview late Thursday to the *Rocky Mountain News*:

> 'What am I going to do? Let him become a cripple for a lousy $11,000?' snapped a rather angry Shaw as the pair told their tale.
>
> 'We were already told Mac would have to win by a knockout to beat Lyle...We knew it would be tough fighting in Ron's hometown, but asking Mac to fight this way is too much. How many advantages does Lyle need, anyway?'
>
> Foster chimed in, 'If my own doctor says I can't fight, then I won't,....but I don't feel their doctor gave me a real exam. If I can't spar, then how can I perform for the public?'

The Boxing Commission had given them only until 9 a.m. Friday to commit themselves on the fight before legal action would be taken. Shaw's response: 'After they kept us from leaving tonight (Thursday) it will be impossible for us to get back by then. And we won't fight without the okay from Dr. Leventhal.' He later told the *Denver Post* that if Foster's doctor gave the okay, they would be willing to postpone the fight to the following Wednesday. It never happened.

Even while the ring and special lighting were being prepared at Mile High Stadium, Shaw contacted the Lyle camp and informed them that, after examining extensive X-rays, Dr. Leventhal had found two bone chips the size of peas in Foster's left shoulder, chips that had not been discovered by Colorado physicians.

Suspension or not, lawsuit or not, Ron Lyle was once again deprived of his chance to meet a highly-ranked competitor. He was quoted by Terry Anderson: 'I was ready for my toughest fight yet, and I'm sorry things have turned out this way.'

Sorry didn't begin to describe the feelings of Bill Daniels and the Denver fans. Daniels told Anderson: 'Of course, we're terribly disappointed by this temporary setback in Ron's career. He was ready for the fight, as he always is. He's shown up for every fight, and he's fought even when he has been hurt. And we'll fight anyone at any time.'

Daniels went on to say that he would begin to search for another fighter immediately, hoping to set a fight in Mile High Stadium before the Denver Broncos opened their home exhibition season. And, of course, the cancelled fight also put an end to any hopes of the September appearance by Lyle in Madison Square Garden.

The frustration Ron didn't allow himself to express in public was starting to show at home. Nadine told him she was tired of acting as Monte's only parent during the long 18-hour days of training, not to mention that much of Ron's free-time was still spent working with other kids. He couldn't understand why she didn't get his frustration - why she couldn't hang in there until he fought for the championship. The marriage was starting to fray, even as his career seemed stalled. Ron didn't foresee that his life would soon improve dramatically on one front, even while he put the rest on hold.

19

*

ON the last leg of his trip home from coaching the Olympic Games, where Duane Bobick had lost his chance for a medal, Bobby Lewis drove straight from Denver airport to the Elks Punch Bowl. Shaken by the massacre of Israelis in Munich, he immediately threw himself into training Ron Lyle.

The Friday before, Lewis had received a telegram from Bill Daniels announcing a fight with Buster Mathis for September 29, only two weeks away. Anxious to make up for time lost after the Rondon fight and the Foster fiasco, he had already decided on sparring partners for Lyle.

Mathis had been sparring up to 15 rounds a day in preparation for the fight, and since Lewis had forbade Lyle to spar when he was not around, Ron had spent his time in heavy training and shadow boxing, not enough preparation for a guy with Mathis' experience and reputation. Three days after he got back, Lewis flew in Mel Turnbow and two guys who had just finished helping Muhammad Ali shape up for what had turned out to be a seventh-round win over Floyd Patterson at Madison Square Garden the previous week.

Lewis was especially motivated to move Ron forward after the Foster defection that had prevented him from appearing on the Ali-Patterson card. Turnbow was the ideal sparring partner, not only because he had boxed both Lyle and Mathis, but because he approached the 260 pounds Mathis was expected to carry into the fight.

'Dancing Bear' Mathis showed his endearing side when meeting with the press in Denver a few days before the fight. Highly successful in the ring, losing just three of 33 professional fights, he was described by Terry Anderson as a boxer who fights on three levels of competition.

Anderson quotes the fighter:

> I've had a lot of problems fighting myself, my own feelings and opponents. But now I understand all three. And now that I understand that, I want to go even higher.....I just enjoy living. I enjoy everything I'm doing. I came to win and I came to live. I just happen to be a boxer in the process.....I want to be happy with myself, so happy that I can sit down and say that I'm happy with myself. I don't want to ask myself what I have to be happy about. I just want to be happy.

Mathis had given up a promising ring career because of personal and emotional problems following a 12-round loss to Jerry Quarry in 1969 and had gained more than 140 pounds while he tried to iron out his personal affairs. His fighting weight of 222 had ballooned to 360 by the time he decided to return to boxing. It took a year to lose the 100 pounds required to hang in with Ali, only to lose a decision in 12 rounds; he lost 20 more and knocked out Claude McBride in the third round barely a month before he was to meet Lyle.

The Lyle-Mathis fight would illustrate the philosophy of Barney O'Grady, the Colorado State University student who kept scrapbooks on Ron's career from his early amateur days: 'Boxing is not a brutal sport, not when match-ups are even. And it's more than a sport when two people like Ron are in the ring. It's one entire life against another entire life - their struggles, their dreams. And those two people understand each other in a way none of the rest of us do.' Ron Lyle and Buster Mathis understood each other, and on September 29, 1972 one ended the career of the other.

A worthy opponent and two years younger than Ron, Mathis looked ten years older when he went down hard in the second round. On a night when heavyweight champion Joe Frazier appeared on the card for an exhibition bout and when the United States Olympic team was introduced to a record Denver crowd that brought in a $100,000 gate, the pivotal moment occurred when Lyle caught Mathis with a left hook to the head that sent him into the ropes for the last time with only a minute left in round two. Mathis had only suffered two knockouts in his entire career, both TKO's, one by Joe Frasier in the eleventh round.

Even better news for Bobby Lewis was that Ron took two good blows from Mathis, one a left hook to the head in the first round and the other a solid shot to the chest in the second. The trainer still didn't know if his fighter could get up off the canvas to come back and win, but he knew that Ron could take hard hits.

From the *Rocky Mountain News*:

> One of the last quotes Buster Mathis gave reporters before stepping into the ring to face unbeaten Ron Lyle was this: 'I'm not underestimating Lyle because I've seen him hit and he can take a fighter out with one punch!'

And although Buster was off in the number of punches - he was right about everything else. For the first time in his career he failed to finish a fight on his feet as Ron Lyle, the unbeaten Denver ex-convict, put him away at 2:59 of the second round of their scheduled ten-rounder at the Denver Coliseum.

Technically, it took Lyle three punches - not one - to put Buster on ice. But to Mathis' credit, the two left hooks and the right cross which embalmed him might have demolished an office building had Lyle been working on a wrecking crew.

Before the bout, Yank Durham, Joe Frazier's manager, said that he and the heavyweight champion decided to make the appearance in Denver to observe possible future opponents. He had been planning to watch Lyle and Mathis fight anyway because he liked personally to scout anyone who could be a future threat to Joe. Since Mathis had defeated Frazier twice in 1964 during the Olympic qualifying competition, Lyle was the one Durham needed to see. And Lyle eliminated any lingering threat from Mathis. Durham was quoted by Benny Deaton as congratulating Ron in the dressing room after the fight: 'Young man, one of these days in the not too distant future, you're going to get a shot at the heavyweight title.'

The *Ring* headlined their cover: 'Ron Lyle, Best of New Breed?' And Dan Levin in *Ringside* called Ron Lyle '....a living monument to the perfectibility of man, perhaps deservedly so. Among Denverites, he can do no wrong....'

Levin went on to quote Bill Daniels:

'We've got a fighter here who doesn't drink, doesn't smoke and doesn't swear.' They also have a fighter who is something of a community phenomenon. This year Lyle was chairman of the 1972 Colorado March

of Dimes Walkathon, which drew the biggest
response in its history. He works with a group called
Partners, in which adults take on problem kids, and a
friend says, 'He's their honorary God.'

In fact, shortly before the Mathis fight, it was announced
that Ron Lyle would lead a 'Walk for the Retarded' at 7 a.m.
Saturday in Washington Park. Sponsored by the Denver
Association for Retarded Children, Lyle had agreed to serve
as chairman of the walk and promised four ringside tickets
to the Mathis bout for the two persons who turned in the
most pledges. It was almost as though Ron Lyle was too
good to be true.

20

*

RON's reputation for superb conditioning, his devastating right hand and early knockout record continued to scare off opponents, frustrating the Lyle camp. In its October issue, *Ringside* quoted Bill Daniels:

> Whenever we approach the manager of a fighter... they merely look at his knockout record and all of a sudden their fighter has another commitment. Ron's reputation has spread throughout the world and not many want to tangle with a puncher of his calibre....We're not going to rush into anything ...Each fight we pick we do so for a purpose. Lyle someday is going to be the heavyweight champion of the world, and each fight is a stepping stone to that goal. Right now not too many fighters want to mix it up with him. So it's a frustrating experience to come up with the right people to [meet him] in the ring.

Vince Boryla, president of the Denver Boxing Club, was

pushing for a system that would be impartial, allowing natural match-ups. He was quoted by Terry Anderson:

> Ron's at a different part of his career right now. We're trying to keep him active, to fill his schedule, but a lot of fighters are leery of him, so it's often difficult to get him a natural match-up. The good ones don't want to fight him for fear of losing and ruining their own records. And beating Mathis the way he did, didn't make matters any easier....Boxing is so hit and miss. It's not like playing a regular schedule.
>
> But a commissioner with enough power could step in and see that proper fights are scheduled between fighters. Then if someone backs out of a fight or turns a fight down, the commissioner could move that boxer down in rankings, put him on notice to either fight within a certain time period or face suspension.[5]

Unfair system notwithstanding, the city of Denver continued to honour its favourite son. Many believed the voters approved a $10 million bond issue for a new Sports Arena because they wanted Lyle to box in a venue that would seat 18,000. In October, Mayor William McNichols agreed to make Ron Lyle and the Denver Boxing Club its first occupants by accepting a cheque from Denver Boxing Club president Vince Boryla at a photo opportunity with Lyle in attendance. Boryla was quoted as saying the Boxing Club wanted to be the first user of the new building '....because by that time Ron will be needing a larger building to defend his World Heavyweight title.'

With all the publicity surrounding Ron, a momentous personal event occurred almost without notice. Bill Daniels's influence on Governor John Love finally paid off - on October 6, 1972, the Governor of Colorado granted Ron Lyle a full pardon. The gift was enormous, the slate wiped clean. Ron hardly had a chance to absorb the news of his pardon when another step to fulfilling his dream was set for one month after the Mathis bout - a bout with his most important opponent so far, Brazil's heavyweight champion Luis Pires.

Pires would afford Ron an opportunity to meet a fighter who had not only boxed many of the top heavyweights in the world, but also a man with the reputation of being one of the most courageous fighters in the business. Eleven months before, Pires had stayed in the ring for two rounds after George Foreman had broken his arm early in the second. The referee had finally stopped the fight on the recommendation of the attending physician. The Brazilian fighter would present Ron Lyle with two other challenges as well. Pires liked to slug it toe-to-toe rather than box, and he liked to brag that in all his 27 professional bouts, he had never been floored. Bobby Lewis warned Ron that Pires would not be a pushover.

But a pushover he turned out to be. The headlines the day after the fight read: 'Lyle Kayos Pires in Third Round'. Ron had done his usual stalking in the first round, even as both fighters exchanged some good punches. The pace picked up in the second as Ron got in a series of lefts to the head and body while taking some shots without flinching. In the third round Pires caught him with a left uppercut, and Ron 'unleashed a two-fisted flurry that alerted the crowd that the end was not far away.' Bobby Lewis had told him before the start of the round to 'be the boss.' And the boss he was, as he knocked Pires to the floor with a lethal right cross. The referee counted the Brazilian out while he was still trying to roll over onto his knees. Mike Hayes wrote in *The Ring* that: 'Lyle did to Pires something that George Foreman couldn't do a year ago.'

Bill Daniels and Bobby Lewis were as happy that Ron had taken some blistering shots from Pires as they were about the knockout. Both were becoming more and more confident that their fighter could take a hit. And a few days later, *Ring* magazine ranked Ron Lyle the seventh heavyweight in the world. All four rating organisations now had Ron Lyle in their top ten.

BOBBY LEWIS moved to Denver and life became easier for Ron. He could spend more time with Monte and Nadine, not to mention his extended family on Hudson Street. And after having established his generosity to the Denver community, he threw himself even harder into what he identified as 'pockets of need.'

The same month he knocked out Pires, he was named the Jaycees 'Young Man of the Year' for his contributions to the community, and his celebrity grew exponentially. *Ringside* published a picture of actors Al Pacino and Gene Hackman accepting tickets from Ron to the Mathis fight, and *Empire* did a cover story entitled *These Kids Give me Something to Fight For*, which carried a seven-picture spread. The image on the first page is of Ron - a huge smile - holding one boy on his shoulder and reaching out to hug another running into the ring after a fight.

The Young Man of the Year award for Lyle came about the same time as Johnny Rodgers of Nebraska University won the Heisman Trophy. Rodgers had been convicted of armed robbery and arrested on possession charges, which prompted a letter to the *Denver Post* protesting a national 'decline in standards' and questioning both athletes as role models for young people. One measure of Ron's popularity was the flurry of angry replies to that letter. The *Post* even published an Editor's Note which introduced a large sample of reply excerpts, including: '....Mr. Lyle is doing a lot to make up for his mistake by helping underprivileged teens, which is more than any rocking-chair critic does.'

Ron is still grateful for the support Denver gave him in those days. 'The people of Denver understood then…. and they understand now. They have always been there for me. They always gave me hope.'

That year closed out as a time of great expectations for Ron. Things were going better with Nadine as he had squeezed out more time for his family. And not only was he to receive even greater community honours, he was also on the verge of gaining the respect his fans thought he deserved by landing a December fight with the sixth-rated heavyweight boxer in the world; one Larry Middleton.

21

*

RON LYLE was about to meet a whole new calibre of fighter in Larry Middleton. Considered one of the finest boxers in the world, his finesse in the ring had been compared to Jimmy Ellis, but his size also gave him plenty of punching power. Middleton had conquered both the European and British Commonwealth champions with ease, and he, too, was frustrated that bouts with worthy opponents were thwarted. Ali had agreed to fight Middleton, then withdrew, as did George Foreman in October, even after contracts had been signed.

The December 9 fight drew international attention. When the bout was announced, both Middleton and Lyle were ranked sixth and seventh respectively by the World Boxing Association and anticipation ran high. Barely a week before the fight, probably as a response to the match-up, the WBA moved Lyle up to number five and Middleton to number four. Besides champion Joe Frazier, the only heavyweight boxers ranked higher were Muhammad Ali,

George Foreman and Jimmy Ellis; falling behind were such names as Oscar Bonavena, Floyd Patterson and Ken Norton.

Bill Brennan, chairman of the WBA Championship Committee, would be in attendance. He stated that the winner of the Middleton-Lyle bout would be 'considered in the near future for a world championship bout.' Ron finally found himself in the big time.

He kept his head. While Middleton tried to provoke Ron with such comments as: 'I've fought better men than Lyle has....All Lyle has whipped is a bunch of washed-out fighters,' Ron kept his mouth shut and quietly trained with Bobby Lewis as they always had - running, conditioning and sparring to meet his opponent's strengths.

Terry Anderson quoted Lewis: 'A boxer never stops learning, not even the champion. Do you think Joe Frazier has stopped learning? The moment a boxer stops learning, it's time for him to quit....' Then Lewis repeated what he said after the Leslie bout: 'Ron and I play a chess game out there....We think alike. He takes a right uppercut and reacts just like I would have told him to. The day will come when I won't even have to think about telling Ron anything in the ring. When that day comes, Ron's ready for a title fight.'

Ron remembers that he and Bobby were always on the same wavelength. 'We thought alike. Before every fight, we both knew what I had to do. It got so we didn't even need to talk about it.' That wavelength was especially important now.

As usual for Denver home boxing events, the amateur Denver Rocks were scheduled against All-Army champions, but Donny Nelson's name was missing for the December meet. Always loyal fans, the Nelson brothers focused their attention on Ron while Donny pondered his decision whether or not to leap into the professional arena. In the meantime, Dennis was confident his friend would beat Middleton. And he wasn't alone.

Off the Ropes

Not since the Muhammad Ali-Joe Frazier championship fight almost two years before had there been a match between two heavyweights ranked in the top five, and Las Vegas took notice. A few days before the fight, the odds were established at 8-5 Lyle. Most of the boxing world, however, favoured Middleton. Third-ranked Jerry Quarry, who had decisioned Middleton 49¼ to 49 points the previous May, stated: 'I know that Lyle has a lot of heart and desire, but it's not enough to offset the great boxing and punching ability that Middleton has.' And Joe Bugner, who had broken Middleton's jaw and still lost, also weighed in. 'Lyle won't be able to touch Middleton,' he predicted. 'Middleton is a very deceptive fighter. He has a difficult style and is very difficult to hit. Middleton will win, most likely by a decision or a late-round knockout.'

Even Bobby Lewis was uncharacteristically cautious: 'I said before and I'll say it again that Middleton is a tougher opponent than George Foreman. Middleton is tougher because he is harder to get to with right crosses and uppercuts. And the uppercut is Ronny's best punch, I think.'

Middleton kept talking. He told Bob Collins, Sports Editor of the *Rocky Mountain News*, that he would stop the Denver boxer: '....in the seventh or eighth round with a left hook followed by a right hand.' Collins commented: 'He may have the rounds for the ending right. But if there's a knockout at this juncture I would expect it to be scored by Lyle.'

Middleton's trainer predicted a 'beautiful fight' since he saw neither as quitter, but also said he would never take Larry anywhere he thought he might lose. And Middleton kept talking. Terry Anderson recorded him thus:

> I'm in the best shape of my life and all my frustrations
> of the past few months will be released when I face

Lyle next week....I know what I can do in the ring because I've done it against some of the best. Don't forget that I busted Joe Bugner's jaw in seven places and knocked out the British champ. I had Quarry whipped, but the referee gave him the win. Just who has Lyle fought? I've looked at his record and all I can see are a bunch of washed-up fighters. I am without a doubt the best fighter he has ever met in his life and he's going to regret it.

I'll be writing a poem soon and I might even paint a picture showing what I'll do to Lyle. My painting of him will probably resemble a machine because that's all Lyle is.

Anderson reported that: 'Lyle refused to be drawn into an argument with Middleton. He just shrugged his shoulders and said: "Let's wait until December 9th, and then we'll see who's better."'

Ron remembers the extraordinary confidence he felt before the Middleton fight. 'Back then, I didn't think I would ever lose.' And he didn't, at least not that night. The headlines the next day read:

'Lyle's left Dominates in Middleton Bout'
'Lyle Comes Into the Title Picture'
'Unbeaten Lyle KOs Middleton in Three'

Larry Middleton had proven no more difficult to knock out than any of Ron's previous opponents. The Lyle record on December 9, 1972 became 19 straight victories, with 17 KOs, 11 in a row. Ron Lyle remained undefeated.

The fight had gone much like the others, Ron stalking in the first round with Middleton winning on points by scoring some left jabs and hooks that were essentially harmless. Midway through the second, though, Ron Lyle took over. He blocked his opponent's uppercuts and scored with some good shots of his own, then floored Middleton with a right-left hook combination in the last seconds of the round. The third round was reported in detail by the *Denver Post*:

> Ron came out punching in the third, pressing in on Middleton, who kept trying to land his uppercuts. Lyle scored with a pair of left hooks to the head, then landed two solid rights that put the shakes into Larry's legs. Middleton tried to move in and clinch behind a left jab. Ron missed a right hand lead, but landed a right uppercut, a left hook and a right cross. As Larry sagged, Lyle pumped in a stiff left jab, then crossed his right, flooring Larry for the mandatory eight count. When Larry regained his feet, he was bowled over by a flurry of lefts and rights, going down face forward. To the surprise of all, Middleton pounded the mat with his right hand in frustration, and when he arose at eight, he was wild-eyed. He lowered his head and charged towards Lyle, who calmly measured him and unleaded a wicked right uppercut that landed flush on the jaw. The power of the punch lifted Middleton off his feet and dropped him flat on his back in mid-ring. Referee Ullmer could have counted to fifty as Larry was out cold. The time was 2:34 of the third round.

ASKED recently whether he had personal feelings about any of his opponents, including Middleton, Ron answered: 'No. It was already personal enough with a guy wanting to knock my head off.'

In 19 fights, Ron Lyle had not only kept his head, he still hadn't been seriously hit. By the end of December 1972, the World Boxing Association had named him Fighter of the Year and moved him to the number four position on the list of heavyweight contenders. *International Boxing Magazine* rated Lyle third among all heavyweights.

Bill Daniels said: 'I'm just tickled to death that Ron was given the award. What's more fantastic is that he got it with less than two years of his pro career gone. Now everyone's thinking what we've been thinking about for a long time - Ron Lyle will soon be the heavyweight champion of the world.'

22

*

BILL DANIELS was not only pushing Ron's career in 1972, he was pushing his own. Described by more than one acquaintance as a 'human dynamo,' Daniels would eventually be married five times to four different women, all the while remaining active in Republican politics. He had begun tuning up to a run for Governor as early as 1971 and had enlisted his friend Bob Cox in the effort. Cox, who was destined to play a key role in the Ron Lyle story, agreed to participate in state Republican politics, likening that decision to 'agreeing to pass the plate at a Baptist Church - you can't get out of it.'

Cox relates a series of events that fall into a kind of inevitable pattern, ending with a lifetime connection. 'My son was born in 1962. Almost from the beginning he showed signs of poor eye/hand co-ordination. When he was about nine, his doctor told me I needed to spend more time with him - some one-on-one sports activity. I was a single parent with a pretty successful business [Cox Equipment] and Bill

Daniels was getting me more and more involved in politics. I was the Financial Director of the State Republican Party. But that doctor convinced me I needed to put Greg first. So since I had worked with the Ft. Collins boxing team, I took Greg to Dave Cook Sporting Goods and got him outfitted with equipment. He made progress. It was a good decision.

'As a reward, I got ringside seats and took Greg to a Ron Lyle fight. It was one of those early knockouts and Greg was an instant fan. Bill Daniels got wind of it and put a couple of things together. His administrative assistant Bobbi Watson had been looking for a kid to model the Ron Lyle tee-shirts, and Bill thought Greg would be a natural.'

As had other kids who were Ron Lyle fans, Greg soon became devoted, especially after the two of them posed for a series of publicity shots. Ron always took the time to talk to the little boy and to show him some boxing moves, a kindness that would eventually change both their lives.

Bob Cox recalls that Ron's influence on young Greg was especially manifested two years later when he entered the fifth grade. Ron had made it a point to touch base with Greg often, and Bob believes that the boxer was a great influence in increasing the boy's confidence. Greg had sometimes been plagued with bullies at school, and Bob had worked with school personnel over the years on seeking solutions. But one day the principal called to ask: 'Has there been a change in Greg?' Bob found himself replying, 'Better or worse?' The principal said: 'Well, this big kid really got in Greg's face today, and the next thing he knew, he was on the ground.'

Bob didn't condone the violence, but he was happy his son had defended himself. When Greg came home from school, he asked what had happened, and the boy replied: 'It just came to a point, I got fed up. So I decided on the biggest guy and used a couple of jabs and then a cross with the right.'

Ron laughed out loud when he heard that story.

ABOUT the same time that the photo of Greg Cox sporting a Ron Lyle tee-shirt appeared, the February cover of *Ring* magazine featured Ron with the article, 'Lyle, Imprisoned for 7¹/₂ Years, is not Bitter as Ring Heights Beckon Him'.

Ron had reached number four rankings in *Ring*, and with the World Boxing Association and World Boxing Council. *Boxing Illustrated* magazine had him in the number six position, but was expected to move him up to number four in the next issue. Ron was finally poised for a title fight. That same week a poll of UPI sportswriters and sportscasters was released which showed the 'Rise of Ron Lyle' as the second top sports story in for 1972, beaten out only by 'Colorado Voters Turn Down Olympics.'

The Colorado Sports Hall of Fame announced a special award for Ron, and, as if that were not enough, the Point O' Pines Corporation, an organisation with social and economic goals in Black development, named Ron Lyle 1972 Humanitarian Service Award, with published remarks by Mrs. Rachel Noel, the previous year's winner:

> This award expresses our gratitude as a community, and especially on behalf of the Black community. We appreciate the many hours you have spent with young people, helping them and leading them. We also want to express our pride, our hope and our certainty that you will reach your goal as the heavyweight champion.

Ron's opportunity for a championship fight improved by mega-leaps with the announcement of his next fight - Jerry Quarry on February 9, 1973 in Madison Square Garden. Quarry, still relatively young at 27, had been dubbed 'Another Great White Hope' during his impressive climb of

43 pro victories, 24 knockouts, against six losses, and the timing of the fight could not have been better. Two weeks before, George Foreman scored a stunning technical knockout over heavyweight champion Joe Frazier, unraveling a two-year-old 'log jam' that had top-ranking heavyweights lined up waiting for Frazier's rematch with Muhammad Ali. Foreman eliminated the rematch, giving the other contenders hope for a chance at the new champion.

Speculation ran through boxing circles that the winner of the Quarry-Lyle match would have an excellent shot at a championship bout. And when George Foreman announced he would attend the Garden fight as an observer, most sportswriters agreed that the winner would probably be the next heavyweight championship challenger.

The pressure was on; the *CSU Collegian* described the stakes:

> Fame is a fleeting thing for any athlete, particularly an ex-con. Everything that Lyle has today he owes to his success in the ring. The ring has given Lyle respectability and hope for the future. On the evening of February 9 when Lyle makes his way down the narrow aisle to the ring, much more will be at stake than a mere victory in the record books.
>
> After the final bell, Lyle will step through the ropes and out of the ring one fight away from his dream of the championship or one step back into the streets of Denver.

Bill Daniels presented an official challenge to George Foreman by filing a $5,000 deposit with the New York State Athletic Commission on behalf of Ron Lyle. The *Associated Press* quoted Daniels:

'What we're trying to do is to force some action. If

Ron beats Jerry Quarry….that means that Ron and Foreman are the only top ten-rated unbeaten heavyweight boxers in the world.' Daniels also went on to state that Lyle should get a shot at the title 'before Muhammad Ali, Jerry Quarry, Jimmy Ellis or even Joe Frazier because they've all either held the title or have been beaten [for it.] We'd like a chance to fight Foreman for the crown.'

Nobody thought it would be easy. Quarry would be the best opponent that Lyle had ever faced, younger, and with 54 fights under his belt. He had a reputation for being a tough, hard-nosed fighter with great endurance and a powerful right hand. Whatever the outcome, the fight promised to be a terrific slugfest. Lyle and Quarry were equally aggressive, never backing off and delivering dynamite in both fists. And both fighters were in great shape. Bob Collins of the *Rocky Mountain News* wrote:

> …Lyle and Quarry have been pronounced fit in such glowing terms that one would think they were matched in a Mr. America contest rather than a 12-round boxing main event.
>
> 'I've never seen an athlete in better physical or mental condition,' trainer Bobby Lewis said of Lyle… 'This is a new Jerry Quarry. He's in the best shape of his life,' said manager Gil Clancy of his tiger…

The Denver Boxing Club and the *Rocky Mountain News* co-sponsored a weekend excursion to New York to view the fight and New York sights, which immediately sold out. Bob and 11-year-old Greg Cox were on that flight. With Quarry always drawing well at the Garden ('…a Garden fighter,' Ron recalls), and the fairytale success story of Lyle, Garden officials predicted a sell-out.

Madison Square Garden was then, and continues to be, the summit for boxers. Terry Anderson compared fighting there as the main event to playing a solo concert at Carnegie Hall. Because the Garden was built for boxing, the history of the sport is centred there, going back to greats like Jack Dempsey, Joe Louis, and Rocky Marciano, among others. But as Anderson reminded his readers: 'It broke more boxers than it made.'

In New York, Ron continued to run his seven miles a day at 5:00 a.m., while Bill Daniels looked beyond the fight. After Muhammad Ali came up with an offer to fight Lyle, Daniels was quoted by Bob Collins as saying:

> We're not interested in Ali - we want Foreman. Foreman is the world heavyweight champion now, so why should we mess around with a former champion? Ali is just trying to add Lyle to his bum-a-month club, and we'll have no part of it.
>
> After Lyle fights Jerry Quarry….we will attempt to negotiate with Foreman for a title fight. We are serious about this.
>
> It isn't that we are trying to duck Ali. We haven't ducked anybody and we never will. Sometime in the future a fight with Ali might be something we would be interested in for Lyle, but not now.

Bobby Lewis expressed more caution. Always realistic, he had watched Quarry for years hang on to win fights other boxers might have written off. He was quoted as saying: 'Quarry is one tough cookie.' Maybe of most concern to Lewis was that Lyle had never had to go the distance, and had never been hit hard enough to test his stamina.

The odds-makers got busy. Las Vegas called it 11/9 Lyle, while New York favoured Quarry 8/5. Jimmy the Greek made Lyle 4/1, convinced Ron had the tools and the determination, but added: 'In these rising times for heavyweights, the fight could mean much to either man, a loss most damaging. Lyle is 30. [Ron was a few days away from his 32nd birthday]. If he can't beat Quarry, he will be at least two years away from a match with another big-name opponent. By then, it will be too late.' A dire prophecy.

The week before, Ron worked out at the Felt Forum and more than 1,000 spectators watched the drill. The director of boxing for the Garden said later that crowd was the largest to watch a workout since Muhammad Ali trained there for his fight with Joe Frazier. And when Ron switched back to Bobby Gleason's gym, some 1,500-2,000 fans were disappointed after showing up at Felt hoping to see Lyle.

Ron promised to return to the Felt Forum the following week, and arrangements were quickly made for young people from Harlem to be on hand. Ron remembers that morning as the most enjoyable and relaxing period during his stay in New York. After a series of light training exercises, shadow boxing, hitting both the light speed bag, and the heavy bag and skipping rope, he paused when the around 3,000 children began to sing 'Happy Birthday'.

Sports reporter Vic Ziegel described the scene:

> At one point publicist John Condon asked the crowd to rate the leading heavyweights with their applause. George Foreman, Joe Frazier and Lyle earned about the same amount of noise. The loudest, longest sounds came for Muhammad Ali. Later, Lyle stepped into the ring to answer some of the kids' questions. Like how did he think he would do against Ali.
>
> 'First, let me say that I share the same feelings you have about Muhammad Ali. He's one in a million,' he told them. 'But time always brings a change and it's my time now. I want to be heavyweight champion and he's in my way. He must go with the rest.'

Ron remembers feeling almost like he was home with the kids in Denver. One asked about his idol and Ron answered that he didn't have one, but said that he most respected Muhammad Ali. When they asked what kind of food he ate, he laughed and said same as them - soul food. His advice to that audience was the same as it always was: 'Don't drop out of school, and try to live a clean life.'

Two days before the fight, New York odds-makers switched odds from 8/5 Quarry to 7/5 Lyle, with Las Vegas and Jimmy the Greek still hanging with Lyle. Bob Collins of the *Rocky Mountain News* quoted Bobby Lewis: 'Ron wants this fight so badly that he can taste it....We're ready for anything and everything. Ron can go 12 if necessary. If he can end it before that, it will just be the gravy on the roast beef.' Collins went on to caution: 'One factor that might prove important is that Lyle has never gone past ten rounds in his career, while Quarry has proved his ability to go the distance.' Lyle was to receive $22^{1/2}$ per cent of the take, with the gross likely to be $200,000; Quarry would get $27^{1/2}$. Up to that point, Ron's biggest purse had been $16,800 for the Buster Mathis bout in Denver, peanuts by today's standards.

Interviews on Thursday, the day before the bout, revealed the intensity of both fighters. Lyle told Terry Anderson: 'My concentration is on Jerry Quarry....I want to destroy him, move him, get him out in front of me. He's blocking my path. The fight is all I have on my mind....When I eat, I think about Jerry Quarry. When I walk, I think about Jerry Quarry. When I talk, I think about Jerry Quarry. So, when I come into the ring Friday night, it's all Jerry Quarry.'

Quarry, for his part, focused on the experience gap, especially the tendency for many fighters to freeze when they box in Madison Square Garden for the first time. 'Lyle is confident, but a man only has confidence when he knows the other man can't hurt him. When he finds out I can hurt him, he won't be so confident. He'll have Garden jitters, too.' Quarry did say, however, that: '....This is a much more difficult fight than my last one against Randy Neuman [Quarry scored a seventh-round technical knockout]. I expect a much more difficult man in front of me.'

In a telephone interview with Bob Collins, Ron denied fear of the Garden. 'I couldn't be better....And tell those friends and fans of mine in Denver not to be fretting about [the fight] with Quarry. Tell them that if I'm not worried, they shouldn't be either.... Oh, I miss the Denver fans. But I'm at home anywhere once I step into the ring. That's where I'm comfortable. You can say that they're putting on Friday's fight right in my front room.' Part of the reason Lyle remained calm was the presence of Lt. Clifford Maddox. Ron had made special arrangements for his former prison guard and mentor to attend.

Harry Markson, the Garden boxing director set up a special news conference to introduce Ron Lyle to the New York and other sports reporters from around the country. Markson told the audience: 'Few fighters have come into New York as heralded as Ron Lyle.' Among the articles that followed that press conference was one by Dave Anderson of the *New York Times*, who focused his attention on Lyle overcoming enormous obstacles, and quoted Lt. Maddox about Ron's prison experience:

> .....He was our best athlete - in boxing, baseball, basketball and football. And now he assists me in a lot of our programs. He's the only civilian who is allowed to go any place in the institution without custodial assistance. Lyle learned to box in a sandstone building that was built in 1934 as part of the prison....It's about

Above: Colorado State
Prison guard Clifford
Maddox trains Ron Lyle
in 1964

Left: Ron plays American
Football in prison in 1963

Left: Ron Lyle, pictured shortly after release in 1969

Above: Ron's beloved mother Nellie Lyle, pictured circa 1970

Left: Ron with Clifford Maddox on a visit back to Colorado State Penitentiary...

Below: ...and feeding baby Monte, 1971

Inset - Tracy and David in 1978

Right: Ron Lyle -
1972 WBA Fighter of the Year

Below left: Greg Cox spends time
with his sporting idol - and
proudly wears a Ron Lyle T-shirt

Below right: Ron works out

Ron Lyle

★★★★
LYLE
1972 W.B.A.
FIGHTER OF THE YEAR

Left: Ron and Jerry Quarry go head-to-head in 1973

Below: Oscar Bonavena reels from a solid right by Ron Lyle in 1974

Below: A spray of sweat flies after Ron Lyle's punch lands during his win over Jimmy Ellis in 1974

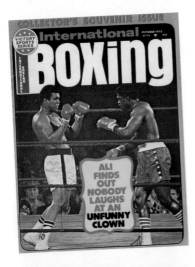

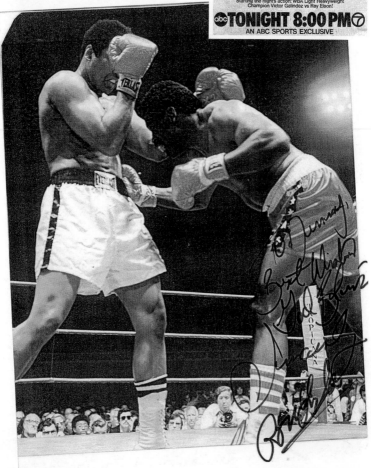

Above: Ron Lyle and legendary world heavyweight champion Muhammad Ali go head-to-head during a brutal bout in Las Vegas in 1975

Above left: Family and friends - Tracy and David, all grown up, in 1997
Above right: Ron and 'Doobie' Vigil pledge their friendship in 1980
Above: Friends rally round - Ron's 1994 boxing comeback receives support from Donny Nelson, Dennis Nelson, Frank Barron, Tony Wu and Dave Kilgour

Left: Ron Lyle and Bert Sugar get together again at the 2007 Lifetime Achievement Awards event. *Right*: Ron and Jill Sellers pose for the camera

Above: The Lyle brothers gather at their father's funeral in 2004. Left to right - Norman, Kenny, Bill, Ron, Ed, Bobby, Mark and Phillip

Above: Mary Kresnik and Ron at her son Michael's wedding in 2002

Right: The Lyle sisters... Marilyn, Karen, Sharon and Donna

Ron Lyle makes a point!

> 40 feet wide and 70 feet long....It's got a 24-foot ring, and everybody works around the ring. Ping pong, a heavy bag, a speed bag, weight -lifting, karate, and a supply area. I go over to the Air Force Academy at Colorado Springs to beg second-hand goods, any old equipment that they don't want.

The *Associated Press* mentioned Ron's impatience with the reporters: 'I hope this is the end of this press interview. I came here to fight.' It seemed nothing was too trivial for their attention. Vic Ziegel of the *New York Post* focused on how poorly Lyle dressed in his New York training days:

> Ron Lyle may someday become the heavyweight boxing champion. What Bob Jackson was certain of was that Lyle would never make the ten best-dressed list. Jackson is one of the owners of the Gramercy Gym where Lyle first began sparring when he became a professional fighter almost two years ago.
>
> 'He used to dress like a bum,' Jackson remembers. 'Always in the same boots, the same overalls....I used to kid him about his clothes, tell him he'd never look good to the women if he dressed that way. He'd say, "There's time for that later." What determination, wow. He always had that.'

Ron Lyle lost to Jerry Quarry in a unanimous decision.

Most news accounts blamed Lyle's inexperience in a bout that had more brawling than boxing. From the very first round, Ron departed from his usual style of stalking his opponent to hurrying across the ring to throw a lunging right hand toward Quarry's midsection, which the veteran dodged. Most also agreed that the younger Quarry fought an almost perfect fight.

Even with that, the winner of individual rounds was a

matter of diverse opinion. The consensus seemed to be that the first six rounds ended even, with Lyle winning two, Quarry two, and two even. Both showed good inside work throughout, and Lyle showed the power in his right hand as early as the second round when he rocked Quarry. In round five, Lyle was working well with quick, short combinations, but Quarry landed a good right that stunned Lyle; even so, most gave the round to Lyle. Round seven was about even when, with a minute left, Quarry landed a good right and left hook, followed another right. 'What are you waiting for?' Vic Ziegel overheard Bobby Lewis shout at Lyle after the seventh round. 'He's playing his game on you.'

The eighth proved decisive, as Ron seemed to be winning when Quarry caught him on the chin. He staggered back and fell against the ropes. Both boxers landed good shots in the ninth round, and Ron seemed to take charge in the tenth, landing well early and following with a good right cross. Ziegel again picked up on Bobby Lewis pleading from the sideline: 'Be the boss, be the boss,' and Ron started round 11 with strong punches; then Quarry peppered him with a series, bloodying his nose.

In the twelfth and final round, Ron needed a knockout. He landed a nice hook, but both fighters were very tired after a long series of gruelling rounds and Quarry's trainer Gil Clancy yelled: 'Don't take chances,' which he didn't.

Ron told Stephen Brunt in *Facing Ali* that the Quarry fight taught him he still had much to learn. 'Eventually I caught up to the pack, but in the meantime I had a lot of tests to take. And I had to pass the tests. Some of them I passed. Some of them, I just missed some of the answers. I mean, I lost fights. The losses are a bitter pill to swallow, but when you swallow that pill, that's what makes you better.'[6]

Ron rode back home in the plane chartered for Denver fans. Bob Cox remembers the defeated heavyweight taking the time to kneel down by Greg and put his arm around him. He recalls Ron's words: 'Sorry you had to come all this way to New York City to see me get beat, Greg. But I want to tell you something. It doesn't matter if it's job, school or sports - you only get out of things what you put into them. I didn't put enough into training for this fight.' Bob says that his son never forgot that moment with Ron Lyle. 'Ron had a tremendous impact on Greg's life.'

Today, Ron looks back at the Quarry fight philosophically. 'It was one of my best fights. At the time, I thought I won it. I figured the Garden promoters were protecting their investments. But I had to learn to accept that part of the game - the hardest part. I learned in prison to forget about those things I can't control.'

Ron says that the Serenity Prayer fits his life, that he learned early on which parts he could control and which he couldn't. He says he fought as hard as he could, but eventually gained the serenity to let go when the fight was over. When asked if there wasn't anything in prison he could control, the famous smile broke out: 'What am I going to do? Say "I'm leaving prison now?",' he laughs. 'I had to accept that I was going to stay there for a long time.'

In February 1973, he had to accept the fact that he would be starting all over again.

23

*

Starting Over

J OYCE CAROL OATES, in her book *On Boxing*, states that
'....boxing is as much about losing as about winning.'[7]
Losing to Jerry Quarry set Ron Lyle so far back that he
felt like he was starting over. It didn't matter. Accepting that
the road would be long and tedious, Ron's dream of fighting
for the heavyweight championship of the world grew even
stronger, and he threw himself back into training.

Dennis Nelson recalls that Ron's focus that year was as
intense as it had been since he was released from prison. 'I
saw Ron a few times after the Quarry fight,' Dennis says,
'and mostly he talked about getting the right opponents. My
brother Donny was training in Phoenix then, and I spent
some time out there, but whenever I was in Denver, I'd
check on Ron.

'I was starting to drink pretty heavy about then, and
even though he didn't say anything, I knew he and Donny
were not happy with me. I feel bad about that. We did talk
some, though. I remember he wasn't too thrilled with his

first fight after Quarry, but at least it got him back in the picture.'

Long Island New Yorker Bob Stallings was so far out of the rankings that even the Colorado State Athletic Commission turned down the first fight Daniels could muster, so the April venue turned out to be Missoula, Montana, with the promoter losing big after taking in barely $13,000 at the gate.

Heavily favoured, Lyle won a unanimous decision over Stallings after chasing the crouching, bobbing 5-foot 9-inch Stallings around the ring for ten rounds. The crowd that did show up wasn't happy. 'Got it figured out yet, Lyle?' a fan yelled midway through the ninth round. 'It's about too late.'

Ron continued to counter with good uppercuts, but couldn't seem to get low enough to make them effective, and he never counteracted Stallings' weaving. The uneven match was hardly an auspicious comeback, but then Bill Daniels came through again. He managed to land a May fight in Denver with Gregorio Peralta, ranked number ten by the World Boxing Council and the only boxer to ever last a total of 20 rounds against world heavyweight champion George Foreman. The Lyle team was back on track.

Peralta was 37 years old at the time and was a veteran of an incredible 107 pro fights, losing only eight, the winningest active heavyweight in the world. *Ringside* recorded Bobby Lewis's typically realistic assessment:

> Peralta's style is one of a boxer....He's a cutie. He's smart, tricky and just when you think you got his style figured out, he suddenly changes to a left-handed stance. He jabs very well and hits hard. ....[Lyle] will have to be at his absolute best to defeat Peralta. Peralta is always in tremendous shape, and Ronny's gong to have to be sharp in order to win.

Peralta was considered a 'spoiler,' specialising in making the best of them look bad, including Foreman, so Daniels pulled out all the stops. He sent Ron to New York for extra training with George (Chickie) Ferarra, who had been cornerman to Peralta for 13 fights, in order to better prepare Ron for his opponent's strengths.

Terry Anderson quoted Ferarra:

> Peralta is faster now than when I last worked with him two years ago, and he hits a helluva lot harder, too. In order for Ron to win, he's going to have to forget about ending the fight with a single punch. Everyone says Foreman is the hardest hitter in the division right now, but he couldn't put Peralta down in 20 rounds. So you can see that he knows what he is doing once he gets into the ring.

Lyle shared some insight into the aftermath of the Quarry fight with Anderson: 'Bobby [Lewis] learned something about me that he didn't know before. It's easy when things are going good and you've got it all together. You don't know how to determine the sincerity of the people involved. I didn't look at the loss itself, but at ourselves. Did we forget our motives? Were we sidetracked?' Lewis added: 'When you're going along and things are clicking, everything's okay, but if you fall off the track, you have to be in a position to pull yourself back on track. And we're the type of people who will pull ourselves back on track.'

The boxing community both inside and outside Denver agreed that Ron Lyle had found himself at the crossroads of his boxing career. A win could put him back in the spotlight, while a loss would most certainly take him out of title contention.

In preparation for the Peralta bout, Ron practiced his own brand of meditation. 'I wanted to be spiritually in tune with the world. I had to tap my inner spirit and ask myself: "What else is there to be afraid of?" The answer was: "Nothing." Then I would ask myself: "Do I really want to win?" And the answer was always: "Yes".'

After the Quarry fight, Ron had been dropped from fifth to sixth in the rankings, right behind Quarry, but most felt he would still have to prove himself all over again, and not all the Denver sportswriters were kind. Jim Graham, who had climbed on the bandwagon late in Ron's amateur career, now seemed inclined to bail. The week before the Peralta fight he wrote:

> Pushed too fast into a bout with Jerry Quarry, an in-and-out heavyweight who put it all together for the best fight in his career, Lyle came out of that fight with a serious credibility gap. To the sceptical New York press and ring-wise Madison Square Garden habitués, Lyle came off as another fighter with an inflated reputation based on a local build-up against pushovers.

Graham did offer some hope to Denver fans: 'However, all hands conceded that Lyle showed he could take a punch, and the set-up merely placed his career in limbo while his handlers worked to correct the Denver boxer's deficiencies.' But his optimism was short-lived: 'Against Quarry, Lyle was exposed as a strong, slow puncher who couldn't throw effective combinations, or handle a fast-punching, experienced heavyweight.' And a low blow: 'Lyle followed up a Quarry debacle with a victory over a hamdonnie named Bob Stallings in Missoula, an opponent so inept that even the Colorado Athletic Commission refused to sanction him.'

But with all that, Graham couldn't seem to help coming back to the home team. In his final paragraph: 'All in all, it's a most interesting match on paper, and a most meaningful one for Lyle, who should win by a decision.'

In the meantime, Denver fan loyalty continued, even as Ron needed it most. He says now that at one of the lowest points in his career, '....they really came through. Denver and I have always had a love affair.'

The Colorado State Athletic Commission chairman Eddie Bohn hadn't given up, either. John Morrill recalled all of Colorado's world boxing champions - Jack Dempsey, featherweight Young Corbett and Max Baer - and quoted Bohn as saying that he thought Colorado's fourth champion would be Ron Lyle. 'Colorado will be just as proud of Lyle as it was of the others.'

Ron returned from New York the Thursday night before the Peralta fight and plunged back into community activities. He drove to Fort Morgan Friday morning to speak before the annual Lion's Club athletic banquet for high school students, then returned to Denver in order to make an appearance at a Lakewood High School fundraiser for a three-year-old boy who had cancer of the foot.

'I owed the Denver community,' he says, 'and somehow doing for kids helped me get ready for a fight, maybe because I was doing what my mother liked me to do, you know, help others.' Community service might also have served to expend some of his nervous energy as he waited around for the next bout.

Even after losing to Quarry, Lyle couldn't get many ranked boxers interested in meeting him. Ken Norton, an upset victor over Muhammad Ali, turned down an offer from the Denver Boxing Club; Quarry hadn't expressed interest in a return bout; and George Chuvalo, Jimmy Ellis and Joe Bugner all just flat refused to consider Lyle.

Ron talked to Terry Anderson about his frustration. 'I've always been active, even in prison. I'm the type of guy that likes to stay active, busy - and when I'm not, it's a drag just sitting around and waiting. I anticipate getting to the top and so prefer to stay active. I'd like to have a fight at least once a month or every six weeks.' He was about to get his wish. Starting with Stallings, Ron would fight eight times in eight months, an astonishing pace for a professional heavyweight.

The cranked-up schedule would not do his marriage any good. Nadine once again felt neglected as Ron spent much of his time in New York and most of his Denver hours in training. But he had to make up valuable time, beginning with Gregorio Peralta.

The decision was a unanimous one. Ron had Peralta in trouble at least five times, but was unable to take advantage. He staggered Peralta in the first round with a right and almost knocked him down with a body blow in the fifth until the bell intervened. Lyle charged Peralta in the sixth, but couldn't put him away, and in the seventh a left hook sent Peralta halfway across the ring and into the ropes, but Ron still couldn't finish it. No matter. Peralta had only been knocked out once in 107 pro fights; beating him by decision was no disgrace.

Even so, Jim Graham managed to put a negative spin on the fight. 'Lyle won the fight all right, but nowhere near as comfortably as his local supporters or myopic hometown officials would lead you to believe....At the finish, Lyle's right eye was swollen and half-closed, while Peralta had only a superficial cut along the left side of his mouth from the heel of Ron's glove.'

His critics notwithstanding, Ron Lyle had managed a toehold on the first step of the comeback ladder to the top.

24

*

ONE month after the Peralta decision, Daniels landed Ron a fight with Wendell Newton in Philadelphia. While not ranked nationally, Newton had an impressive record, losing only three times, including once to Oscar Bonavena. He had physical advantages over Ron - three inches in height, five pounds in weight, three inches in reach. Newton wasn't a great opponent, but he could keep Lyle in the picture, if just barely.

After letting reporters know he wanted a knockout, Ron won an unimpressive split decision. He spent most of the bout chasing Newton around the ring and trying to get past his grabbing, wrestling strategy. What was worse, Newton raised an egg-sized lump on Lyle's forehead and opened a cut over his right eye with a right uppercut in the first round. It was the first time Ron had been cut in his pro career. There were no knockdowns in the fight, and several times the Philadelphia crowd booed both boxers for lack of action. Oh, well. Ron shrugged it off and went on.

His next fight, with Lou Bailey in Oklahoma City, was even more forgettable. Bailey had been around a long time and hadn't accomplished much in the past couple of years, losing seven out of 16 fights, but he did have one claim to fame - being knocked out by George Foreman in 1970. In July's bout, Ron knocked him down six times, but couldn't manage to put him away, winning by a ten round decision.

Then Daniels pulled off a bigger one - José Luis Garcia for August in Denver. The Venezuelan fighter was ranked 13th, having a career record of 22-4-1 with 14 knockouts, a record not unlike Lyle's own. In fact, he had been ranked number five and scheduled to go after Jerry Quarry when he met one Joe Alexander in a 'warm-up' one month earlier. In the first round of that unheralded fight, Garcia caught Alexander with a right uppercut, causing Alexander's head to rebound from the blow directly into Garcia's face. The force of the head butt almost knocked out Garcia and Alexander went on to record a win - a bizarre moment that Ron understood as 'just part of the fight game.'

Physically, the two fighters were almost identical in size with powerful right-hand punches and exceptional knockout records; Garcia, however, was six years younger than Ron. Terry Anderson quoted Eddie Futch, trainer to Ken Norton whom Garcia had knocked out: 'This will be a dangerous fight for Lyle. He will have to be careful all night. Garcia is big and has a great right hand. Lyle will have to buckle down for him.'

The card for the night promised to be a great one, with Oscar Bonavena going against what *Ringside* called a 'durable' Lou Bailey; Duane Bobick, recently undefeated as a new pro, taking on Chuck Borden; Denver two-time Golden Gloves Champion welterweight Larry Bonds versus Ward Jones; and, most significant to Ron, his buddy Donny Nelson, who had won five of his first six pro fights coming up from Phoenix, against Heinz Klein (3-0) from Vancouver, B.C.

Denver Post Sports Editor Bick Lucas caught Ron in an uncharacteristic reflective mood as he prepared for the Garcia bout. But first Lucas tried to draw him out about possible future opponents, including a rematch with Jerry Quarry. 'Right now I'm trying to get ready for Garcia. My mind is not on anything else. Quarry's not even in the picture. I can't get my mind to go back that far.'

Lucas asked about Bonavena, and Ron replied patiently: 'There you go again. I'm not planning past. I'm only planning to. I don't make the matches. I don't pick the opponents. All I do is fight 'em.'

Lucas described Lyle as 'an outgoing person concerned about his fellow man, particularly those who have fallen on hard times as he once did, and Ron offered insights he hadn't shared with the press before.

> If giving my time means anything, right on. The press says Ron Lyle digs young people and I do. But I dig going to juvenile homes, reformatories, industrial schools. The kids really need somebody to rap to, that they can confide in and identify with. If I go rap to a kid in a regular school and I tell him what it means NOT to get a Christmas card from home when you're in an institution, he can't identify with that and consequently he doesn't even know what I'm talking about.
>
> But when you're talking with guys who're in that spot and they know you've been in that spot, too, that's different. That's why I'd rather go around to institutions. Not to change their lives, but simply to let them know that somebody is thinking about them. The average kid in an institution, his thoughts are, 'Who cares?' Some of them are 12, 13 years old. And they grow up with the attitude that nobody cares. I

care what happens to them because I've been there. That's one of my hang-ups. You can't change the world, but you might be able to shed a little light on some of the problems.

As ever, the kids helped Ron keep his mind clear as the days moved down to the fight with José Garcia. He remembers feeling calm and confident even after listening to Garcia's remarks to the press the Tuesday before the fight: 'I hit harder than Lyle. He's easy to hit. My right hand is too strong for Lyle and my speed will be too much for him. Lyle has never met a fighter who can hit as hard as I can. Lyle won't last ten rounds against me.'

Garcia didn't last three rounds against Lyle. The headline in *International Boxing* read 'Lyle Scores First Kayo Since Quarry Defeat', hitting on the real significance of that fight. The picture in that magazine was the same as the one in the *Denver Post*, albeit from a different angle - a small, wiry Bobby Lewis lifting a 215-pound Lyle up above his head. The Lyle camp hadn't experienced such jubilance since the Middleton fight back in December. And, in fact, Ron did something he had only done once before - in the Middleton fight; that is, he 'danced' in the first round. No more stalking.

The August 15 card in Denver turned out well all around. Bobick decisioned Chuck Borden, Bonavena easily whipped Lou Bailey and, especially gratifying to Ron and the Denver crowd, Donnie Nelson knocked out a tough Heinz Klein. But the night belonged to Ron Lyle.

At a Monday press conference after the fight, Bobby Lewis said the first round was the key to Wednesday's bout. 'Just by moving around in that round, Ron got Garcia to show him every punch in his arsenal. After that, it was easy because we knew what we had to do.'

During the first round Garcia had landed several right

jabs, Lyle easily casting them aside. In the second round, Ron began going on the offence after Garcia got in a good punch with a right to his head in the first 45 seconds. After that, Ron came at him with three rapid rights and had him on the ropes for nearly 30 seconds near the end of the round, railing him with uppercuts and body punches.

In round three, Lyle charged, pinning him almost immediately against the ropes again. He used a left hook, a short right and another right to batter Garcia through the ropes and onto the canvas. As Anderson put it: 'It was all Garcia could do just to roll back into the ring.' The Venezuelan didn't make it to his feet before the referee finished the count at 1:10 of the third.

The typically sceptical Jim Graham appeared to come around. 'The bout was a crucial one for Ron, and Lyle needed a convincing one to re-establish his credentials as a top heavyweight contender. Although Lyle is unlikely to move up in the ratings, he once again proved his tremendous local charisma at the box office provided he is matched with a name opponent.'

Graham was wrong about the ratings. Both the World Boxing Council and *Ring Magazine* moved him up to number five after the Garcia knockout.

25

*

I N the *Denver Post* piece before the Garcia fight, Bick Lucas described Lyle as smiling 'serenely' when discussing his wife Nadine and two-year-old son Monte. 'I spend as much time with them as I can. We talk about our home, what we're going to do for Monte, how we're going to rear him, what we have to do to provide him with a sound education....

'Boxing means everything to me. It has provided me with a beautiful family. We're building a home in Lakewood with a view of the mountains. Something could happen. We might not even get this home, but boxing has given me the opportunity to look in that direction. It has given me a purpose in life, the chance to turn my dreams into reality.' The house was never built, and a few months later, the marriage would be over.

In the meantime, the Denver press was starting to repeat itself. Once again, it seemed that Ron Lyle needed to beat his next opponent if he wanted a shot at the fighters ranked above him. When his next fight was announced for October 4 with Jurgen Blin of West Germany, a local headline read: 'Lyle Needs Win for Shot at Best'.

A veteran of 46 professional fights, Blin was two years younger than Ron with an impressive 30-10-6 record. Regarded as an excellent counterpuncher, the German heavyweight champion also had a long reach and an effective left hook which staggered Muhammad Ali several times during a 1971 slugfest. To make Bobby Lewis even more nervous, Gregorio Peralta, defeated by Lyle the previous May, was helping Blin to prepare for the bout.

As a counter-measure Lewis brought in Lou Bailey as Ron's sparring partner, the fighter who held out for ten rounds in July, even after Lyle had knocked him down six times. Terry Anderson got a rare glimpse of Lewis's style during a training session at the Elks Punch Bowl the week before the fight. He first quoted Lewis: 'How can you call a fighter like Bailey a sparring partner? The guy's fought every top heavyweight in the world, dating back to Sonny Liston. There is just no such thing as a sparring partner. A sparring partner? That's the heavy bag over there. It doesn't hit back.'

Anderson went on to describe the sparring bout:

> Lewis wanted Lyle to concentrate on combination punching in Monday's workouts, and he particularly wanted Lyle to set up a right hook coming off two left jabs. For two rounds, Lewis and Bailey knew what they wanted to teach Lyle, but the lesson wasn't coming through. Finally, at the end of the second round, Bailey took matters into his own gloves and took Lyle off into a corner.
>
> 'Look,' he said, breathing heavily, 'you're trying to set yourself before you throw the left jab. Don't do that. Do it this way.'
>
> Bailey threw three imaginary blows at Lyle,

showing him how he thought Lyle should throw the punch. Lewis nodded his approval.

The advice worked, much to Bailey's delight - and chagrin - midway through the next round, Bailey had taken out his mouthpiece so he could talk to Lyle and offer advice as the two traded blows. Then came the perfect combination Lewis was looking for.

Obviously shaken by the blows, Bailey stood off and said: 'Yeah, right on. That's it. I felt that one in my knees.'

As usual, Lewis's training paid off, this time with a smashing two-round knockout. The German moved in fast, fists churning, but Ron countered with shots to the stomach. Blin back-pedalled as Ron continued his relentless assault. In the second round, Lyle continued to target the body, but while the German champion was protecting his mid-section, Ron threw a right uppercut, stunning Blin, who went down with a follow-up left hook. At the nine count, he managed to get to his feet, but the referee rescued the defenceless fighter and called it off at 1:01 of the second round.

The press couldn't wait to speculate on bigger and better fights. The subtitle to a story about the Blin fight read, 'Does Foreman Fear Denverite?' The call-out may have been premature but confidence ran high in the Lyle camp. Daniels and Lewis, not to mention Ron Lyle, were well aware of the seven rounds it had taken Ali to knock out the same German fighter. Speculation in the locker and press rooms, and among Denver fans, was all about Foreman, Ali, Bonavena, Norton, Frazier and Quarry. Big fights were looming, but first, two previously scheduled commitments had to be fulfilled, one a rematch in Baltimore with Larry Middleton in three weeks, then another with Gregorio Peralta in Frankfurt, Germany, three weeks after that.

Ron remembers how hard it was to focus during that period, knowing he had to get through the next fights while mentally preparing for the final steps to the crown. He flew to New York to work with trainer Chickie Ferrara, trying to improve on what he did best. He had started to believe that his best chance would be to put pressure on the big players, force them to make mistakes, rather than waiting for the other guy to make a move and counter-react. But the biggest distractions were outside the ring - the departure of Bobby Lewis and the increasing deterioration of his marriage.

The Denver Boxing Club had decided to replace Lewis as Lyle's primary trainer with Ferrara. Ron tried to accept the news philosophically, telling Terry Anderson: 'I can't let personal feelings interfere with my career. They told me what had to be for me to be the champion. I'm a pro now. I've got to accept the change.'

Ron was well aware of Chickie's sterling credentials; he had trained Rocky Marciano, Ezzard Charles, Floyd Patterson, Nino Benenuti, Muhammad Ali, Jimmy Ellis, Oscar Bonavena and Gregorio Peralta, among others, with extraordinary results. 'We [Lewis and Lyle] both have to look at it that way. As pros. The people who are putting up the money for me didn't get rich by making mistakes. I know that Bobby is in my corner, and he understands the move. This move won't change the way we feel about each other.' And then, as though unbidden, his real feelings slipped out. 'I want to be the world champion, and I won't let anything get in my way, even if it means living by myself. In my heart, I was by myself for $7\frac{1}{2}$ years. I was surrounded by associates in the penitentiary, but I was alone.' Ron was thinking of his troubled marriage. He knew Nadine was often lonely for weeks at a time, but didn't even consider compromise. Rightly or wrongly, he had made up his mind years before. His dream came first.

THE Middleton fight ended in a Lyle decision. The *Associated Press* reported that: 'Larry Middleton didn't dispute his defeat, but he resented the contention that winner Ron Lyle avoided going for a knockout and used the ten-rounder as a mere tune-up for tougher opponents.'

Ron confirmed that he wanted to knock Middleton out as early as the third round, just as he had ten months earlier, but that Chickie Ferarra had wanted him to go the distance. However it happened, the decision was unanimous.

Ron went back to New York to train for the upcoming fight with Peralta in Frankfurt, even as the Denver Boxing Club worried about Peralta's 'unorthodox' style, which included thumbs and laces in opponents' eyes and face. Ron knew that style first hand; he had suffered a thumb-in-the-eye injury in his May decision over Peralta. The Lyle camp was also concerned about the Frankfurt venue favouring Peralta, the most popular fighter in Germany, and they worked to find a 'neutral' referee.

In the meantime Bill Daniels was doing his thing, going public with his many offers to fight George Foreman for the championship. He told reporters: 'We have always been on record as saying we'll fight Foreman anytime he wishes to give Ron a chance....Foreman's going to have to do something soon because the World Boxing Association will withdraw recognition of his title unless he defends it against a legitimate top-ten contender before January 22, 1974,' which was only two months away.

Ron tried not to think about Foreman or anyone but Peralta when he flew to Frankfurt four days before the fight. He continued training hard, using Vicente Rondon as a sparring partner even as the discussion of a neutral referee continued. It seemed that promoter and Peralta manager Fritz Weine hired a French referee, who turned out to be a long time friend of Weine. Ron tried to ignore the sideshow, but he knew the fight game.

Today he talks quietly about that game. 'Promoters set up bouts, managers agree, and fighters fight. That's the way it was in the seventies and the way it is now.' Ron says he had to remember the serenity prayer while he waited for opponents. 'It was all in the political and financial area,' he says, 'And I had to accept that. A promoter would own one contract, then get a piece of another boxer when he set up a fight. I saw that more and more while I was climbing back up the ladder.'

The outcome was probably as good as it could have been, given the circumstances - after ten rounds, the referee and judges called it a draw. Officials refused to release the scorecards of the group of German judges, but Ron was certain he had won at least seven rounds. The *Associated Press* scored the fight six rounds for Lyle, three for Peralta and one even. But the fans were the biggest surprise. After cheering for Peralta throughout the fight, at the announced draw, the crowd turned into one gigantic boo. Even Ron's opponent seemed startled by the draw. Prior to the announcement, Peralta crossed the ring and raised Lyle's hand in victory.

Chickie Ferrara said: 'Anytime they [German officials] bring you over here and spend a lot of money on you, they aren't bringing you over here for a win.....But you got to be glad you got the draw here. Anyone with common sense has to figure your fighter must have won if we got the draw here.' And Ron knew he had to accept what he couldn't control and move on.

26

*

A FOUR-month hiatus set in, while Bill Daniels and the Denver Boxing Club conducted frenetic negotiations for a fight with Foreman, or at the very least, one of the top contenders. After winning the crown from Frazier the year before, Foreman had turned elusive; except for one first-round knockout of a Puerto Rican named José Roman, memorable as the shortest title fight on record, he had fought only exhibition bouts. The Lyle camp was relentless in issuing challenge after challenge, reminding Foreman of his obligations while appealing to his pride.

Leaving the negotiations to his managers, Ron and his brother Phillip decided to take a road trip to San Diego, not only to visit their sister Donna, but to reconnect with each other. Ron's troubling relationship with Nadine had triggered a need for family that went beyond deposits to his parents' bank account and occasional visits to their home. His brother Bill was often on hand to support Ron in strategy meetings with the Denver Boxing Club, but that

November, boxing would be put on the shelf, just for a little while.

The visit with Donna and her family brought back simpler days, and Ron remembers feeling truly relaxed for the first time in months - years even. One evening after what felt like a very short week away from all the pressure of the boxing game, he and Phillip set out for the drive back to Denver, setting in motion another of those uncanny Lyle family events that would turn out to fortify an already solid friendship.

Donny Nelson recalls the incident well. 'It was cold that night,' he remembers. 'I was headed from my training camp in Phoenix to a fight in Santa Fe when my car broke down near the Arizona-New Mexico border. It was getting late, maybe 8:00, and I walked to a gas station a couple of miles back. I called my wife in Denver, and she said she would bring my mother and drive out to pick me up. My wife drove pretty slowly - for her it would have been about an eight-hour drive - so it was almost 2:00 in the morning when they ran out of gas miles from the nearest town. There weren't any cell phones in those days and they had no choice but to try and hitch a ride. My mother sat on the side of the road while my wife waved at drivers going in both directions. Finally, a dark coloured car stopped a few feet ahead and my mother watched my wife run up to the passenger's side and stand talking to the driver for a couple of minutes.

'My wife didn't wave her forward; rather, she ran back to where my Mom was sitting and said: "There's good news and bad news. The good news is they will take us into town. The bad news is they are the biggest, blackest guys I ever saw." My mother was cold and tired and thought the only choice was to take the ride. After they had gone a few miles down the road, my mom noticed the driver kept looking at her in the rear-view mirror. Finally he said: "Mrs. Nelson?" And my mom said: "Ronny Lyle?"'

Ron remembers how, in those days, it was foolish to pick up hitchhikers anywhere in the open stretches of the Southwest. 'Drivers would pull over for somebody innocent- looking, like a woman, and guys would jump out from behind a rock or something and rob them. The only time I ever stopped for a hitchhiker was that night we picked up Mrs. Nelson and Donny's wife. When I saw that white woman in the road I thought I should drive on by, but something made me slow down and finally stop. God must have been telling me to help them.'

Back in Denver, Ron and the Nelson brothers marvelled at the twist of fate that put Mrs. Nelson on the same spot on the same road at the same time as Ronny. They all agreed that more than coincidence had to be at work - that their friendship was meant to last. And lasted it has, even though unconditional trust took some time to solidify. Back then Dennis was becoming known as a hard drinker and Ron still wasn't ready to confide in anybody about his personal life. If problems with Nadine bothered him he didn't let on, and Dennis remembers that he still had Monte around much of the time.

In December Ron went back to Canon City to do some general training. He worked from 12 to 18 rounds a day to keep his fighting trim, shadowboxing four to five rounds, working on the heavy bag two to four rounds and spending another three or four rounds on the speed bag, taking time out to work on the sand bag for timing, and winding up a day's session by skipping rope another three or four rounds. In between he helped boost the morale of the inmates.

Terry Anderson spoke to Lt. Maddox, who told him Ron had the run of the institution. 'That's because he's in here trying to help the inmates. The attitude of the inmates seems to improve every time he shows up. By Ron's just being there, it doubles the number of guys who show up to box.'

In the meantime the posturing of Bill Daniels went on, with public statements that George Foreman owed fifth-ranked Ron Lyle a shot at the title. Ron's manager took issue with an *Associated Press* story that Foreman hadn't had any luck in getting a bout with a top ten contender, including Ali, Oscar Bonavena, Jerry Quarry and Ron Lyle, and had been miserable and disillusioned since he captured the title from Frazier.

Daniels was quoted as saying that the Foreman group '....hasn't tried too hard to get a fight with Ron. In fact, we're the ones doing all the work right now....We are prepared to sit down and negotiate for a title fight at any time or place they choose.'

Early in 1974, *Boxing Illustrated* would carry the cover story 'Foreman tabs Lyle Dynamite Foe' and quote the champion as saying: '....the top contender is Ron Lyle. After him, they are all in the same class - one big group.'

Most sportswriters agreed. A fight between the unbeaten Foreman and the once-beaten Lyle would have been a natural, since both were sluggers who were having trouble getting fights with reputable top ten challengers because of their punching power. Ron remembers how much he would have welcomed the chance to fight Foreman. 'That was my greatest ambition, to fight for the title. I was always ready for the chance.'

While Ron continued to train for whatever opponent Daniels could dig up, the Denver Boxing Club put out a press release - 'Ron Lyle Honored for Work with Children' - which listed all of the honours Ron had accrued over the past year, including the Point O' Pines Corporation of Colorado naming him recipient of its annual Humanitarian Award and the chairmanship of the March of Dimes 'Walk-a-thon,' in which he had personally led thousands of teenagers and volunteers on a 20-mile march through the streets of Denver to raise more than $100,000, the biggest net in the organisation's history. Officials attributed the success of the march to Lyle's speaking efforts before various high school groups.

The Denver Association for Retarded Children had staged a similar walk, and again Lyle was asked to be chairman. More than $10,000 was raised, the most ever earned by the local ARC. The press release listed that event along with all the occasions Ron had spent with underprivileged youngsters and his active work with Partners, the group dedicated to matching adults with kids who had been in trouble with the law. Fighting in the ring and good works outside had become the rhythm of his life.

In January of 1974, the boxing logjam began to break up, first with Ali beating Joe Frazier in a grudge match decision and George Foreman agreeing to meet Ken Norton in March. Ron was frozen out of the championship bout, but Daniels hoped that at least he could lure Jerry Quarry into a rematch, since Quarry, too, had lost a shot with Foreman. But Quarry backed off, and Daniels took his second best shot, landing a fight with sixth-ranked Oscar 'Ringo' Bonavena for February 28. Bob Collins of the *Rocky Mountain News* expressed relief that Ron had a decent bout coming up. 'So the machinery rusts and time marches on with the latter of some concern in that Lyle will be 32 in February and can't afford inaction.'[8]

Right after the Bonavena fight was announced, Ron left for New York City, and very specific guidance from Chickie Ferrara who had trained Bonavena a couple years before. While Lyle trained, the Denver Boxing Club was far from inactive. The group sent a telegram to Gil Clancy, Jerry Quarry's manager, offering third-ranked Quarry $50,000 to fight the winner of the Lyle-Bonavena bout in Denver. Vince Boryla, president of the club, said he had read where Quarry was bitter because Ali and Foreman wouldn't fight him. 'We want Quarry and Clancy to know that Ron Lyle is not a part of any conspiracy keeping Quarry out of action, and that we want a fight in Denver with him. Even if Ron loses, we'll still put on the Quarry-Bonavena fight here.' But Boryla had spoken too soon.

One week before the scheduled fight, the Denver Boxing Club received a telegram from Bonavena's handlers saying that the boxer was suffering from a liver ailment and wouldn't be able to fight for at least three weeks. Disappointment blanketed the Lyle camp. Ron remembers that just when they thought all the postponements and 'injuries' were finally over, Bonavena had pulled the plug.

Daniels kept trying to reschedule the fight, and the Denver Boxing Club even told the fans who had bought tickets for February 28 to hold onto them, promising a new date. After a few anxious days, Oscar Bonavena came through. A new fight date was set for March 19.

27

*

AT a press conference a week before the fight, Ron Lyle and Oscar 'Ringo' Bonavena went through the verbal sparring that had come to characterise the seventies boxers, great and small. 'Don't get locked in your room,' Lyle reminded his opponent, referring to a Madison Square Garden bout in which Bonavena refused to leave his hotel room for a fight against George Chuvalo until the promoter handed him an advance of 25 $100 bills. 'Make sure you show up. The fight starts at 8 p.m.' To some gathered reporters, Ron's jibe also sounded like a reaction to Bonavena's 'three-week liver ailment.'

In response, Bonavena pulled out a rubber chicken and told Lyle the chicken was like him and his trainer, Chickie Ferrara. 'You'll never forget me,' he laughed as he dangled the chicken in front of Ron's face. I'll see you in the ring - on the floor....'

Ron came back with: 'Bonavena can't fight me like he fought Ali, Frazier or Ellis. He'll have to take me differently.

You have to take a fighter as he comes.' Still stinging from media reaction to his previous opponents, he spoke directly to the gathered reporters: 'I just hope that Bonavena has passed the test for the press and meets with their approval.'

The sports stories and headlines had repeated over and over, 'Lyle Needs a Big Win.' And Ron wasn't particularly happy with the speculation that he might have lost his big punch. 'Funny thing,' he mused, 'when I first started out and was knocking everyone out, you all said: "He isn't learning anything." Now that I'm learning something in there inside the ring, I've lost my punch....I'm preparing for Bonavena. I'm getting up emotionally for one guy. To me those other fights aren't that important.'

Ron's old nemesis Jim Graham concluded his column that week with: 'On the face of it, Lyle needs a big win, an important win, against a sound Bonavena if he's to get back on the track of his self-imposed timetable of winning the heavyweight championship of the world inside of the next two years.' As usual, the press got the last word - at least before the fight began.

Another irritating sideshow threatened the fighters' concentration when Pat O'Grady, an Oklahoma sports promoter, petitioned the Colorado State Athletic Commission to suspend Oscar Bonavena and prevent him from fighting Ron Lyle 'until disputed contracts have been adjusted or legally adjudicated.'

O'Grady contended that he had a contract for Bonavena's services which took precedence over the one the Argentine fighter had with the Denver Boxing Club for the Lyle fight. The flap came to nothing when the chief judge of the Denver District Court denied the O'Grady motion, but the legal action symbolised the tortured complexities of promoters-managers-boxing clubs that hovered over professional boxing.

In the meantime, Ron had no choice but to train for the

sixth-ranked boxer on his own terms. 'Ringo' Bonavena had fought 59 bouts, lost eight and only been knocked out once - by Ali in 1970. A puncher-boxer with a reputation for dirty blows, Bonavena had fought big names in the heavyweight division, including Jimmy Ellis, Joe Frazier and Muhammad Ali, and he was always considered dangerous.

Chickie knew both fighters very well and didn't seem worried before the fight, although he limited his comments to Ron's character. 'He's very dedicated and determined. His family and his fighting, that's all he has on his mind. He gives up everything as a fighter. He [lives] a clean life and that's in his favour, too.'

Ron remembers the pleasure he felt when he knew that not only Chickie Ferrara would be in his corner, but that Bobby Lewis would join him there. He thought having the two trainers together would be just the added bit of support he needed before this most important bout. And he knew that even though many of the pre-fight bets were even money, he was slightly favoured to win. That helped, too.

One more hurdle remained. A collective breath was held by the Denver boxing community as Oscar Bonavena went through his physical exam. Not only had his liver condition worried fans, but also his left hand, which had been broken two years before and re-injured in the Denver fight with Lou Bailey seven months before.

On the eve of the big fight, the physical pronouncement was made by Dr. Sam Ozamoto, the Colorado Commission-attending physician who pronounced the Argentinian boxer had passed with flying colours. 'His hand is healed and very strong. As far as I'm concerned Bonavena is in fine physical condition and more than ready to fight Lyle.' First the postponement, then the lawsuit and finally the physical. Three down and none to go.

As the fight neared, Chickie Ferraro became more vocal.

He told *Rocky Mountain News* sports editor Bob Collins: 'Lyle has been looking very sharp the past few days. He has been throwing beautiful combinations and his jab, which must be effective Tuesday for him to beat Bonavena, is getting better all the time.'

Ferrara went on to tell Terry Anderson: 'Bonavena doesn't know what a combination is. He relies on brute strength and those hard rights and lefts. Ron is okay if he can keep Bonavena in a defensive shell.'

Chickie had asked the Colorado State Athletic Commission to watch Bonavena's tactics. He had the reputation of using illegal means to win a fight, including hitting below the belt, biting an opponent and hitting a man while he was on the canvas, having hit Ali below the belt five times in their 1970 encounter.

The Argentinian was often described as 'bull-like.' At five-feet 11-inches tall and 207 pounds, his weight was concentrated from the waist up, making him one of the hardest boxers in the world to knock down. And his style was to charge his opponent and intimidate him from the opening bell. He swarmed over his foes, constantly throwing body shots and overhead rights and lefts. And he was motivated. Bonavena had been offered a fight against Muhammad Ali if he won, not to mention the $750,000 the Denver Boxing Club had offered George Foreman to fight the winner. Ron had no doubt that he would be up against the strongest opponent of his career.

By most accounts the fight was the most exciting in Denver history. Bonavena came in strong, as expected, throwing lefts fast and furiously as Lyle dodged and got in a few shots. In the second round 'Ringo' tried to keep up the pace, but a Lyle left jab drew blood on the ridge of his nose, and the round was even.

Ron came in fast in the third, scoring well before

Bonavena could go into his clinching tactics. But in the fourth Ron ran into his opponent's right hand, which shook him up for a few moments until he rallied to even the scoring in the round.

Lyle landed hard right uppercuts to the body in the fifth and then hurt Bonavena with a right to the chest on the ropes. 'Ringo' was in trouble midway in the round but survived by clinching, and Ron 'couldn't pull the trigger on his knockout punch.' In the sixth a left uppercut by Lyle knocked out Bonavena's mouthpiece and he slipped to the floor, the first of three slips in the fight. Lyle stalked his man in the seventh and scored big with right hand shots to the head and a left uppercut to take command.

The crucial eighth round saw Lyle coming back to score with some good early flurries, but with 50 seconds left in the round, Bonavena got off a solid left hook to Lyle's head and had him so dazed that Lyle had to go into a clinch to clear his head. Bonavena went on to win both the ninth and tenth rounds, mostly by tying Lyle up. Ron did manage one good blow early in the tenth with a left hook to the head that had Bonavena reeling against the ropes. Late in the round, however, the referee deducted one point from Ron's score for a low blow and gave Bonavena a one-minute rest period.

Not only the Denver fans, but the Lyle corner continuously yelled at their man during the last two rounds as Ron kept up the pressure during the 11th which prompted Bonavena to open the 12th with a hard charge; in his hurry to punch Lyle around the ring, he slipped to the floor, not once, but twice. When the bell rang, ending the bout, the referee and judges huddled for only a moment before declaring Ron Lyle the winner in a unanimous 12-round decision. Ron had just won the most important fight of his career.

Chapter 28

*

KAREN remembers the Bonavena fight vividly. With a ringside seat arranged by Bill, Ron's ten-year-old sister spent most of the night standing, shadow boxing along with her brother Ron's punches. 'At the end I was screaming and crying. Ronny looked at me, then leaned down and lifted me into the ring, just like he had Gerry at an earlier fight. It was a great moment in my life.'

The scene in the dressing room afterwards illustrated the extraordinary bond between boxing adversaries. As Terry Anderson reported:

> Ron Lyle sat back in a chair, sweat pouring down his face, and drank water from a taped quart bottle. Next to him sat Oscar Bonavena, amused as he watched Lyle. He faked a punch at Lyle's chin.
>
> 'Hey,' Bonavena said quietly as he turned to Lyle. 'You look happy. Do you feel all right? A little tired?' He grinned. 'You no chicken....You no little boy. I couldn't believe how strong and tough you are.'

Lyle poured some of the water down over his head and then looked back at Bonavena. The Argentinian motioned for the other quart water bottle and the two toasted one another.

'I hope you win the championship of the world,' Bonavena said. Lyle raised his bottle in toast.

The caption on a photo of the fight showing Ron reaching with his right, as Oscar avoided the punch read: 'Ron Lyle didn't look good defeating Oscar Bonavena. But nobody ever does. More important, the bout drew the best gate in Denver boxing history.' More important to some people, maybe.

The big players in the boxing game dictate the financial winner of a bout, regardless of who beats who; the Lyle-Bonavena fight was a case in point. Oscar Bonavena was guaranteed $18,000 tax-free, plus expenses, including hotel and three round-trip tickets from Buenos Aires. Ron Lyle was guaranteed 20 per cent of the gate, less all expenses, which included Coliseum costs, along with paying trainers and sparring partners and other training costs, not to mention taxes on Bonavena's $18,000, for a total of approximately $75,000. The Denver crowd paid a record $109, 000 for the privilege of watching their local guy beat a major contender in a honey of a fight. Subtract expenses and the net was $34,000, of which Ron received his 20 per cent, or $6800. Bonavena took home $28,650, including expenses. Boxing was a lucrative investment in the 1970's, but not often for boxers, win or lose.

As the dust settled after the fight, the pundits began to view Ron Lyle with more respect. Leonard Cahn wrote: 'Ron Lyle has paid his dues as the number five heavyweight of the world.' Ron was finally getting the respect most of Denver thought he had deserved for a long time, and he had decisively put to rest the question as to whether he could take a punch. What next?

Harry Barnett, attorney for champion George Foreman, had watched the Lyle-Bonavena fight and was impressed with what he saw. 'A Foreman fight against Lyle is inevitable,' Barnett said. 'Those two are on a collision course and George has never ducked any opponent.' Barnett failed to answer follow-up questions with specifics.

Then there was Jerry Quarry. At a Golden Gloves banquet in Denver a week after the Lyle-Bonavena fight, also attended by Ron, Quarry made it clear he was personally ready for a rematch. 'I haven't been able to buy a fight,' he said. 'All they have to do is talk the right price and I'll listen about a Lyle fight - yes, right here in his own hometown.' He smiled when told that Lyle and Bonavena had drawn a gross gate in excess of $108,000, and his interest 'perked up considerably' when told the financial possibilities of an outdoor rematch with Lyle that summer at Mile High Stadium. 'I'm not disappointed in anything Lyle has done since we met the first time, and I'm sure as heck not disappointed in myself. We had a good fight when we met in the Garden.'

But whatever the other contenders said, they continued to duck Lyle, and another dry spell set in. Except for older brother Bill, who was often in on strategy meetings, the Lyle family could hardly tell the difference between those times Ron was frustrated in his quest and when things were going well. They only knew that he was always there for them, even in 1974 as he wondered if he would ever get a chance at his dream. Gathered together to talk about those times, the family speaks with one conviction.

Karen says: 'Ronny is a hero, like nobody else I know. His faith in God must have carried him through times that hurt him, but he always was there for me.' 'He always protected us, always,' says Marilyn, 'whatever he was going through.' Sharon remembers that 'No matter where he's been, he always included his family.' Kenneth says simply,

'Ronny's a champion.' Bill stands up and with tears in his voice says: 'Ron taught me much more than I taught him. He taught me never to quit, however many times you fall. And he taught me not to blame anybody else for the hard times.'

But in 1974, even as he supported his family, Ron was unable to sustain any kind of familial understanding in his married life. The fights with Nadine grew more frequent and more intense. Ron had started to feel that not only would she leave him, but that whatever love had been between them had been eaten up with the angry words and long silences. He had hung on only because he didn't want to part with Monte. Things got worse when Ron accused his wife of not being supportive during the hard times and she accused him of neglecting their marriage. Their arguments escalated, and Ron knows he discredited himself during an incident that occurred in May.

The Lyles got into a physical fight when Nadine hit Ron with a frying pan and he shoved her toward an open window. She fell to the ground, unhurt but furious, and ran to a neighbour to call the police. One short newspaper item reported that a shot had been fired. Ron was charged with second degree assault and menacing, charges which were eventually dropped, but not for many months, during which period he experienced the peak of his boxing career.

Twenty-five years later, when asked by sportscaster Peter Boyles about the hardest hit he had ever taken, Ron replied: 'The hardest hit was from my wife. And it broke my heart.'

A couple more newspaper pieces about his fight with Nadine appeared, although the Denver press chose not to sensationalise the incident. One caption on a picture of a smiling Ron and Monte read: 'Although beset by domestic strife with his wife in recent months, Lyle wants another crack at the heavyweight championship to build financial security for his son.'

Off the Ropes

Until his next fight could be scheduled, Ron tried to fall back into an old waiting pattern, dividing his time among his family, general training at Canon City, and Denver kids. Photos of Ron with his son Monte appeared frequently, and at all encounters with the press and public, he appeared relaxed, smiling as he teased Monte and whatever other kids happened to be around. He hoped, but didn't really believe, that his troubles with Nadine were behind him - that the marriage could somehow work.

In response to a question from Kay Gilman of the *News*, he spoke of how Nadine had grown accustomed to marriage with a boxer:

> I'm the onliest guy she's ever been married to, so she don't know any different. Why should she object to it? She's got to eat, doesn't she? She used to get nervous before we were married, but now she takes it in stride. She believes in me like I believe in myself. My son knows what his father does. He's seen films of me fighting and I explain what I'm doing. But I'd never take him to see me fight....he'd probably think daddy was mad and that I was trying to kill the guy in front of me.

After going over Ron's prison history, a story which had appeared in print many times, Gilman went on to conclude: 'His exposure to the raw edges of death, both on the giving and receiving ends, have made Ron Lyle intensely aware of the quality of his own life.' But even as Gilman wrote, the quality of Ron's life was on the verge of disintegrating. Nadine had tried, but going for long weeks without seeing her husband, caring for three-year-old Monte, all alone in a neighbourhood where she didn't know anyone, had been wearing on her for a very long time. The physical confrontation was the final straw. Only a couple of weeks later, Nadine called it quits and returned to East Denver and her own family.

The impending divorce worried Ron's mother, and not only because Ron would be separated from Monte. She feared that without the stability of a family, Ronny might slide back into the kind of trouble he had engage in during his teenage years. She needn't have worried. Even in the midst of his collapsed marriage and waiting in limbo for his next bout, Ron Lyle would let nothing distract him from the dream. He simply took a deep breath and settled down, falling back on the serenity prayer and accepting the way things were as Bill Daniels worked on a strategy to get him a title shot.

As though to mitigate the turmoil in his personal life, Ron started to appear even more frequently at schools and detention centres and, responding to invitations, added youth groups, boys clubs and one day shortly after his win over Bonavena, a junior boxing club in Denver. As usual when he was around kids, he didn't make speeches, just conversation. He rapped about training and school and friends - whatever the kids wanted to talk about. One of the boys asked him what his record was and whether he would get to fight Ali and if he did, could he beat him. As reported by Terry Anderson in the *Denver Post:*

> Lyle laughed softly and told him to sit down. 'You know what? You learn as you go along. Boxing is just like any other sport. The better the competition, the better you fight. You have to be an athlete and to be an athlete you have to think that you are the best to be the best. You are just as much a man as anyone else. You must learn to think like that.'
>
> He told them he had lost to Jerry Quarry and had a 30-1-1 record. Lyle also said, if given the chance, he

thought he could beat Ali. He had to think that way, he said, because you always have to think positive to accomplish something positive.

Ron went on to rap with a number of the kids one-on-one, ending up with advice about listening to their coach. Anderson closed the piece:

> Lyle told the group that they also could learn from one another, but above all else, he told them that they had to respect each other.
> 'That's the thing about boxing,' he said. 'You learn to respect each other. Remember, if someone is boxing and gets hurt, don't laugh at him because it could happen to you, too. Do you want him to laugh at you if you get hurt? Instead, learn to respect what each of you is doing.' That is Ron Lyle, the man.

It was about this time that Barney O'Grady, the young man who had started the comprehensive scrapbook collection finally met the man he so admired. An undergraduate in science, Barney had conceptualised a kinesiology project involving movements in boxing. He had arranged to observe a Ron Lyle sparring session but, by the time he arrived, Ron had already showered and dressed. When told the young student who had missed his opportunity was still in the gym, Ron re-dressed in his boxing trunks and went back into the ring, earning another lifelong fan.

While Ron waited and trained, the hearing on the assault charge against his estranged wife had been held over to be finally dismissed in August, but Ron knew he wouldn't get another chance with Nadine. In November, impatiently waiting for a new opponent, feeling restless and very much alone, he sought the company of a woman, hoping to relieve the intensity of the moment.

His first thought was of Patty Jordan, a strikingly beautiful woman he had met a few months before while training at the Albany hotel where she was an employee. They had spoken a just few words, but her image had drifted in and out of his thoughts ever since.

Patty was of mixed heritage, Native American and African American, and her father was in the Army. Like Nadine, she was from a respectable family that would pass muster with Nellie, and Ron took the plunge. After only a couple of dates, he learned that her fiery temperament was equal to his own and it wasn't long before sparks started to fly between them, both in private and in public. But both Patty and Ron found themselves increasingly intrigued, and they continued to find ways to see each every few days.

Always maintaining as much of his privacy as he could, Ron even kept his family and the Nelsons in the dark regarding his intentions for weeks - until one day he moved Patty into the Green Mountain house, introducing her first to Sharon who came over one day when Monte was visiting. Nellie might have objected to the living arrangement 'without benefit of clergy' since Ron's divorce was not final, but by then the couple had already committed to parenthood, with Patty expecting in October. Budda boom, budda bing.

29

*

SPORTSWRITERS grew more restless as the weeks went by. They reminded readers of such worries as '....this fan favourite is growing no younger and needs heavy action against a top-ranked opponent before summer gives way to fall.' If the Denver Boxing Club couldn't get Quarry or Foreman, most of the pundits wanted Lyle to meet either former heavyweight champion Jimmy Ellis or always-in-the-running Ken Norton, who had fought well twice against Ali.

In March, Norton had shown a feeble effort against Foreman, losing with a TKO in the second round and, in May, the Lyle camp went after Ellis. After brief but intensive negotiations, they got him - a Lyle-Ellis bout was scheduled for July 16, and Ron immediately headed to New York for intense training with Chickie Ferraro.

Excitement grew when on June 17, Jerry Quarry lost on a TKO to Joe Frazier in the sixth round and Ron Lyle moved to the number-three position in the World Boxing Council rankings. Even though he remained number five with the

W.B.A., local fans were adamant that their homeboy was ready to be champion. They were reminded that while Muhammad Ali, Joe Frazier and George Foreman had kick-started their professional careers on Olympic gold medals, Ron Lyle served his apprenticeship in a cell block. And now only those three - Ali, Frazier and Foreman - were ranked higher than Lyle. Denver wanted the championship bout almost as much as Ron did. As one bold headline put it: 'As Ron Lyle Goes, So Goes Denver'. It was as though the whole city had already put the Ellis fight behind them and moved on to a championship bout. But the Lyle camp knew the staying power of Jimmy Ellis should never be discounted.[9]

Ron returned to Denver after just two weeks, eager to get into the hometown groove. The week before, he had joined with Colorado State Athletic Commission chairman Eddie Bohn to establish a fund for Ham Jenkins, a blind ex-boxer whose home had been damaged by fire, and he went out of his way to personally present a cheque to Jenkins shortly after his flight landed. Then it was all business - back to the Elks to prepare for Mr. Ellis.

Angelo Dundee had been training Jimmy Ellis for years, along with Muhammad Ali and other great boxers, and he was adamant that his man would knock out Lyle within seven rounds. Never mind that Lyle was slightly favoured by the bookmakers, and that he was only a few steps from a championship fight, Dundee managed to sober the Denver fans.

Rocky Mountain News sports editor Bob Collins described the stakes:

> ....the 34-year-old Ellis knows he's got to win Tuesday or likely face the end of his big money fights. It's also do-or-die for Lyle....If he can handle the classy Ellis, Lyle will remain a 'contender.' If he can't, then he'll

have to run out the string as a trial horse for younger prospects.

In an odd twist Jimmy Ellis would be using as a sparring partner Ron's friend Donny Nelson, who had his own important fight on the card against Duane Bobick.

Nelson had never been resentful of Lyle coming onto the Denver Rocks and usurping his place as the number-one heavyweight of the team, even when he was forced to relocate to Phoenix in order to schedule fights in such venues as San Diego, Las Vegas and Tucson. He had gone on to win 12 of his 13 professional bouts and was looking forward to meeting Bobick, undefeated after 22 fights. The fighters had met once before as amateurs and Donny Nelson had won in a close decision. In the meantime Donny was picking up extra cash and more valuable experience sparring with former champion Jimmy Ellis. Neither Ron nor Donny took any of it personally - boxing had to be perpetually separated from friendship.

Two weeks before the scheduled card, all four boxers were working long hours to prepare. The usual hoopla prevailed, with special sparring sessions scheduled here and there around Denver, and Mayor William McNichols proclaimed the Thursday before the fight as 'Ron Lyle Day' in tribute to Ron achieving number three in the rankings.

Another interesting aside emerged in pre-fight news stories - the long-standing relationship between trainers Chickie Ferrara and Angelo Dundee. Between the two, they had trained, worked with or managed 12 world champions, but had never before matched wits in opposing corners. Dundee called Ferarra his 'professor,' having taken 'lessons' and served as Ferrara's assistant 25 years before. Both were cautious and deferential of each other's ability, but each also had a few things to say about the new rivalry. Ron Lyle, respectful of Angelo Dundee ever since the trainer had replied to his letter in prison, kept his distance from the ensuing exchange.

After watching Lyle spar, Dundee said to a reporter: 'You can see the magical touch of Chickie there in a couple of things. There is no better trainer than Chickie.' He also took a shot: 'But I liked what I saw there. In fact, I loved what I saw because Lyle is going to complement everything my fighter does.' For his part, Ferrara stated that Ron had an important advantage going for him in the Ellis fight: 'Angelo says he knows a lot about Lyle, but he's never worked Ron's corner. I know Ellis like the back of my hand.'

Two days later tension between the two trainers heated up. It seems Ferrara had booted Dundee from the Saturday sparring session between Ron and sparring partner Leroy Jones. 'I don't come to watch his fighter work out, and I expect him to observe the same principles,' Ferrara said to Terry Anderson. 'After all, this is a gym and trainers have a rule against anyone bothering their fighter by staying around.'

Dundee responded: 'All I said was that Lyle has some bad habits that will make it easier for Jimmy to whip him. I admit I shouldn't have been at Lyle's workout, but it doesn't hurt if you get away with it.' Dundee did admit to having other things on his mind. He would shortly be off to Zaire in to head Muhammad Ali's corner against George Foreman in what would be known as the 'Rumble in the Jungle.'

Still smarting over the loss to Quarry 18 months before, Lyle admitted it was 'do or die' with Ellis. Everyone agreed the fight would come down to Ron's punching power versus Jimmy's vast experience and ability to move. In Bob Collins's uncharacteristically lyrical language: 'It is man against man, will against will, emotion against emotion and gloved fist against flesh inside the ropes - which accounts in part for the fascination of this most primitive of sports.'

Off the Ropes

The gruelling fight took place in over 100-degree heat under the Coliseum ring lights. After the excitement of the Bonavena bout, a new record crowd of standing-room-only brought in a $120,000 gate; the fans were rewarded with an even better fight, the best in Denver history.

Neither boxer gained an advantage in the first round, but Ron picked up punching in the second and third, even while Ellis held and dodged, inserting his left hook whenever he could land it. With one minute left in the fourth round, the pattern for most of the rest of the fight was struck as Lyle put Ellis on the ropes with combinations to the head, but couldn't put him away. Lyle would move out early with flurries that often had Ellis in trouble, back off momentarily as Ellis held on to regain his composure and finally wind up back in command. It happened over and over in the fifth, sixth, seventh and eighth rounds. Then came the ninth.

The round started out ordinarily enough as Lyle put Ellis on the corner rope early with a good left-right combination that left Ellis' eyes glassy. But Ellis came back with a crunching left hook to the head and a right uppercut. In the neutral corner, he managed to land a tremendous right hand to the jaw, a left uppercut and another right. Ron was dazed. He managed to keep his record of never having been floored intact, although he absorbed at least two more smashing left hooks and four rights to the head before the bell sounded.

Ron recovered. Under punishing heat and surrounded by screaming fans, he came back strong in the last three rounds and might have put Ellis out in either the 11th or 12th, but the former champion managed to hang on. Thirty seconds into the 11th, Lyle used a right-left combination to daze Ellis and then came back with a good left uppercut. Somehow Ellis stayed on his feet and survived. In the 12th, Ellis's knees twice started to buckle, but he was standing at the end of the fight.

The headlines ranged from 'Lyle Wins, But it Wasn't All That Easy,' to 'Lyle Wins Unanimous Decision' to 'Lyle Wins Decisively Over Ellis.' The score favoured the latter point of view with the referee's card 59 to 55, and both judges voting 58 to 52. The *Rocky Mountain News* sports editor, a highly respected authority on boxing, called it seven rounds for Lyle, three for Ellis and two even.

However the sports reporters rated the fight, for the fans and Lyle's corner it was an evening of unadulterated joy. And there was no question that Ron had dispelled one lingering myth - that he wasn't a defensive boxer. Jimmy Ellis himself put it best: 'People say that Ron is easy to hit. That's a lie. Man, he knows what he is doing in the ring and is hard to put down.' With Ken Norton in attendance, the press box was unanimous in predicting a Lyle-Norton bout within a few weeks. As usual, they were wrong.

Once again Ron's prospects entered a holding pattern, even after his great victory over Jimmy Ellis. The same old system prevailed - the top contenders avoided fighting the top contenders, and for the most part, they got away with it. Jerry Quarry was recuperating from cuts he had suffered during his June bout with Joe Frazier, and Ken Norton, rather than face Lyle in the ring, set about making *Mandingo*, the first movie in what would turn out to be a minor acting career. Both Ali and Frazier camps talked a good game but neither followed up Daniels' advances. While Ali prepared for the 'Rumble in the Jungle' with George Foreman, Frazier chose to meet Oscar Bonavena for the third time in December.

As number three Ron knew he had to stay sharp, not to mention keep the pressure on the other top contenders to put up or shut up. Bill Daniels finally settled for a respectable bout with 11th-ranked Boone Kirkman, a former National AAU heavyweight champion with a 31-4 professional record. Kirkman had beaten many of the same opponents Ron had put down and also had the distinction of being beaten by George Foreman and Ken Norton, who had chosen to meet him rather than Ron in June. The fight was set for September 17 in Kirkman's hometown of Seattle.

Ron prepared for the Kirkman fight with an intensity that his trainers compared to fighting for the world championship. He sparred with a strong, unbeaten Leroy Jones for two weeks in Denver, then flew to Seattle for the remaining four weeks when he inflicted a severe cut on Henry Culpepper, his local sparring partner.

Ron remembers feeling like he was in the best shape of his life that September, following a near perfect six weeks training. Jones had provided major challenges in the ring, and Ron had progressed significantly in his ability to jab. For his part, Boone Kirkman worked hard under Eddie Futch, former trainer of Ken Norton and Joe Frazier, and felt equal to the challenge of fighting Ron Lyle.

It wasn't even close. That night in Seattle, Ron scored his first knockout in 11 months. He body-punched Boone Kirkman at will while getting in a fair number of punishing head shots. Kirkman had already begun to bleed from the nose and mouth in the second round, and was staggered by uppercuts in the third, sixth and seventh. By the time the ring doctor stopped the fight at two minutes into the eighth round, the Seattle boxer was bleeding profusely and his eyes were cut badly, nearly closed. He was immediately taken to the hospital. In the locker-room after the bout, Chickie Ferrar told reporters Lyle had fought perfectly against Kirkman's infighting style and his tendency to fight from a shell.

Third-ranked Ron Lyle had been the most active heavyweight in the top ten for three years, gaining a record of 29 wins, one loss and one controversial draw. He had never been knocked out or even knocked down and barely cut. He had earned the right to a heavyweight championship bout, and still it eluded him as time moved relentlessly on. Ron would be 34 years old in February.

Then, on October 30, Muhammad Ali stunned the world by knocking out George Foreman in the eighth round of the 'Rumble in the Jungle,' winning back the heavyweight championship of the world, an event that would change everything.

In spite of his recent loss in the primary race for Governor, Bill Daniels hadn't taken his eye off the Lyle ball for an instant. And he didn't waste any time. No sooner had the referee declared Muhammad Ali the winner than Daniels fired off a telegram to Ali in Zaire which read: 'Congratulations for a great victory. Two million dollars guaranteed for title fight in Denver against Ron Lyle. Fight to take place indoors or outdoors in 1975.' Feverish negotiations ensued, with even Madison Square Garden representatives entering the picture, stating the Garden wanted Lyle.

Asked at a Colorado State Booster Club dinner how he would do against the champion, Lyle said: 'Yeah, I think I could beat Ali....because I can move from side to side and I can take a good punch. I'd fight Ali in his own style. When he talks, I'd talk. When he dances, I'd dance. And when he's slugging, I'd slug. That's the only way to fight Ali....there's no sense in trying to punch him out.' Six months later everyone present that night would remember his words.

Ron recalls those days as just 'biding my time.' By then, he was confident he would get a shot at the championship; it would just be a matter of when. But it wouldn't be easy. After Ali recaptured the crown in Zaire, the 1974 rankings held firm:

George Foreman
Joe Frazier
Ron Lyle
Oscar Bonavena
Joe Bugner
Ken Norton
Jerry Quarry
Chuck Wepner
Henry Clark
Larry Middleton

None of the top ten would agree to meet Ron Lyle in the ring. But Ron made it clear to Daniels that he wanted and needed to stay busy, so two fights were scheduled - one with Al Jones in New Orleans on December 13 and the other with Mac Foster in Houston on January 28. Ron hoped that after two more decisive victories, albeit over unranked opponents, Ali would agree to give him a shot at the crown.

30

*

ON knew he was close to fulfilling his dream in the winter of 1974. He could almost reach out and touch Muhammad Ali. But first he had to travel to New Orleans and tackle Al Jones, an unpredictable heavyweight who had won all six of his fights that year, including a three - round knockout over Boone Kirkman, after a miserable 4-20 record in his seven years of professional fighting through 1973.

Jones attributed his turnaround to a new manager and Ron did not take him lightly, with the stakes again very high. The Denver Boxing Club announced a few days before the fight that it was 99.9 per cent certain that a victory over Jones would clinch a Garden fight with Ali in early March.

As usual, no problem in the ring. Lyle was never in any difficulty, dominating the fight throughout and knocking Jones down six times, including a knockout in the fifth round. That didn't stop the New Orleans crowd, who had been told to expect a second or third-round knockout, from beginning a raucous booing demonstration starting in the fourth round up to the knockout. Ron wasn't in Denver anymore.

But the press saw it differently. After the Jones fight, not only the local newspapers, but the *Associated Press* stories started pushing for an Ali-Lyle bout. The most objective envisioned a good fight, one in which Lyle, slower than Ali, would outlast him. They pointed out that the Denver boxer could take a punch and had proven beyond a doubt his patience, discipline and ability to be dangerous in late rounds. One *Denver Post* story even compared a Lyle challenge to the 'Cinderella Man' meeting with Max Baer:

> Certainly [Lyle] would have as good a chance as did the late James J. Braddock when as a 10-1 underdog, he upset Max Baer and won the title on June 13, 1935, two years after his career was thought to be over and he took a job on the New Jersey docks to feed his family.

The comparison was a stretch. Lyle and his camp knew he had a much better chance of beating Ali than Braddock had of outlasting Baer, but they let the speculation continue, hoping the underdog image would fuel the imagination of fans as the march to the championship fight continued.

The Denver Boxing Club told the press that arrangements for the Ali-Lyle world championship fight were expected to be completed in a few days and announced in New York the following day. The Lyle camp had accepted terms and signed their end of the contract with Madison Square Garden the day after the Jones victory, and officials of the Garden were said to have received Ali's verbal agreement to terms.

Ron waited only for final negotiations - which would involve the closed-circuit aspects of the fight - with Herbert Muhammad, who handled Ali's business dealings. And the *Associated Press* reported that: 'boxing insiders feel that Ali will defend against Ron Lyle of Denver in Madison Square Garden in March. As usual, the 'insiders' were wrong.

ROCKY MOUNTAIN NEWS, Tuesday, January 7, Denver, Colorado - four column headline: 'Ali ducks Lyle, decides to fight Wepner.' The Lyle camp was devastated and Bob Collins spoke for the rest of Denver:

> The only conclusion that one can draw is that Ali, the idol of so many after having regained his crown with an eighth-round KO of George Foreman on Oct. 30 in Zaire, Africa, prefers to fight a sure thing in Wepner, rather than take the risk of fighting Lyle, a rock-hard 215-pounder who has a 30-1-1 record.

Ron was packing for his trip to New York where he would have appeared at a press conference announcing the fight, when he got the news. The '99.9 per cent certain' March championship fight was off. Speculation ran rampant that Ali had been under the influence of promoter Don King or his manager Herbert Muhammad in electing to take a half-million dollars less to fight Chuck Wepner in Jamaica. Nobody outside of Denver wanted to believe that the great Muhammad Ali was afraid to take on Ron Lyle.

But the President of the Denver Boxing Club Mike Hayes expressed his bitterness in the Collins piece:

> We're very, very disappointed, especially in that Ali always has made such a big thing out of his wanting to be fair with his title and to give deserving boxers a chance at it. Who is more deserving than Lyle, a legitimate contender who has lost only one fight, by a decision to Jerry Quarry two years ago?
>
> If Ali gives the fight to Wepner, it's got to be because he wants a soft touch and wants to avoid

Lyle, especially in that the fight will bring him a cool $500,000 less.

Wepner is a nothing, a nobody. It will do nothing but hurt boxing....Nothing could be closer than this fight was. We were sure we had it. The shame of it is that nobody in this world is more deserving of a title fight than Lyle. It's been a ten-year goal for him ever since he started boxing seriously back in 1965 while in the Colorado State Penitentiary.

He's worked like a dog and trained so hard. He's fought everybody we could coax into a ring with him and no one in the top 10 is more decent or dedicated in his desire to upgrade the sport. Then they pull the rug from under him like this.

Maybe because of all the disappointments Ron had experienced, he expressed a more philosophical view; he found himself consoling Hayes when the Boxing Club President brought him the news. 'Hey, don't worry,' Ron told Hayes. 'We've been down this road before. Lots of people have ducked us, but they can't keep ducking forever. It's taken ten years to get where I am now. If it takes a little longer, it still doesn't change the goal. If Ali takes the easier route now, it will just make it more difficult for him when he does have to fight me.' Then he added: 'We've just got to pick up the pieces and continue our efforts. Get me the fights and I'll win them. This thing isn't going to ruin my determination.'

Ron was even more generous in his take on Ali with Chet Nelson of the *Rocky Mountain News*. He said he was sorry he didn't get the Ali match in March, but added: 'I've been waiting for a championship fight since I met with you fellows five years ago when I started my career. So waiting won't be anything new for me. I'm not going to let it blow my mind.' He went on to say he had a 45-minute talk with Muhammad Ali in Philadelphia back in June of 1973 and had impressed upon Ali that he would someday be fighting for the title and he expected Ali to be the champ when the time came. 'Ali knows what I want and he also knows that it will be a long, hard night. I feel that I am where Ali was when he was waiting for Foreman. I realise Ali just came down after reaching a peak for the Foreman fight and he needs this Wepner fight to get himself back together.'

In his conversation with Hayes, Herbert Muhammad had thrown out the comment 'Wepner is white,' creating another disturbance among Denver press and fans. Speculation that Ali wanted to beat an easy white guy, passing over the white contender Joe Bugner, was rampant, but again Ron refused to criticise the champion. He saved his energy for whatever was to come next.

Denver fans knew that Wepner's only claim to fame in his 30-9-2 career was the time he got an unpopular decision over Ernie Terrell. He had been knocked out by Jerry Judge and Buster Mathis, among others, and had lost a lopsided decision to Randy Neumann in 1972. Since then he had beaten eight undistinguished opponents. But all of that was water under the bridge for Ron. When asked how many years he could possibly have left to box, he replied: 'I feel ten years younger than my age. I will keep boxing until I reach my goal of the heavyweight championship. It's within my reach. I can taste the title now.'

After taking a breath Daniels began again to negotiate with the Ali camp. Back in September, he had already obtained a verbal agreement for an Ali-Lyle match-up in June if Ron could win his next two bouts, and his efforts were to hold them to that agreement. History repeating itself.

Step one was getting past 'Memphis' Al Jones, which Ron did spectacularly, knocking Jones out in the fifth round. Step two was doing away with Mac Foster, the guy who had withdrawn from a scheduled fight with Lyle in 1972, pleading an injury. Foster copped out again. Daniels didn't give up. He managed to land a fight with ninth-ranked Jimmy Young for a February fight in Honolulu. Once again, Ron prepared for the fight at Canon City. A heavy favourite to dispose of Young, Ron didn't take any chances. He continued his fitness regimen and sparred with anybody and everybody who showed up at the prison ring - whatever it took to win a shot at the heavyweight championship of the world. But once again, maddeningly, he was stopped in his tracks.

The headline read 'How to Lose $1,000,000 in One Night', with a lead by Mike Hayes. 'The chances of third-ranked Ron Lyle's title hopes suffered a severe blow when the Denver heavyweight dropped a ten-round decision to ninth-rated Jimmy Young in Honolulu, Hawaii.'

Even today, Ron finds it difficult to reconcile his loss that night. He came out strong and won the first round with bone-jarring body shots that began to take their toll on Young midway in the bout. However, Young's exceptionally quick hands soon began causing trouble for Lyle and gradually the fight momentum swung in Young's favour.

During the many clinches Young got the best of the stronger Lyle with quick, snappy left hooks. Although Lyle was never hurt or stunned, the punches did much to throw off the Denver heavyweight's timing and enabled Young to dictate the flow of the match. And whenever Lyle cornered him against the ropes, the 26-year-old Young would hang on until the referee broke in. Lyle constantly forced the action, especially in the last three rounds when he realised Young was ahead and a knockout would be the only way he could salvage a win and his No. 3 ranking.

But Young never got careless and he withstood Lyle's awesome punching power. Admitting that his body absorbed tremendous punishment, Young later stated his excellent conditioning prepared him for the body-shots.

Promoter Sam Ichinose stated: 'It was simply a matter of timing and styles. Young fought a good fight and had a good night. Maybe Lyle, on another night, could win.' Ron knew then and knows now that he could have beaten Jimmy Young, but the truth was, he didn't. Ron Lyle had to start all over again.

In his book *The Fight*, Norman Mailer maintains that boxing is a vanity sport - that because so many boxers are there to attract admiration, they will suffer the greatest humiliation. A headline that had appeared after the Bonavena fight came back to haunt the Lyle camp after the loss to Jimmy Young. 'As Ron Lyle Goes, So Goes Denver' translated into humiliation for a handful of fair-weather Denver boxing fans, and for the first time in a long time, Ron started to take some flak for losing a fight. His ability to absorb bad news faltered and he momentarily lost the knack of publicly shrugging off criticism. He not only lashed out at a few fans, but found himself raging at a reporter who did not write about the incident. Jimmy Young notwithstanding, Ron knew he would get his chance at the heavyweight championship and he temporarily lost patience with anybody who doubted him.

For a time, Ron retreated into what felt like safe haven with Patty. The other saving grace during that period was Monte, who often stayed at the house in Green Mountain. But soon, even that pleasure would disappear.

31

*

The Big Three

VI

MUHAMMAD ALI met the low-rated Chuck Wepner in March and managed only a technical knockout in the 15th and final round. In the meantime, headlines regarding Ron's lost chances proliferated, some in excessive hyperbole: 'Ron Lyle apparently had a match with Muhammad Ali in the bag. But that was before unknown Jimmy Young emptied the bag.'

Behind the scenes, the Lyle camp continued its pressure on the Ali camp and Ron's closest fans rallied around, calling and stopping by the Elks Gym just to let him know they still believed in his dream. Other signs of Denver support appeared as well. A photo of Ron at a fund-raiser is captioned: 'Despite his upset to Jimmy Young this spring, heavyweight contender Ron Lyle is still a popular figure wherever he goes, and he is never too busy to sign an autograph.'

Two weeks later, it happened - Muhammad Ali signed a contract to fight Ron Lyle for the heavyweight championship of the world.

While the win over Jimmy Ellis had helped position Ron for a shot at the title, what helped even more, as it turned out, was the loss to Jimmy Young. As Stephen Brunt put it in *Facing Ali*: 'It's reasonable to surmise that Ali and his handlers, watching that fight [Young vs. Lyle], figured that the aging champion still had enough guile and experience to get past a relatively raw opponent.' The 15-round title bout was scheduled for May 16, 1975 at the Las Vegas Convention Center and would be carried live on network television.

Ron finally had the chance he had dreamt about since that day in the prison hospital, and it had come, not because of all the hard-fought wins, but because of a single loss. Ron didn't care how it happened; he was determined to make the best of what might turn out to be his only chance at the heavyweight championship of the world.

The fight was no sooner announced than Ron suffered a personal blow. In April, after spending more time with Monte that he had in years, Nadine moved away - disappeared - with Monte in tow. Her family either didn't know where they were or wouldn't tell Ron. Believing Nadine would return, he didn't try to find her at first. He would never see Nadine again and it would be years before Monte came back to him. But in 1975, he moved the pain of losing his son to the back of his mind and focused on the immediate future - Muhammad Ali and the heavyweight championship of the world awaited.

Ron began hard training, first in Denver with Bobby Lewis, then to New York and Chickie Ferraro. Chickie had studied Ali's moves for years; now he watched and re-watched the Ali-Foreman tape frame by frame. Bobby, Chickie and Ron all knew what it would take to defeat the champion. And all knew it wasn't going to be easy.

Boxing enthusiasts still remember that fight. Bloggers on fight websites still write about it. And interviewers still ask Ron Lyle how he remembers it.

Off the Ropes

Philadelphia disc jockey and boxing fan Roland Riso was recently invited to write a series for Ringsports.com and chose the Ali-Lyle bout as his opening subject. The first prize fight he had ever viewed on television when he was eight years old turned out to be the most memorable and solidified his belief that boxing alone represented the romance of the: 'individualistic mano-a-mano, with no other team-mates on the field to take the blame. At the end of the night, the referee would raise only one man's hand.'

Ali was 33, Ron 34. Ali had reached the pinnacle, twice, and had nothing left to prove; Ron was still a relative newcomer and had everything to prove. Ali had lost three-and-a-half years when his license was suspended for draft evasion; Ron lost seven-and-a-half years in prison. Ali's record was 46-2; Ron's was 30-2-1. The two fighters were close in height and only five pounds difference in weight (Ali weighed 224, Ron 219). They were identical in sizes of biceps, forearms and waist, but Ali had a four-inch reach advantage.

Interest in the fight was universal. Because Muhammad Ali was no longer at his peak and because Ron Lyle had proved so dangerous, the odds were close to even in Vegas. And as Stephen Brunt put it: 'The anticipation was not so much that Lyle would win, but rather that Ali would lose.'

Brunt wrote that Lyle understood well that he was a bit-player, stepping into the ring against an icon. In his interview with Ron at the Canastota 2001 Boxing Hall of Fame gathering, he asked how it felt to meet Ali in 1975. Ron said:

> At a time when America - when black America - was in the revolution of equal rights, Ali was at the forefront. Not only am I fighting a fighter, I'm fighting against a guy that represents freedom for

black people in America. Now, was I aware of this? Absolutely. I've always been aware. I've always been politically aware. I never said nothing, because no one's ever asked me. No one ever asked me my opinion about it until now. Yes, I knew. I understood. Was it hard? Yeah, it was hard. Was I trying to win? Absolutely.

Ali was a guy that I admired, that I have always admired from a distance, because he represents a lot of things to a lot of people. But I had to fight this guy. I think getting to that point was rough because of the people we live around and the emotional feelings about this same guy. It was like you against the world. He was the world's symbol. Did I make the best of it? I think I did. Did I win? In my own mind, in my own self-satisfaction and well-being, I thought I upheld my ability as well as any man could against the obstacle that was ahead of me.[10]

Howard Cosell called the fight. He began the broadcast with interviews of both boxers, beginning with a conversation he had conducted with Ron Lyle weeks before in Denver right after the bout had been announced. They were seated on a park bench, Ron looking relaxed and dapper in the style of the day with plaid pants and a coordinated suede coat, trimmed in white fur. Cosell had introduced the interview by referring to 'the nature of Lyle's sordid past' and proceeded to delve into the shooting and prison years, including the stabbing and Ron's subsequent commitment to competing for the heavyweight championship. In a soft voice and with a smile, Ron predicted that: 'He [Ali] is going down, and so are you.'

The second interview had taken place just hours before the championship bout, Ron in a tee shirt and wool cap, still relaxed, but responding with something of an edge. He said he wouldn't be caught in the 'rope-a-dope' [the technique Ali had used to conquer Foreman, whereby he leaned back on the ropes to conserve strength, allowing Foreman to be a 'dope' by punching himself out]. Ron maintained that it wasn't his job to worry about the ropes. In response to another question from Cosell, he said that he wouldn't try and kill Ali like Liston and Frazier and other fighters had, that the champion was defensive, but not completely, and not completely offensive either. 'He will have to come to me.'

Cosell remarked: 'I believe that you believe in yourself,' but pointed out his loss to Jerry Quarry and an 'unheralded' Jimmy Young. Ron responded: 'Show me anybody who hasn't lost. I've been in 36 fights and lost two.' He ended the interview by holding up his fingers an inch apart, saying: 'It only takes that much to win a horse race, only one point in basketball.'

In the Ali interview, Cosell's banter typified their long-standing friendship, starting with the introduction: '....the heavyweight champion of the world, perhaps the most visible figure in the entire world these days.' Ali went on to predict a knockout between the first and the eighth round and added: 'This man's never been knocked out. George Foreman had never been knocked out. Chuck Wepner had never been knocked out, and this man's never been knocked out, so it gives me something to fight for.'

Ali said he would use the 'rope-a-dope' and when Cosell asked about a 'Plan B' in case Lyle refused to play the part of the 'dope,' Ali demonstrated the 'mirage,' where he will walk to the centre of the ring, cover his head with his fists and block Lyle's punches from 'the vulnerable areas.' He said: 'Watch this carefully, how I wear this man down. I'll give him an offer he can't refuse.'

Having earlier characterised Lyle as 'confident,' Cosell tried to close the interview with Ali: 'Obviously, the champion enters tonight's fray shaken, with a loss of confidence.' Ali responded: 'Shaken? You be there. And after the man rings the bell, I'm gonna jump over the ropes and slap Cosell!'

THE night opened with the standard ring introductions, including a roar for former champion Joe Louis and boos when George Foreman stood up. Then, after a short period of time, Ron moved towards the ring, accompanied by both Chickie Ferrara and Bobby Lewis, to loud cheers and applause throughout the auditorium.

Next, Ali entered with his enormous entourage, a chant of 'Lyle! Lyle! Lyle! Lyle!' overwhelmed the cheers of the Ali fans, and the camera zoomed in on a huge Lyle banner in the centre of the hall. The Denver fans were out in force.

As the two boxers danced in their respective corners, the camera moved in low to Ron shadow boxing, his face turned to Ali with eyebrows raised and a big grin on his face. Cosell called it a 'leer.'

Many of Ron's friends were there, including Jimmy Farrell, who remembers the ringside introduction of Howard Smith, the heavyweight Ron Lyle had defeated back when the Canon City Rock Busters met the U.S. Army.

Seated in a prominent row were three former convicts Ron had arranged to attend the fight - Albert Johnson, Corny Cruz and 'Rip' Clark. In the Cosell interview, Ron had mentioned their names, saying that he hoped to inspire them to do something with their talents. That film clip would be replayed many times over the next three years.

32

*

'Champions aren't made in gyms. Champions are made from
something they have deep inside them - a desire, a dream,
a vision.' - Muhammad Ali

ALI might just as well have been talking about Ron
Lyle as himself. From the time they met at Ali's
training camp during the *60 Minutes* taping,
Muhammad had treated Ron with respect; he hadn't
indulged in what had become his pre-fight routine of taunting
and labelling his opponent with insulting nicknames.

To this day Ron believes Ali treated him with respect
because he understood the long struggle that brought him to
that world championship fight. At a reunion of former
boxers in 2001, Ali's Parkinson's Syndrome was well-
advanced, and he recognised few of his old adversaries, but
when he spotted Ron, he made an effort to smile and
immediately moved in for a hug with the man he had met in
Las Vegas 26 years before.

Ali was there to be beaten that day. From the moment the
bell rang for the beginning of round one, with the ongoing
'Lyle! Lyle! Lyle! Lyle!' chant in the background, Ron
punched while Ali covered up. Even Howard Cosell had to

admit that Lyle was fighting smart, refusing to be drawn in to the 'rope-a-dope.' At the end of round one, Ali had a bloody nose. In round two, Ali kept trying to use his 'rope-a-dope' strategy - Cosell called leaning against the ropes 'a strange posture for Ali' - but in the words of Ali's physician, Ron was 'too smart to go for it.'

By the third round Cosell started expressing his concern that Ali must be feeling the contrast between Lyle and George Foreman, who had fallen for the 'rope-a-dope' and used himself up. He declared: 'Lyle has no fear of this man.' Round four was much the same, other than a quick left and right by Ali and Ron following through with a hard left. First four rounds to Lyle. Cosell: 'Ali is doing virtually nothing.'

Ali started dancing in round five and got in a few punches. But Cosell cautioned: 'Lyle is not afraid; he looks quite strong.' Ali goes back to the ropes and a right by Lyle gets to him. In the sixth round, Ali kept dancing and talking, and Ron kept chasing; neither put together combinations that did any real damage. Cosell: 'One has to wonder if Ali can continue dancing...they're not kids, anymore.' Lyle looked even stronger and more confident in the seventh round. He got in some good combination punches and Cosell said that he thought Ali must be 'concerned.' The faces of both fighters were studies in intensity. Ali had long since stopped his dancing and chatter. He hit Ron after the bell had rung for the end of the round.

Round eight had been predicted as the knockout round by Ali and, as it began, the Denver fans once again chanted, 'Lyle! Lyle! Lyle! Lyle!' Ron came out strong, but Ali inflicted some hurt with a couple of right leads. Cosell told his viewers: 'Lyle is a powerful man. He can take a punch,' but after winning the first seven rounds, Ron appeared to have lost the eighth to Ali.

The champ looked tired as he came out in the ninth,

having expended much energy in the previous round. He retreated to the corner ropes and Ron gestured at him to come out. Ron got in some punches, but didn't do much damage. Just before round ten, Chickie Ferrara told his fighter that all he had to do was stay with it, and Ron nodded. Right off the bat in round ten, Ron got in a hard hit to the middle. After some circling and thrusting, Ali retreated for the ropes and stayed there, covered up, for most of the round, but Ron managed to land a solid right to Ali's left side, a hard left uppercut and a punishing right slam on the side of Ali's head.

Both fighters looked tired as they moved slowly to their corners at the bell, but Lyle was ahead on all scorecards. He had Ali on the ropes. Round eleven. It looked like more of the same until, suddenly, Ali started punching hard. Cosell hollered: 'He hurt Lyle! He hurt him with a right!' Ron was up against the ropes, trying to cover from a flurry of shots, then moved across the ring against ropes on the other side. Ali continued the onslaught, then stepped back and motioned the referee in.

With no knockdown and no mandatory eight count, the referee called the fight at 66 seconds into the eleventh round. Ron protested, and Chickie Ferra hollered: 'Why stop it?' But Ali had already lifted his arms above his head, mouthing the words: 'I'm the greatest.' The fight was over.

THE spectators seemed surprised; even Howard Cosell hesitated to endorse the technical knockout call. Ron put his hand on Chickie's shoulder and said: 'It's okay. I know how I got here.'

Long time Muhammad Ali watchers saw his explosion in the eleventh round of the Lyle fight as the most spectacular assault in his career, but Chickie Ferrara, Bobby Lewis and virtually all of the Denver fans were outraged the fight had been stopped. Ron Lyle had won nine of the first ten rounds; it wasn't until the eleventh that Ali even demonstrated much punching power. But the unwritten rule prevailed - the only way to beat the champion is decisively, punctuating it with a knockout.

Ron was clearly disappointed but his reaction was mild compared to his lead trainer's. Ron recently told Roland Riso that in the eight years he and Chickie were together, 'That was the only time I ever heard him [Ferrara] raise his voice. [Usually} you couldn't hear him speak - barely above a whisper.'

Riso wrote about the heart those 'great gladiators' displayed that evening: 'There were no knockdowns - just ten-and-a-half rounds of world-class boxing at its sweetest.' He went on to describe the bout as the vintage heavyweight challenge:

> In Lyle's case, his performance left no doubt that he belonged in that ring with Ali. He made fighting Ali appear a lot easier than it was. And Ali always made boxing look a lot easier than it is. That's because a Ron Lyle will always be difficult to come by, and a Clay/Ali will be impossible to duplicate. Students of the Sweet Science need to learn from the past in order for the noble, good stuff to be, well, at least emulated.

Many years after his championship fight, Ron watched the 1975 tape with a *Denver Post* reporter. He said: 'One night back in '64, I had a dream that I fought for the title. The fight I eventually had with [Ali] was exactly the fight I dreamed - except the referee took it away from me.' He raised his fists and began to shadowbox. 'I had all the punches, and I could put 'em together in series. Hard left jab to the head - Bop! Right uppercut and left hook to the body - Boom!'

But Ron's failure to win the heavyweight championship of the world that night was not a story of regret or bitterness. In a response to a question from Peter Boyles, he remembers that his biggest purse, $175,000, was for the Ali bout, and shrugs that off as unimportant. The fight was the thing. 'I wasn't afraid of the Ali fight. I was relaxed and knew my skills were coming to a peak - I prepared for a moment. When the moment came, I gave it my all. It didn't work out, and only God knows why. But the greatest challenge in boxing is accepting the results, win, lose or draw. Come to peace with it.'

He told Stephen Brunt that he was never bitter about the fight. 'No. I was glad for the opportunity. Was I disappointed in the judge's or the powers that be, decision to stop the fight? No, because...it wasn't my time.'

THE Denver press reflected most fans' reaction to the fight, emphasising Ron's refusal to act as Ali's 'dope'; his clear victory through ten rounds; and the referee stopping the fight earlier than necessary. A headline: 'Nobody Loves an Unfunny Clown.' And another: 'Ron Lyle Must Begin Again.'

33

*

BETWEEN the May championship bout and Ron's next
fight, which would finally be scheduled for September,
he tried to balance his life, as he always had, among
family, friends, training and working with the kids he
thought needed him. Even as he struggled with his own
alcoholism, Dennis Nelson once again supported his friend
without reservation, frequently working the corner as Ron
shadow-boxed in the Elks ring. And when Donny was in
town, Ron would offer support to the other Nelson brother
who, like himself, had a long way to come back after a
devastating loss. And then another character reappeared in
his life.

Vernon 'Rip' Clark came directly to Denver after having
been one of the 'special guests' Ron invited to the Ali fight.
At 5 foot 7 inches, 'Rip' had been too small to play on the
prison athletic teams and he hadn't been a particular friend,
but he did represent a whole population of former convicts
Ron perceived as needing a step up, a reason to go straight.
So when he walked into the Elks Gym, Ron invited him to

stay around while he worked out with some of the younger children.

For several weeks Clark would drop into the Elks and hang around whenever Ron was training or working with the kids. Soon it became apparent that the ex-con was using hard drugs and Ron told 'Rip' to stay away, especially when youngsters were there. Clark had come around to Ron's house a couple of times to touch him up for 'loans,' but stayed away from both the Elks and his house after having been so summarily dismissed. For a while, Ron forgot about his old prison-mate. Then, after what seemed like a long two-month wait, the right fight came along at the right time.

Heavyweight contender rankings that summer were:

Ken Norton
Jimmy Young
Joe Frazier
George Foreman
Ron Lyle
Earnie Shavers
Duane Bobick
Joe Bugner
Chuck Wepner
Randy Neumann

Unable to arrange a bout with any of the top four, the Lyle camp landed the next best opportunity in Earnie Shavers. The match-up would be good for one or the other of the fighters. Shavers sported a record of 49-4-1 with 48 knockouts and had just come off three wins; beating Lyle could get him a crack at Ali. For Ron's part, a decisive win over Shavers would keep him in the game. The fight was scheduled for September 8, in Denver.

During the previous year, Ron's brother Bill had started

getting more actively involved in the Denver Boxing Club and had spent as much time as both could manage in dialogue with Bill Daniels. Always protective of his younger brother, Bill researched the nuances of the boxing game and came away surprised and disillusioned that most boxers had less input and control over their careers than did managers, clubs, promoters and even, on occasion, trainers. He began to gradually edge into the role of Ron's advocate, gently, to be sure, but unmistakably assuming the role of protecting his brother's best interests. That role had been solidified by the eve of Ron's battle with Earnie Shavers.

THE Lyle-Shavers bout opened to a raucous crowd of Denverites, determined to yell their favourite son to victory - if that's what it took. The absolute war that followed the opening bell astonished even the most knowledgeable fight fans and press. Both fighters demonstrated that they could hurt the other with almost any punch, and they bombed away at each other with downright recklessness.

In round one, Shavers came out strong with Lyle, uncharacteristically, moving backward. Ron said later that he was well aware of Earnie's huge power and wasn't about to be slammed right off the bat. Shavers got in a nice right and some follow-up blows, but Ron came back with a small flurry at the end of the round.

In the second round Ron opened with a pawing kind of jab, and Shavers backed away, seemingly wary of Lyle's strength. Then Earnie delivered a devastating left hook and Ron went down, obviously shaken when he finally got to his feet at the count of nine. The round was over - saved by the bell.

Shavers' expression and body language strongly indicated he was determined to end it in round three, as he pounded away at Lyle who was already covering up and on the ropes, trying to clear his head. Then out of nowhere, Ron started fighting back and stunned Shavers with a quick left-right combination. The crowd roared.

In round four, Lyle came out the aggressor for the first time, and Shavers retreated to the ropes. Lyle hurt Shavers again and Earnie came back with a huge right that nearly sent Ron down. Members of the press in the front row scribbled madly, trying to capture the extraordinary action.

Lyle came out strong and fast again in the fifth round, making Shavers retreat for the first time. Ron started punching more, gaining confidence. He scored a punishing combination and Shavers was hurt again from another right. Earnie started to look like he was running out of gas.

In round six, Shavers came out of his corner and swung at Lyle and missed; Ron immediately countered. Thud. Ron landed what one sportswriter called a 'lightning bolt' right. Shavers staggered, then was hit with six straight punches, going down and not getting up - knocked out cold. The Denver fans screamed, whistled and pounded each other until they, like Earnie Shavers, were totally spent. Ron Lyle was still alive and in the game.

As one sportswriter put it: 'When Ron Lyle's losing streak stood at two, his career stood on the brink of oblivion. But his recent starching of Earnie Shavers shows it would be a mistake to dismiss him as a power in the heavyweight division.' And a headline read, 'Iron-jawed Lyle regains stature, coming off deck to stop Shavers.' That night Ron Lyle was called the King of Denver.

Earnie Shavers went on to complete a remarkable record of 88 fights, winning 73 with 67 of those by KOs. But he still remembers Ron Lyle as the hardest hitting fighter he ever met in the ring. He talks about their slugfest as 'just a job' and describes how the two eventually got to know each other through their mutual friend Dennis Nelson.

'Nobody ever hit me that hard. No question about it. I'll

remember that punch on my deathbed. Ron was a great puncher.' Recently Ron Lyle returned the compliment: 'Nobody ever hit me as hard in the ring as Earnie Shavers.'

In 2005, Jess E. Trail wrote a piece that covered Ron Lyle's boxing history. He captured the Lyle-Shavers fight: 'After being decked in round two by one of the best left hooks Earnie Shavers ever threw, Ron Lyle got up. At the end of the bout, he walked away with Shavers lying face down on the canvas.'

Denver fans thought they had seen what would have to be Ron Lyle's greatest fight, but, as Dennis put it: 'They hadn't seen nuthin' yet.'

34

*

TRACY LYLE was born in October, one month after the Shavers fight. Ron and Patty were both delighted with the bright-eyed, animated baby girl who smiled almost from the very first day, and Ron found himself in a rare contented state of mind, just the place he needed to be before his next challenge. But once again his peace was short-lived.

The win over Earnie Shavers triggered two events that dramatically impacted Ron's life. His brother was primarily responsible for the first and, for almost thirty years, Bill Lyle has wrestled with that decision. He broke the long-standing contract with Bill Daniels.

It was no secret that Daniels had a taste for politics, spirited women and fast cars, and although Bill may have felt a level of discomfort with that lifestyle as a possible influence on Ron, he had a different reason for advising his brother to change course. While in retrospect, severing ties with Daniels might seem shortsighted, at the time Bill Lyle presented a practical rationale. It had always bothered him that while standard contracts for the time provided the manager $33^{1/3}$ per cent of the purse, Daniels had always split 50/50 with Ron. They shared the cost of trainers, sparring partners, travel and other expenses, and so Ron realised a significantly smaller net profit than he should have been entitled to.

With the Shavers win, Bill thought it was time to recover the most they could from Ron's upcoming opportunities - to seek a greater share of revenues, especially since they were still providing financial support to the family. He knew the time would come when purses would be smaller and money tighter. When Daniels refused to modify the contract, citing the trust he had set up for Ron, Bill hired an attorney, not only to end the contract, but to file a lawsuit against the Denver entrepreneur to recover past profits. Enter Walter Gerash.

Bill Lyle had met Gerash back in 1963 when he was a maintenance worker at Denver Law School where Gerash was teaching. An attorney with a national reputation, Gerash had successfully taken on civil rights and anti-war cases, not to mention celebrity criminal defence cases. Almost by accident the Lyle brothers had found the arguably best attorney in Denver. Ron formally requested his services, and, after finding the 50/50 agreement to be in violation of Colorado statutes, Walter Gerash agreed to take the case. He immediately brought court action to invalidate the contract and won easily. He also prepared a lawsuit on behalf of Ron Lyle and a settlement was quickly reached. The era of Bill Daniels was over.

A few years later, Ron and Bill Lyle sought help from media journalist Peter Boyles to make amends with Bill Daniels, sending word that they had 'made some big mistakes.' Expressing feelings of betrayal, Daniels replied that he didn't want to be involved anymore.

Bill Daniels also apparently found it difficult to forget the role Walter Gerash played in breaking up the partnership that had worked so well for so long. In March of 1986 he framed a magazine cover with Walter's picture and sent it to the attorney with a letter taped on the back.

Dear Walter,

Although I, to this day, think you gave Ron Lyle some very bad financial advice as to his trust I set up for him, and although at the time I personally resented your hostile attitude toward me, I do admire you as a defence attorney. I wanted this permanently preserved for you and your heirs. I hope it brings you some moments of reflection - a hell of an article.

Respectfully, Bill Daniels

Today Walter Gerash likens his relationship to Bill Daniels to that between boxers: 'You can be friends out of the ring, but when the bell sounds, it's another story.'

Ron says now that if he had to do it over again, he wouldn't have filed the lawsuit against his manage-promoter-protector. After all, Daniels had helped get him out of prison and obtain his pardon, had supported him during his amateur years, and promised him a salaried job for life. But he doesn't blame his brother Bill for the decision. 'Bill and I both decided to do what we did,' Ron says. 'And I meant no disrespect to Bill Daniels. It was about my family - bringing us together and keeping us together. We started Lyle Enterprises, and that was a good thing since we gave a percentage of every fight to our parents who always supported our brothers and sisters.'

At the time of the legal action, Ron had also remembered losing a job that had meant a lot to his family's finances - the time he threw C.L. Patterson's golf bag into the creek. He was only 13 years old, but still felt a sense of responsibility for the loss of revenue. Bill Lyle says: 'We probably made a mistake leaving Daniels, and it was my idea, but Ron never blamed me. He never blamed anybody for anything. That's the thing I most admire about my brother.'

Ron expresses an enduring respect for both Bill Daniels and Walter Gerash. 'You make a decision, and sometimes it's the right one and sometimes it's wrong. Bill did a lot for me, and Walter only did what we asked him to do. I have been lucky to have both men in my life.'

THE Shavers win also apparently triggered the re-entry of 'Rip' Clark. The ex-con showed up in Green Mountain a month after the fight, professing his admiration for Ron's performance and proclaiming his own reformation. Ron hesitated for a moment, then did something he profoundly regrets. Once again, he invited Clark inside his home.

Clark started coming around regularly again, sometimes asking for 'loans,' even while following Ron's edict to stay away from the kids at the gym and to leave his drugs behind.

Patty didn't like or trust 'Rip' and was uneasy at having him in their home. Bill urged Ron to '....get rid of him. He's bad news, doing drugs.' But Ron's loyalty to former prisoners took precedence. He doesn't regret that loyalty to any of the other Canon City alumni, only to 'Rip' Clark.

Ron soon learned that 'Rip' wanted something more than just handouts - he needed a guarantee of employment so he could stay on parole and out of prison. Ron agreed to use him as a 'road man,' a guy who would drive the car when he ran in the morning and keep him supplied during sparring sessions. He also continued to lend the ex-convict money, none of which was ever repaid.

In the space of three months, Ron Lyle had made two mistakes - he fired Bill Daniels and he let 'Rip' Clark back into his life. The enormous consequences of both those actions would soon be apparent. But first he would live out the greatest fight of his life.

35

*

RING magazine's 1976 'Fight of the Year,' variously tagged 'The Greatest Fight in 30 Years,' 'Everybody's favourite Fight,' and 'The One for the Ages,' took place at Caesars Palace in Las Vegas on January 24, 1976, between Ron Lyle and George Foreman.

Three months after Ron devastated Earnie Shavers and only one month out of the contract with Bill Daniels, Walter Gerash helped Bill Lyle land the former heavyweight champion, who finally agreed to the match-up, believing that if he could beat Lyle decisively, he would have a shot at winning back the heavyweight title. The Lyle camp was ecstatic, knowing a win over Foreman would give Ron his own best opportunity for a rematch with Ali.

Immediately after the fight was announced, Ron again focused his attention on the ring, his training regimen more brutal than ever-with daily running, push-ups, shadow-boxing, heavy and speed bags and sparring under the direction, once again, of Bobby Lewis.

He cut down on his visits to youth centres during this

period; hoping to avoid the mistakes he had made with Nadine, he spent the little spare time he had with Patty and his new baby girl. But his primary focus was on Mr. George Foreman.

The Foreman fight, more than any other, represents what Ron faced every time he climbed into the ring. All boxers go into fights knowing they will either hurt or be hurt, or maybe both, but Ron Lyle was more powerful than most heavyweights, more likely to inflict serious damage. He never wanted to be responsible for causing another boxer permanent injury or, God forbid, death in the ring. But while he monitored the strength of his own punches, he had to be ever aware of the damage that could be inflicted on himself, and he believed nobody could dole out as much pain in the ring as George Foreman. Ron knew he had to pull out all the stops in this fight - hurt and be hurt.

Howard Cosell was again calling the network-televised fight, with Ken Norton by his side doing co-commentary. Cheers greeted Lyle's entry into the ring, and boos followed Foreman, still stinging from his loss in Zaire to Muhammad Ali one year earlier. During the pre-fight instructions at the centre of the ring, the fighters' noses practically touched as each gave the other man a stare-down calculated to terrify.

In round one, Ron came out at the bell and swung a right that George dodged. Both fighters jabbed, with Foreman taking a shot to the body. Lyle landed a right to Foreman's ear, but Foreman came back with two good jabs. With 20 seconds left, Lyle landed a big right hand to the side of Foreman's head, which momentarily rocked Foreman and drove him back into the ropes. In commentary, Cosell yells: 'You see George in trouble....he's wobbling to his corner.' Then: 'Ron Lyle has no fear of Foreman. There is no fear in Ron Lyle.'

Ron opened up, seemingly looking for the one big punch

that could bring an early end to this night. Foreman survived the remainder of the round without getting caught by anything significant, but he looked hurt as he went to his corner. First round to Lyle.

Ron came out swinging wildly in round two, but George was more aggressive in this round, throwing his left jab and pushing his opponent away with both hands as Lyle continually came forward. Midway through, Foreman stunned Lyle with a four-punch combination, driving his man back into the ropes, and Cosell hollered: 'Now Lyle is hurt.'

Ron spent the remainder of the round with his back to the ropes and then in a neutral corner. An odd quirk in the fight was that the round only lasted two minutes due to an error by the timekeeper, probably a good thing for Ron, as George was unloading straight rights and left hooks as the bell sounded. To his credit, Ron was throwing back valiantly. Round to Foreman.

At the beginning of round three, Cosell informed the television audience that the fighters were using eight-ounce gloves, less padding for greater damage from the blows, '....more punishment, more knockdowns likely.' Ron immediately landed a right to Foreman's face, then kept pressing forward. He hit Foreman with a left hook and a right, but Foreman came back with a nice right hand and Lyle found himself on the ropes again with Foreman pressing in, landing good body shots that Lyle effectively countered off the ropes. The round could have been scored for either man, with Foreman clearly the aggressor, but Lyle did some very effective work with his back against the ropes.

The fourth round would prove to be, unequivocally, the most exciting in heavyweight boxing history. First Ron came out and connected with a good straight right. No more than

20 seconds later, a right followed by an uppercut wobbled and dropped George hard to the mat as Cosell shouted: 'Foreman is down. It started with a right, then a left.'

Reminiscent of the Ali fight, the roar of the Denver fans drowned out all other sound in the Las Vegas arena. Foreman rose, his senses apparently intact, and took a standing eight count. Lyle put on pressure, trying to end it, but was held by Foreman. Ken Norton said: 'Both are working very hard. Both are using their powers.' The fighters exchanged huge hooks in the centre of the ring, and it was difficult to determine who was getting the better of the exchange until Foreman landed a crisp right that dropped Lyle to his knees. Cosell roared: 'Now George struck back... now.... now... George fought back with a magnificent right!'

Lyle rose to his feet and Foreman, looking to end the show, backed him against the ropes. Ron slugged valiantly off the ropes, hitting George flush with a few counter-lefts. Near the end of the round, an uppercut stunned Foreman, who returned fire, but then a huge Lyle right hand connected squarely with Foreman's chin, and big George was down for the second time in the round. *Boxing Illustrated* described the scene: 'Foreman dropped with his posterior in the air and the left side of his face glued to the canvas, looking like a man resting his head on a railroad track listening for an oncoming train - and not quite realising the train had already run over him. At the bell he staggered up and reeled instinctively to his corner.' Round to Lyle.

Round five began with Ron swinging two big lefts, stunning Foreman who almost fell forward into the ropes. Lyle landed another big left followed by a right as Foreman tried to push away from him. Cosell: 'Foreman is in bad trouble now.' Then George landed two good shots of his own to slow Lyle down for a moment. Lyle sneaked in a right that appeared to badly hurt Foreman. Norton opined: 'Lyle has the mental edge.' Then Ron landed a big left, and Foreman tried to stick the jab. They exchanged rights in an all-out war to rival any seen before. An uppercut from Lyle and Foreman was badly staggered. Cosell again hollered: 'Foreman is in bad trouble now.'

George struck back and landed a vicious four-punch combination, pushing Ron into the corner and unleashing 30 unanswered punches on his opponent. Lyle finally dropped both hands to his knees, then began to slump over as George continued to fire right and lefts. Lyle's knees hit the canvas and he fell flat on his face, as the crowd rose to its collective feet. Lyle tried to rise at the nine count, but fell over onto his back and was counted out.

Cosell said in an uncharacteristically quiet voice that the fighters had shown 'total guts and power.' In the immediate post-fight interview, George Foreman said: 'All credit should be given to Ron Lyle. He took some hard punches and gave some - a tremendous fighter.'

Many have written about the Foreman-Lyle fight, but none of the articles or essays can begin to reflect the sights and sounds preserved on tape, the amount of punishment dished out by each fighter and the amount of punishment each absorbed.

Admiration and analysis of the fight continues to this day, even by the combatants themselves. George Foreman still tells sportswriters that it took his greatest act of will to get up after being flattened by Lyle. He remembers lying on the canvas in that epic fourth round, vowing to himself that *this time, if I get counted out, I'm going to have to be dead.*

And Lyle says: 'When George Foreman hit, it felt like the house fell on me.' As late as 1995, Ron still wanted another crack at George. He told a reporter: 'I want George Foreman. If I could fight him again, I'd fight exactly the same way.'

Whatever boxing fans think of either fighter, none doubts that both gave their all that day in January, 1976.

Ian Haas, contributing writer for PrizeFightNews.com recently wrote: 'Foreman-Lyle. The mere mention of this legendary slugfest elicits nods of approval from true boxing fans the world over.' Peter Boyle said that in the Foreman fight, Ron Lyle had shown he had 'a heart like a lion.'

Jess Trail wrote: 'I can still hear the crack of the first hard right hand [Ron Lyle] landed on George Foreman in round one of the Super Brawl in Vegas in 1976.....The brawl with Foreman was a classic for the ages. It pitted two of the biggest, strongest men ever to lace on a boxing glove, teeing off on each other with no regard for defence. It was a brutal war of attrition. Although Lyle lost, he probably gained more fans in defeat than in all of his previous victories.'

But maybe Hall of Fame sportswriter and historian Bert Sugar, who ranked the fourth round as one of the three best rounds of all time, said it best in a 2006 piece for ESPN. Sugar described the fight as falling '....somewhere in between the manly art of self-destruction and a down-and-out-bar fight, tempered in part by a hint of something right out of an old Laurel and Hardy film clip.....It was, in short, a marvellous mélange of mayhem, with Foreman and Lyle playing it to the hilt, turning it from a comedic sketch into a war, a war in which neither side was seeking survivors.'

GEORGE FOREMAN once said: 'There is never a loser. No fighter should be a winner. Both should be applauded.' But the 'One for the Ages' won Foreman a chance to fight Joe Frazier, which began a quick four-win streak before a loss by decision to that spoiler Jimmy Young, after which Foreman retired.

And for Ron Lyle, it would nine long months before he fought again.

36

✳

The Long Struggle

VII

ITH the well-connected Daniels out of the picture, bouts would be harder to come by and the fight purses would be smaller, but Ron refused to give up on his dream. Unable to keep up the salary Bobby Lewis required, the Lyle team hired a new trainer, one Sam Boardman, a journeyman fighter from the 1940's whose son Larry had been a world-ranked lightweight in 1957.

Out of the old Jewish Chicago school of training, Boardman focused on taking the fighter's power and refining it with technique, teaching him not just to attack an opponent, but to observe him. He told Ron always to look for angles, defend himself, then go for the kill. That strategy fit Ron's style and the relationship worked.

With Ron dropping only one slot to the number four contender after the loss to Foreman, Bill Lyle and Walter Gerash managed to hook up with Main Event Boxing Corporation, a promotional company out of Utica, New York. They promised Lyle a fight in September.

In the meantime, Ron and Patty both vowed to keep their

family together, even after Boardman started him on the old-fashioned regimen of staying away from any physical relations with women prior to a fight. Boardman later told a blogger that he believed a heavyweight should not have sex for six weeks prior to a fight, but that Ron Lyle, as he did with all his training, took this advice to the extreme, refusing to have sex for ten weeks before the scheduled September bout, becoming so 'surly' in the process that Boardman had to break the regimen for the fighter's own good.

On September 12, 1976, Ron Lyle restarted his professional quest for the fourth time. He was a 35-year-old 'antiquated veteran' facing a 21-year-old hot shot by the name of Kevin Isaac from Brooklyn, who in three short years had built a record of 10-4-1. But just as he had in his other 'comebacks,' Ron took care of business decisively. He knocked Isaac out.

The bout took place in Utica and the 'tough' Isaac went further than expected. He held his own, exchanging jarring blows with Lyle for five rounds. In the sixth, Ron caught the young fighter against the ropes and rained a flurry of punches on him. Early in the seventh, Lyle knocked Isaac to the canvas and seconds later, knocked him down again. The fight was halted at 1:14 of the seventh round, and the Denver press rallied, predicting that with Ali's retirement from the ring, their favourite son would soon have another shot at the heavyweight championship of the world.

Ron had taken 'Rip' Clark to Utica for the fight, only to learn later from Don King that the former convict had verbally attacked the promoter, 'cussing him out.' King advised Ron not to trust the ex-con, who was probably trying to scare King and give himself more influence in the Lyle camp. Ron says: 'That's when I started watching 'Rip'.'

TWO months later in San Francisco, Ron was again stopped cold by the exasperating Jimmy Young. Just as had happened in their February '75 match-up, the loss was to a ten-round decision. Having given Ali a run for his money in April, Young had ascended to third place in the rank of contenders while Ron, who had dropped to number five, had earned his way back to fourth with the Isaac win. The odds were close, but just as before, Jimmy's speed thwarted Ron's major weapon, the knockout punch.[11]

Ron remembers that 'Rip' gave him an orange before the fight. 'I believe he injected something into that orange, trying to hook me into drugs,' Ron says, then hastens to add: 'That didn't have anything to do with me losing the fight. I felt something affect my strength. I was determined to overcome that feeling and I did. But I knew there was something scary about the guy.'

Sportswriter Bill Verigas postulated that the way Lyle lost to Young eliminated him forever from the heavyweight title picture. Still, the Denver fans were not disheartened. A headline read: 'There's Still a Future for Ron Lyle.'

Boxing historians believe that Young served as the primary spoiler to Ron achieving the status of world champion, but Ron brushes those conjectures aside, speaking of Jimmy Young with great respect and expressing sorrow at his early death. And in 1976 he blamed only himself, resolving to work his way back up the contender line once more.

While Ron waited for Bill to find him another worthy opponent, the rest of the family rallied around their special son and brother. Just as he had contributed to their financial support for the six years he had been fighting professionally, so now they provided much needed moral support during the days and weeks following the loss to Jimmy Young.

Ron remembers feeling the loss of Monte sharply in those days, reinforced by the joy he felt when he held his daughter, and he appreciated Nellie making time, not only for him, but for Patty and little Tracy. Sharon, too, was often at the Green Mountain house, cooking and staying over. And Ron found himself spending more and more time with his younger brother Phillip, who provided the kind of easy, non-judgmental companionship Ron needed.

Dennis Nelson, too, tried to be there for Ron, not only in the ring, but when he needed to talk to a friend. With Frank Barron - who had left the Navy a couple of years before - in his corner, Donny Nelson was hanging on in the ring, still winning more fights than he was losing. Dennis ended up splitting his time between his blood brother and his adopted brother, but both were starting to get seriously concerned about his drinking. More and more often, Dennis appeared inebriated in public, even at some of the fights.

Ron remembers another old friend re-entering his life about that time, his former Rock Busters team-mate Doobie Vigil, who had been released from prison. By the time he ran into Ron, Doobie had already found a job at a Mexican restaurant, which he would eventually own, along with a small corner grocery store. As with all the real friends Ron made along the way, Doobie, too, would stay in his life off and on for decades. And Ron remembers that shortly after his old friend got back to Denver, Doobie made a point of warning him about 'Rip' Clark. 'Doobie was always a stand-up guy,' Ron says. 'I should have listened to him.'

A tiny glimmer of the satisfying life that might await the boxer beyond the ring was ignited with all the good will of his friends and family, but it had not yet been fanned into any real blaze and wouldn't be for a long time. First he had to discover whether his dream was still alive.

TWO good fights followed the loss to Young. Ron's win over Britain's Joe Bugner in March was especially sweet, as Bugner was one of the crowd of contenders who had refused to fight him in '74 and '75. And he was a worthy opponent.

Jim Amato is just one of many boxing aficionados who declared Joe Bugner the best white fighter since 1960: '....Joe turned pro in 1967. He was still fighting well into the nineties. His record is a 'Who's Who' of the heavyweights of that era. He went the distance with Muhammad Ali - twice. His second encounter was a losing effort for the championship. In all he travelled 27 rounds with the Greatest. He also went 12 rugged rounds with Joe Frazier, losing a close verdict....He was tall and well proportioned. He was a smart boxer with a good left jab. He was very mobile for a man his size and he had a pretty fair right cross. He also had a solid chin.'

Nine years younger, Bugner gave Ron a run for his money that March night in Las Vegas - 12 rounds worth. In fact, Ron was behind on points midway through the fight. In the fifth, he was momentarily stunned at the bell when Bugner got in two quick rights. For a moment after the bell rang, Lyle appeared unable to locate his corner. But he held on. In the tenth round, he managed to bloody Bugner's nose with a right-hand punch and that seemed to bring him back to life. Using fierce rights to the body and left uppercuts to the head along the ropes, Ron tired Bugner, who began holding to stave off the blows. The decision was split, but the win was real. Jess Trail wrote: 'I remember the angry red welts on the sides of Joe Bugner as Lyle ruthlessly pressed the tall and talented Brit. Bugner was as durable as they made them during the greatest and most talent-laden era in heavyweight boxing history. Very few could have concluded that bout on their feet. Lyle said of Bugner: "He could box, he could punch and he could take a punch. And if you weren't on your game, guess what - you got an ass whuppin'."'

As for Bugner, years later he added his voice to that of Earnie Shavers and George Foreman in declaring Ron his toughest adversary: 'The biggest beating I took was from

Ron Lyle in 1977.... He was one of those tough dudes that just kept coming. It was the only time I thought to myself, "What am I doing this for?" Going the distance with Ali, Frazier, was not near as bad. I had busted ribs, a sore jaw, you name it. For weeks I was hurting.'

The victory over Bugner energised Lyle Enterprises. Ron and Bill expressed even more confidence in Sam Boardman, and they set up a general training routine for whoever the next fight would turn out to be. Ron also settled into his most comfortable routine, dividing his time among family, visiting youth centres and hard training. Dennis recalls Ron as optimistic at that time, confident that he would get another shot at the title. The only jarring note came in June when Ron woke up in a sweat, recalling a particularly vivid dream in which he was fighting some guy for a gun when it went off. Even today he remembers every detail of the dream, which he shrugged off at the time. He now believes that vision was a warning from God that he failed to heed.

In September, Ron met an even younger boxer, Stan Ward, in Las Vegas. Ward had turned pro in 1974 and quickly established himself as a heavyweight of promise. After a number of impressive wins, including four knockouts, he entered the world ratings with a decision over Mac Foster and a stunning knockout over Jeff Merritt. He lost the gruelling ten-round decision to Ron Lyle, returned to California and continued as a strong contender for a number of years. But like most good heavyweights of the 1970's 'when giants walked the earth' in the ring, Ward never got a title fight. Ron Lyle, on the other hand, was on schedule for a second chance at the championship, starting with Larry Holmes in February.

In the meantime, Patty and Ron managed to get pregnant again, and all seemed right in the Lyle world. Until, three months later, the unthinkable happened. Ron Lyle was charged with murder for the second time.

37

*

NEW YEAR'S EVE, 1977. A small Lyle family gathering including Sharon and her family, Joyce, Robert, Phillip and Bill, were quietly celebrating in Ron's Green Mountain home. As non-drinkers they followed their tradition of a late dinner and a quiet evening leading to the New Year. Tired from a day of training, Ron went upstairs to his bedroom and lay down around 8:00, shortly after the kids were put to bed, while the rest of the family talked quietly in the family room.

At around 11:00, the doorbell rang, and Sharon walked through the front room to the door. 'Rip' Clark stood on the porch. 'Just wanted to wish you all a happy new year,' he said. Sharon backed up, not inviting the former convict into the house, but called out to Ron: 'Rip's at the door.' Ron woke immediately, alert and on his feet. He ran downstairs and confronted Clark. 'It's late, man, the party's over.'

'I need to use the bathroom, Ronny,' 'Rip' said, and Ron hesitated a moment before he stood aside to let him pass. Clark knew the layout of the house, but passed by the hall bathroom and climbed the stairs to the master bedroom, apparently to use the master bathroom. Ron remembers wondering why 'Rip' went upstairs out of his way. He didn't even think of the loaded nine-millimetre pistol he kept on the top of his chest of drawers, out of the reach of the children - the gun 'Rip' knew was there - until it was too late.

The former convict came back into the living room, holding the pistol at his side, and brushed past Sharon to stand a couple of feet away from Ron. He raised the pistol. 'Man, you owe me,' he said. Sharon ran to the family room.

Describing the scene 27 years later, Ron's eyes smoulder at what happened next. 'I looked at the gun and realised he didn't know how to operate the safety. I snatched it from him and looked him in the eye. He reached for the gun, the safety went off and he grabbed my hand. The gun fired and the bullet hit him in the head.'

Ron stands up, points his finger towards the ceiling and raises his voice. 'I believe in God,' he says. 'I had a dream that was exactly like that night. I can still see it happening in slow motion. I had been training, and when a fighter is training and living right, he finds his spiritual side.' He sits back in the chair, voice still booming: 'God forewarned me, and I didn't pay attention. Look what happened.' He lowers his voice. 'It happened just the way God told me it would.'

Ron had become acquainted with a Lakewood policeman by the name of David Dahl who lived just around the corner. David knew that fans and detractors alike sometimes came around the Green Mountain house, and he had told Ron to call him if there was ever any trouble. Within seconds after the shooting, Ron went to the family room and picked up the table phone. David Dahl's number was in the drawer. 'Come to my house,' Ron said. 'I have something important to tell you.'

Off the Ropes

THE *Associated Press* headline on January 1, 1978 read: 'Ron Lyle, Boxer, Is Held in Murder,' and described Ron's life in a very small nutshell:

> Ron Lyle, the heavyweight boxer who once spent seven years in the Colorado State Penitentiary for second-degree murder, was being held on first-degree murder charges today in connection with the shooting death of a friend.
>
> Joe Busch, a spokesman for the Lakewood Police Department, said that the 35-year-old Mr. Lyle was arrested late last night in connection with the fatal shooting of Vernon Clark, 30 years old.
>
> Mr. Clark was shot once in the head with a handgun, the police said, apparently after a fight at a small family gathering at the Lyle home in an upper-middle-class section of this Denver suburb.
>
> Mr. Lyle, ranked among the leading heavyweight boxers, was being held without bond in the Jefferson County Jail and was scheduled to appear for arraignment Tuesday morning.
>
> Two of Mr. Lyle's brothers and his sister and brother-in-law were questioned and later released, the police said. They added that three children had been in the Lyle home when the shooting occurred, but apparently had not seen it.
>
> Mr. Lyle began his career as a boxer while serving his seven-year-prison sentence. He was [paroled] in 1969. Mr. Lyle quickly became the Amateur Athletic Union heavyweight champion and turned professional in 1971. He rose in the rankings until he fought Muhammad Ali on May 16, 1975, in Las Vegas for the heavyweight crown. He was defeated on a technical knockout in the 11th round.
>
> Seven months later, George Foreman knocked him out in the fifth round. But last March, he won a

12-round split decision over the British champion, Joe
Bugner, in Las Vegas.

He is scheduled to fight Larry Holmes in Las
Vegas in February.

After the shooting, Bill immediately called Walter Gerash,
who accepted the case for a $30,000 retainer, a substantially
lower fee than would be expected for such a high profile
client. Gerash immediately went to work. He visited his
client in jail, listened to Ron's story of a struggle, then looked
for and found bruises on the base of Ron's thumb. He had
photos taken and dated of Ron's hand, then contacted the
pathologist for a viewing of Clark's body. 'The decedent had
similar marks on his hand, which we also photographed,'
Gerash recalls. 'That turned out to be one of the most
important pieces of evidence we had in the case.'

ON Wednesday, January 4, 1978 the *New York Times* carried
a photo of a handcuffed Ron being led into the Jefferson
County district courtroom by a police officer. With Gerash
by his side, Ron pleaded not guilty and was released on a
$10,000 bond. That Bill and Ron had already established a
working relationship with Walter Gerash would turn out to
be their greatest stroke of luck or, as the Lyles might put it,
'God's will.'

'Gerash, in the courtroom, is a modern day William
Jennings Bryan, an orator....' wrote syndicated columnist
Alan Prendergast in 1998:

> He lurks in the bad dreams of hungry prosecutors and
> hidebound judges, a caped avenger in bolo tie and
> maroon beret. The cameras catch him exiting the
> courtroom in the eye of the media whirlwind, a feisty
> bantamweight with a large voice--a voice so

thunderous when raised in outrage that one frazzled judge felt compelled to note for the record that defence counsel was bellowing. But if you're in trouble with the Man, there's no sweeter sound than when he stands before the bench and introduces himself: 'Walter Gerash for the defence, your honour.'

While the Lyle side was preparing its case, the fight with Larry Holmes was cancelled and would never be rescheduled.[12] Bill managed to find a mediocre opponent in a boxer known as 'Big City' Robinson for June, but mostly, he focused his attention on helping his brother's defence, and by the time the case came to court for a continuation of the preliminary hearing in May, any chance at a major contender seemed unlikely.

The *Rocky Mountain News* photo on page five of the May 11, 1978 edition shows Ron sitting at the defence table with his brother Bill looking on while Walter Gerash made his argument. The story was written by Steve Chawkins:

A professional killer was asked either to collect money from or murder heavyweight Ron Lyle by the man Lyle has been charged with slaying, the boxer's defence attorneys said Wednesday in Golden District Court. It was the continuation of a preliminary hearing begun in March.

The dead man, Lyle's ex-roadman, Vernon 'Rip' Clark, discussed the pay-or-die proposition with David Bufkin, a self-described soldier of fortune, in the bar of the Holiday Inn in downtown Denver during the first week of December 1977, a private detective testifying for the defence said.

The detective, Dean Leiser, said Bufkin lives near Fresno, California and flies crop-dusting planes. But he has also fought in Angola and elsewhere, and is apt to undertake paramilitary missions in far-flung regions of the world on short notice, Leiser said. The investigator testified that Bufkin told him and defence attorney Walter Gerash about Clark's alleged offer in March.

Clark died in Lyle's Lakewood living room December 31 of a single gunshot wound in the head. At a start of the preliminary hearing in Jefferson County Court in March, a Lakewood policeman said Lyle admitted at the scene that he and Clark had been arguing over money Clark claimed he was owed by Lyle.

Lt. David Dial said Lyle admitted the shooting at the time. At the same hearing, Lyle's brother Phillip testified Ron told him he was 'in danger of his life,' but the cause of that fear wasn't revealed during later testimony.

District Judge Joséph P. Lewis ordered Wednesday that Bufkin give a deposition in Golden June 12. Lewis quashed a defence motion to have a Jefferson County district attorney's representative fly to California for the deposition immediately.

'This witness travels around the world engaging in activities dangerous to his longevity,' said Gerash. 'If he's still alive and available, we'll call him as a witness. But we fear he won't be available.' Gerash said Bufkin's testimony would be 'devastating' to the DA's case against Lyle because it would prove Clark's 'propensity for violence' and 'planned assassination.' Gerash said his trial efforts will center on a claim of self-defence. But Gerash said he isn't certain the case will come to trial.

Gerash argued Wednesday that the case should be dismissed because Lakewood police destroyed records of smudged fingerprints on the pistol alleged to be the murder weapon.

The fingerprints, Gerash claimed, could have been crucial evidence supporting the defence contention that Lyle and Clark had struggled before the pistol went off.

Gerash spent about three hours Wednesday questioning Douglas Monsoor, the Lakewood officer who said he shredded a set of latent prints taken January 2 from the weapon. Monsoor, supervisor of police technical services, also said he did not photograph the prints before destroying them.

He testified the five prints lifted from the pistol and one from a cartridge casing were too blurred for positive identification. He said it is 'departmental policy' to destroy such apparently unusable prints because keeping them would crowd police files.

Gerash, however, contended the prints were destroyed in a willful cover-up by Lakewood police. Gerash said material in the Lakewood police evidence locker related to the Lyle case includes carpets, sweatshirts, bags, shoes and garbage. 'Six possibly significant prints on pieces of cellophane tape shouldn't have presented a storage problem,' he said.

'Nobody can contest Monsoor's opinion that those prints were of no value because he destroyed those prints,' said Gerash. 'He didn't consult anybody in his own department about the prints, or anybody else connected with the investigation. We can never resurrect the evidence which might have acquitted the defendant. The only remedy is dismissal - and if this court doesn't want to stick its neck out, maybe the Colorado Supreme court will.'

A fingerprint specialist presented by Gerash, James W. Blake of Idaho Springs, testified that standard procedure in virtually all police departments calls for saving even illegible prints in homicide cases, and photographing them at several phases of the investigation.

SEVENTY-NINE years old and still practicing law in the only Victorian house left in downtown Denver, Walter Gerash recalls almost every detail of the case. Listening to his former attorney talk about the missing fingerprints today, though, Ron says he doesn't remember any of that testimony. 'In fact, I don't remember much of anything about that time.'

Gerash says: 'It was like Ron was in a whirlpool - the vortex - his life and his career being sucked down into oblivion.' He turns to Ron, 'You were in a kind of shock.' Ron replies: 'I couldn't believe it was happening. I couldn't believe this guy I tried to help .....' He trails off, then: 'It still doesn't seem real.'

The case went to trial seven months later, almost a year after the shooting, with much the same evidence as had been presented at the preliminary hearing, but with the added cross-examination of the pathologist, who agreed that the bruises on Ron's and Clark's thumbs could be the result of a struggle over the gun. Ron took the stand in his own defence and gave passionate testimony, in both direct and cross-examination. 'I was almost worried, Ron was so emotional,' Gerash says. 'I was afraid the jury might conclude that he could get out of control.'

The trial only lasted ten calendar days, and court records show: 'At the conclusion of the people's case, the Court granted defendant's motion for judgment of acquittal as to count two, first-degree murder.' After only one day, the jury returned a verdict of 'not guilty' on the remaining two counts - second degree murder and a violent crime. It was over.[13]

By December 18, 1978, Ron had lost almost everything he owned defending himself, including the Green Mountain house. He still counts Walter Gerash as a friend and doesn't blame his lawyer for the cost of acquittal. 'He didn't charge me that much,' he says, 'especially with the experts he had to call.' He adds: 'I only wish I'd had Walter in my first trial,' he says.

Ron's old Rocks team-mate Jimmy Farrell has spent his entire career in law enforcement. He hasn't studied the facts of the shooting, but relies on his years of experience with criminals. 'A lot of guys present themselves well, but you can look past that and know they are not good people. Their criminal natures give them away,' he says. 'I have no doubt Ron is a decent person, a good human being - he is not a criminal. It's a mystery to me how he could have been involved in two killings.'

An ironic footnote: During the trial, Ron won two unrelated judgments. A Federal judge awarded Ron Lyle $15,000 damages for breach of his contract to fight Ken Norton the year before, and he won a $22,000 decision in a lawsuit against the Denver Boxing Club for owed compensation. It all went for his defence expenses.

38

*

DURING the year Ron fought the murder charge, his career almost ended, but not quite. He says now that it was too early to give up on a dream that had kept him going for so long, and so he had continued working. Building on the wins over Bugner and Ward, he once again began to accumulate a string of victories, surprising even his staunchest fans. A shorter streak, but encouraging nonetheless.

Walter Gerash had officially joined the Lyle Enterprises team, and one month after the preliminary hearing, even while he was preparing Ron's defence, he and Bill landed a heavyweight with only 12 fights under his belt, New Yorker Horace 'Big City' Robinson. Robinson's record was 7-4 with three knockouts, including the likes of Ron Stander, and he had been given an opportunity Ron had not, a shot at Larry Holmes, who TKO'd him the year before.

The June 1978 fight with Robinson turned out to be an effective warm-up. Ron knocked him out in the eighth round in front of still loyal and enthusiastic, though slightly fewer Denver fans.

Exactly one month later, one day before the fourth of July, 1978, Patty gave birth to a boy they named David, and the couple once again vowed to hold the family together even as the murder trial loomed. Ron, in the meantime, also tried to keep doing the only thing he knew how to do.

In August, he was given permission by the court to go out of state to take on a boxer from the South Pacific archipelago known as 'Tonga,' one Fili Moala, who fought out of San Diego. Moala had boxed for barely two years, knocking out his first five opponents on his way to accumulating a record of 9-2. His last fight with Leroy Jones ended in a decision loss. In a repeat of the Robinson bout, Ron knocked Moala out in eight rounds. Remarkably, it was enough to retain his number-four ranking.

But with Ron turning 38 in February, an age when most boxers are considered over the hill and advised to retire, sportswriters had already begun to view him as a trial horse for up-and-coming fighters to beat. One called him an 'old man.' Even though neither of the new fighters had been able to prove themselves against the tough Lyle, his age was working against him, and a couple of months later, he was finally removed from the top-ten contender list.

Bill Lyle worked hard to keep Ron in the game. Sam Boardman departed, and Bill hired Bud Gordon as manager, along with trainer Eddie Futch, considered one of the greatest trainers in boxing history, not to mention, as Ron puts it, 'a real gentleman.' Futch trained some of the best, but his greatest claim to fame was training both Joe Frazier and Ken Norton for the wins over Ali. By the time Bill Lyle decided to invest in Futch, the trainer was 68 years old.

Ron felt an almost immediate respect and affection for Eddie, partly because he reminded the boxer of Bobby Lewis, both physically - Futch was short and dark complexioned - as well as in his highly professional approach to the ring. Once again, Ron's loyalty to his trainer was unquestionable.

'A fighter is no better than his corner,' he says, 'and you end up feeling closer to your trainer than almost anybody else. You're putting your life in his hands.' But in spite of good intentions, Ron was unable to preserve that same kind of closeness in his personal life. He and Patty kept trying to rebuild their relationship, but the going was getting tougher. It didn't take long after the birth of their second child before they started arguing more frequently. Patty found caring for two small children overwhelming at times and demanded that Ron be home more, while he grew more impatient with her demands for attention. The same old state of affairs.

Memories of Nadine and how she couldn't get it either - that he had to do everything in his power to fulfill his dream - reinforced Ron's often irrational anger at Patty. Over the next year and a half, even as his chances seemed to be fading, he lashed out at anyone who suggested he give up the dream, especially his woman. And the more they argued, the more he stayed away. But he almost always took Tracy with him, and often he would tote baby David along, as well. 'I took her everywhere,' Ron smiles, and Tracy remembers her daddy as always there - a loving force in her early childhood.

'We were together most of the time,' she says. 'I remember sitting in a boxing ring somewhere with my dad putting gloves on me, just for fun. When we took trips to Las Vegas, he would always park in front of the strip and say, "Tell Daddy where you want to stay," and I would always choose Caesars Palace because it was so pretty. My most vivid memories are when I would fall down and get a little scrape or cut myself on something, my daddy would put his mouth over the wound before he cleaned it. He called it daddy's blood. And you know, I do the same thing with my son.' She adds: 'He was a great dad.'

His own children usually within reach, Ron continued to work with kids in trouble and spent some time with Abby Espinoza and Dennis Nelson, in spite of Dennis's escalating drinking problem. His days were full, but he was beginning to know he would never have the kind of marital bond with Patty that his parents had sustained for more than 40 years. He held on only because he didn't want to lose Tracy and David the way he had lost Monte.

When, in December of '78, Ron was acquitted of the murder of Vernon 'Rip' Clark, he was finally free to concentrate on the life he wanted to lead - whatever that life might turn out to be. 'I was publicly declared 'not guilty' by a jury of my peers,' Ron says. 'But I didn't know what to do next, so I kept on fighting.'

An almost year-long hiatus followed the Moala win, broken at last by a May 1979 fight with 'The Fighting Frenchman' Scott LeDoux in Caesars Palace. The fight was billed as 'the battle for survival,' and most fight fans thought it had the most furious action since the Lyle-Foreman fight in 1976. LeDoux had a respectable 26-6-3 record with 18 knockouts. Howard Cosell, who was calling the fight on national television, said: 'Whichever one loses can expect his career to be thoroughly ruptured.'

Described as a 'blood and guts brawl all the way' with both men fighting for what one sportswriter called 'their fistic existence,' the last eight rounds were filled with action. LeDoux started his attack in the third round, sending Ron to the ropes twice - first with a straight right, prompting a standing eight-count, and then with a left hook. After the bell, Eddie Futch laid out a new battle plan, and the fourth and fifth rounds saw Lyle pounding LeDoux with brutal head and body shots.

LeDoux recovered enough in the sixth to stalk Lyle into the ropes, but was unable to land any impressive punches.

The seventh round was all Ron's as he delivered a series of stunning blows to LeDoux's head, forcing him into a corner and almost sending him down just before the bell. The eighth round was more of the same, and LeDoux sustained a severe cut over his right eye, which was swollen shut by the end of the round.

In the ninth round, LeDoux hit Lyle with a shot that dislodged his mouthpiece, but Lyle recovered quickly and went on to win the round, leading to the final brawl in the tenth with both fighters obviously desperate for the win. LeDoux's relative youth had held him through the gruelling rounds and he won this latest, but not the final decision, which was split and as close as a fight can be without calling it a draw. One judge scored it 45-44 LeDoux, while the other two called Lyle the winner at 45-44 and 46-45, respectively. With Gerash and Futch, not to mention both brothers Bill and Phillip sticking with him, the 'old man' had managed to pull out yet another win.

Most boxing historians believe Ron's next fight ended any chance he might have had for a title fight. Lynn Ball was an unheralded boxer with a very short record when he met Lyle. Ball's entire career was comprised of only 19 bouts with unknowns; he would be forgotten now except for one fight. On December 12, 1979, in Phoenix, Arizona, he knocked out Ron Lyle in the second round. What was supposed to have been another warm-up for a contender effectively ended Ron Lyle's boxing career. The brief UPI piece said it all:

> Ron Lyle's hopes for a title bout virtually ended last night when Lynn Ball scored a knockout of the veteran heavyweight in the second round of a scheduled 10-round fight.
>
> The [39-year-old] Lyle, attempting a comeback

> after having been acquitted in a trial resulting from a
> fatal shooting in Denver ...., had been headed for a
> title fight with the World Boxing Association's
> champion, John Tate, provided he beat Ball.

Although Ron wouldn't admit it at the time, even to himself, the chance to fulfill his dream had ended.

IN February of 1980 Nellie Lyle was killed in a car crash caused by a drunken driver. Tears well up in Ron's eyes, even now, as he talks about his mother. 'She was saved at eight and died at 58....she died a saint, and the things I did broke her heart.'

Members of the Lyle family remember the devastation caused by her death. They had lost their bulwark against evil, their place of refuge, and for a while the family broke into fragments. Nobody had the strength to hold them all together.

Attendance at the funeral was the largest anyone in the church had ever seen. Old friends from the projects were there in great numbers, as were friends of all the younger Lyles, not to mention congregations from two other churches. Nobody left for hours, until it was time for the regular church service.

The grief at losing Nellie seemed a precursor to other sad events. Ron's younger brother Raymond, who had long suffered from mental illness, lost control and ended up attacking a woman during the funeral service. After being detained by the police, Raymond was eventually diagnosed with paranoid schizophrenia and institutionalised at the state hospital in Pueblo, where he still resides.

Sharon had been in the car when it crashed and was almost killed herself. She spent weeks in the hospital with a broken pelvis and when she was released, took her children to live with William and the siblings left at home. But her father quickly remarried and found it difficult to accommodate the large family without Nellie. Gradually they all found themselves on their own, and Sharon took the youngest Karen to live with her. The family fell apart and the rift lasted for a very long time.

It would be years before Sharon heeded three signs that occurred just before and just after Nellie's death. A week before the accident, a voice came to her in a dream, saying over and over: 'Every one of your brothers and sisters will come to you.' Then the night before her mother was killed, on a day the two spent sewing, Nellie told Sharon: 'You're the one. You're the strongest in the family.'

After the accident Sharon heard Ron whisper in her ear, 'You're the one now.' She couldn't remember whether she was still in the hospital, but Ron remembered: 'Sharon was home. She couldn't walk, but something told me I had to let her know she was the one now. I told her: "All the responsibility mother had, you have."' It would be some time before either brother or sister knew what those messages meant.

Ron retreated into himself. After he lost the Green Mountain home, he rented a house in Thornton, a suburb north of Denver, but didn't spend much time there. After his mother's death, he found himself pulling further away from Patty, even when he was home. And she was growing more and more restless in a neighbourhood where she didn't know anyone. Marital history was about to repeat itself.

With his corner still intact, Ron kept training, but he had begun to lose faith in the dream and he couldn't seem to find anything else to fill that hole. So he went through the motions. When Bill landed a bout with Gerry Cooney for October, Ron rallied briefly, intensifying his training regimen as he always had before a big fight.

In March of 1980 Patty departed - without Tracy and David. Perhaps she was trying to demonstrate to Ron how difficult caring for two small children could be; for whatever reason, he was left with sole responsibility for his children. Ron was immediately jerked back into reality and a goal even more important than another championship bout - caring for four-year-old Tracy and little David, not yet two.

Ron asked Bud Gordon if he knew anyone who could help out, and Gordon called an old friend, district attorney Paul Beacon, who immediately thought of Mary Kresnik, the wife of a colleague who worked in the Adams County D.A.'s office. He knew Mary as a loving woman, with a son of her own and two foster children, who also kept a day care centre in her home. Beacon called John Kresnik, who had followed the Ron Lyle career for years, even travelling to Omaha to watch the decision over Lou Bailey. The next day Ron got a call that Mary would be happy to care for the children.

For Ron and the Kresniks, it was love at first sight. He went to their house the evening John called, and they spent a couple of hours talking about children, with the Kresnik's son Brad and their two foster children looking on. A little foster girl named Cassie climbed on the couch next to Ron, scooted close to him and proceeded to twirl her own hair with her left hand and his with her right, a practice she continued whenever the 'giant' would visit.

Ron was eager to bring his children to Mary and they immediately set a schedule of Tracy and David staying with Mary during the day while Ron trained and on those nights he had to be away.

Ron still counts the Kresniks among his closest friends and remembers them as being there for him when he needed it most. John had been in the Catholic priesthood for 11 years, but his relationship with Ron was not so much that of a counsellor as that of a friend. Ron told them about the death of his beloved mother earlier that year, and before long, Mary was thinking of Ron as a kind of adopted son.

She recalls the time a father came to pick up his child from day care when Ron was there, and she introduced him as her 'oldest son.' A half hour later the man's wife called. Upon returning home, he had immediately asked her why she hadn't told him that Mary and John had a black son.

For the first time in months, Ron felt like he had his life under control. His primary responsibility would be to his children, and he would keep trying to conquer the ring - for a while, at least. Then he met the woman he would ever after call 'the centre of my soul.'

39

＊

JILL SELLERS grew up on a ranch in Nebraska. Not unlike William and Nellie Lyle, her parents lived a strong work ethic and expected the same from Jill, her two-year-older brother and baby sister. Their father would not hesitate to administer a whipping with a willow stick if the situation called for it.

As a very young child, Jill would escape in dreams - day and night. Almost as though she was meant to be a part of the Lyle family tradition, at age five she dreamt of marrying a boxer. She might have fixated on the sport because her father had boxed when he was younger and talked about his fights now and then. In any case, as sometimes happens with childhood dreams, she never forgot that image and came to believe that it was a premonition of her life with Ron Lyle.

Chafing under what she came to view as impossibly tight restrictions on her behaviour, Jill left home at 14, determined to be her own person. She always kept in touch with her family, but would never again allow anyone to take control of her life.

Jill moved from place to place, working sometimes, finding rooms to rent, until she landed in Denver in 1973. She was 18 years old. For a few months, she couldn't find any kind of job that would pay her enough to rent a decent room and she ended up in a very tough neighbourhood, not far from where Ron Lyle grew up. Having already stacked up almost 20 knockouts, Ron was already making his mark in those days, and not just with the Denver elite and boxing fans. Many young people from poorer neighbourhoods were already starting to idolise the boxer as one of their own who was making it on his own terms.

Because Jill knew something about boxing and enough of the terminology to impress the people she met in the neighbourhood, early on - a full eight years before she met Ron - she invented a very effective strategy against being hassled by any of the 'bad characters' on the street. She would say: 'You better leave me alone. Ron Lyle is my boyfriend.' It seemed they didn't dare doubt the pretty white girl's claim and, within a few weeks, Jill had created for herself an airtight safety cocoon, not dreaming she would ever meet the heavyweight.

Eventually, Jill landed an entry level job in retail sales, and started what would be a successful climb up the ladder of the highly competitive clothing business. She dated a few guys along the way, but nobody quite made the mark, and she focused most of her attention on her work.

In 1974 she met the best friend she would ever have, an attractive young African American woman named Jackie Johns. Jackie was working as a personal secretary for Pat Schroeder, the Democratic member of the U.S. House of Representatives, a woman both Jill and Jackie admired for her strong feminist positions.

Though Jackie was six years older, the two were practically inseparable for the next six years; whether with boyfriends or during dry spells, they served as each other's primary support system, seeing each other through major milestones.

In 1978, Jill was ready to put down roots in Denver and bought a three-bedroom brick house in one of Denver's graceful old neighbourhoods on Bellaire Street. A year later, Jackie started dating a young man she thought might end up being her life's partner. That young man was Phillip Lyle.

Phillip got to know Jill well during the year he dated Jackie. He often talked about his brother Ronny and how it felt to work in his corner. Phillip was impressed with this smart white girl who knew a lot, not only about boxing, but about his brother's career. Jill told him how she invoked Ron's name years before as a protection from tough guys and Phillip passed that story on to his brother.

After Patty left Ron in March of 1980, Phillip and Jackie both thought of introducing him to Jill, but they decided to wait until the moment was right. Ron was not only caring for his young children, he had two fights lined up before he was to meet Gerry Cooney, and Phillip knew how important it was for his brother to keep his focus.

That same spring Ron learned that his young brother John John, who had been ill for some time with cerebral palsy, was dying. Devastated, he went to Mary Kresnik: 'He's so thin, Mary. How do I support him?' She didn't have to think about her answer. She took Ron's hands in her own and said: 'Just love him. And remember, all of us are on loan from God.' His mother used to say the same thing.

And so Ron fell back easily into the care-giver role he had assumed after getting out of reform school. He took turns with his brothers and sisters at his 25-year-old little brother's bedside, changing his diapers and providing whatever comfort he could. He remembers that time as an inkling of something that could be more important than boxing.

That summer Ron knocked off - and knocked out - two more young fighters, Al Neumann in Tacoma, Washington and George O'Mara in Inglewood, California, but both fighters had lost more bouts than they had won, and the wins did nothing to boost Ron's rankings or reputation.

In September he made special arrangements with Mary Kresnik to keep Tracy and David for six weeks while he trained for the Cooney fight at a camp set up as a kind of retreat in California. Bill and Phillip phoned Ron often, and during one conversation Phillip casually mentioned that he thought Jackie's best friend Jill, the beautiful young boxing fan, might be interested in dating him. Ron thought about it for only one day, then skipped training camp and headed back to Denver. For the first time since he got out of prison, Ron put training on the back burner.

Jill remembers their first date as lasting a week, during which she met Ron's children and most of his scattered family. Ron remembers telling her more about his thoughts and feelings than he had ever told anyone. And so it began. Within two months, Ron, Tracy and David all moved into Jill's house on Bellaire Street.

IN October of 1980 Ron fought his final battle in the ring. All the great heavyweights Ron had known through the seventies, most younger than Ron, were out of the picture by then. Larry Holmes was the champion and the top contenders were new names: Gerry Cooney, Mike Weaver, Leon Spinks, Michael Dokes, and Gerrie Coetzee.

The Lyle team managed to get Gerry Cooney, who had a sterling 23-0 record, 21 by knockouts and was coming off a TKO victory over Jimmy Young. The *Associated Press* headlined, 'Lyle's Career on the Line,' and quoted Ron: 'If I prevail here, I can't be denied a championship fight. I'm fighting the No.1 ranked heavyweight in the world....I would identify myself with someone like Jersey Joe Walcott. They're the people who give me hope.'

Walcott had won the title in his fifth try at age 37, and Ron was close to 40, fighting during the era recognised by virtually all boxing experts as having the toughest competition in heavyweight history.

Denver fans found the bout hard to watch. Cooney hammered Ron into a corner with eight or nine hooks to the body late in the first round, then caught him with a thunderous hook to the body and followed it with a hook to the head. Ron fell through the ropes and was counted out by the referee. It was over.

Even after such a beating, Ron retained the respect of his adversary. Gerry Cooney waited an hour for him to come out of the dressing room just to shake Ron Lyle's hand. The win took Cooney to a heavyweight title match with Larry Holmes, which he lost in a TKO. The loss took Ron Lyle out of the ring.

He had lost most of the money he had made boxing, and the $200,000 purse he was promised for meeting Cooney turned out to be less than $20,000 after the first-round loss. But he knew it was time to quit. He recalls an old Denver fan named 'Cheet' saying: 'Out of respect for you, Ronny, I tell you to quit fighting,' and believes now that the old-timer's message came from God.

Unique in sport, boxers form an unbroken line from the very beginning to the present day. From John Sullivan through Jack Johnson through Joe Louis through Muhammad Ali through Larry Homes through Evander Holyfield and on and on and on, when a fighter touches gloves with a champion, he has touched all of them. Ron Lyle never won the heavyweight championship of the world, but he earned his legacy in the unbroken line.

40

*

IN 1980, Ron Lyle began the odyssey that would last almost 20 years. Always looking for something to replace the great meaning he had found in his dream of a world championship, he took many wrong paths and ignored some important signs along the way. Sometimes Jill accompanied him on his journey; sometimes he had to go it alone.

The couple barely had time to settle in with Tracy and David when two deaths intruded, once again blanketing the Lyle family in a heavy sadness. Cerebral palsy had so weakened John John that he died of heart failure in late Spring. Only two months later, the lupus Jackie Johns had thought was under control caused a massive infection and kidney failure which ended her life.

At a memorial service for John John, the family came together for the first time since Nellie's funeral and took some tiny steps toward what would be a long, slow process of healing. It was particularly difficult for Sharon as she had felt betrayed by William, first when he asked her to leave the home she had known so long and later, when she was literally stranded along the road with nowhere to go.

Sharon had managed to find an apartment large enough to accommodate Karen and the children and close to the church she wanted to attend. The apartment cost more than she could really afford, though, and after falling behind in the rent for two months, they were evicted. That afternoon, surrounded by her scattered furniture out front, she looked up to see her daddy driving up the street. He slowed down only long enough to say: 'I have to go to prayer.'

Sharon remembers feeling deserted and fearful of caring for the fragments of her family, when a guy in a U-Haul drove up, asked her what was wrong and offered to carry her furniture to an apartment he knew was for rent at a reasonable rate. She ran to collect her family, and he piled them all into the truck. The stranger not only moved them into the apartment, he talked the landlord into giving her a lease with a minimal deposit. She remembers holding out all the money she had, about $200 in small bills. He picked out $100, gave it to the landlord and told her to keep the rest - that she would need it to start over. She never even got the guy's name and he smelled strongly of marijuana, but she believes he was God's messenger that day - that his kindness gave her the impetus to keep going.

A few months later on the day of John John's funeral, as she watched her family all praying together for their brother's soul, Sharon remembered her mother's messages and vowed to take on responsibility for healing family wounds. It took a very long time, but whenever Sharon became discouraged, she would think of how her mother always managed to hold the family together and of God's messenger coming along when she needed him.

Phillip had suffered another loss at least as devastating as the death of his little brother - he had lost the woman he loved, the woman he thought he would be with for the rest of his life. Only Jill could come close to sharing his sorrow at Jackie's death, and he found himself spending more time with Jill and Ron.

Jill had already begun a lifelong ritual of writing poetry whenever she had strong emotions to express. After the death of her friend, she wrote a poem entitled 'Jackie,' not only as a memorial, but also as a lament for the loss of the only person she felt could tell everything there was to tell about herself.

It was the season for passing. Ron was still grieving the loss of his brother when he heard about the death of his young protégé Greg Cox in a Wyoming highway accident. Only a few days after his son was killed, Bob called Ron to tell him that 19-year-old Greg had continued to think of the boxer as his hero - that the young boy's admiration had never diminished. Ron's voice catches as he describes his feeling at losing not only the symbol of his career and dedication to young people, but more significantly, his special little buddy.

And so Ron, Jill and Phillip shared their losses and once again the family, battered and bruised, moved on.

IN October, Jill invited a few family members and the Kresniks to celebrate Tracy's fifth birthday, an event that seemed to mark a happier beginning to their new lives together. Mary Kresnik still laughs when she remembers her ten-year-old son Brad walking up to Ron and asking: 'If I pull one of the hairs on your head, would it all unravel?' Ron said: 'What are you talking about?' And Brad said: 'Look, Mom, he has three little springs in his hair,' and tugged on one. Ron laughed, realising that his first physical signs of middle age - three grey hairs - were visible even to the little boy.

Ron divided his time after retiring between trips to Phoenix, where he gave Dennis Nelson a hand in training

Donny, and sporadic visits to youth centres. But Dennis was approaching the depth of his drunkenness, no longer useful to his brother, and Ron found himself moving away from his old friend. In the meantime, the money left over from the Cooney fight was quickly running out, and he still hadn't decided how he would put his life together to support his family.

His old training regimen faded gradually, and he began to put on weight. Jill waited, not always patiently, for him to find a new way, but he continued to flounder. What had seemed like a new beginning on Tracy's birthday began to feel like 'a train going nowhere,' and occasionally the couple's arguments turned into fights. The worst occurred one night after the children had been put to bed. The police were called by a neighbour because Ron and Jill were yelling at each other on the front lawn. Jill remembers that one of the cops gave Ron the keys to her car and told him to leave. She told them he couldn't have the car and they called him a cab.

She pressed charges, and although she later dropped them, it was too late. The story ended up in the newspapers and on a local television news show. Jill was temporarily let go from her job, and the news piece ended up in a Nebraska newspaper which her parents read. Jill asked Ron to move out, triggering the first of many separations, all of which were followed by reconciliations. But that first break-up resulted in a great loss, not only to them, but to Tracy and David.

As long as Jill stayed with the family, Ron was allowed to remain the custodial parent, even with his criminal record and even though he had never married Patty. But he could not continue to serve as their sole care-giver. Even though Ron never gave up his parental rights, when social services learned that Tracy and David were living alone with their father, they immediately placed the children in foster care. Ron was devastated - the nightmare was happening all over again. And this time he had no custodial rights at all. 'I remember thinking how afraid I was to let them go to foster care. I was scared to death of losing them.'

Jill spent the next few weeks trying to convince the social worker that she could make a good home for Tracy and David - that she had cared for them as her own and would immediately apply to adopt them. But as a single, white woman in the early-1980s, she had little chance of adopting black children and the social worker elected to continue foster placement. A short time later, Patty Jordan found out where Jill lived and went to Bellaire Street, demanding to know where the children were, but by that time, Tracy and David had been absorbed into the morass that was state social services and they were lost, even to their mother.

Four months later Jill reconciled with Ron and together they tried to regain custody of David and Tracy. But it was too late - the system had taken hold, the children had been placed in a foster home, and the rules of secrecy operating at that time would not allow Jill and Ron to see Tracy and David, let alone learn where they were living. It would be 16 years before either of them saw Tracy again, and even longer before they would finally be reunited with David.

Years later, Tracy talked about how she always remembered her father telling her to never let herself be separated from David - that they belonged together. 'He told me never to let anybody split us up, no matter what. I had to take care of my little brother.' So the little five-year-old girl tried to do just that; for two years in three unloving foster homes, whenever one or the other was up for adoption Tracy would 'act up' and tell her brother to do the same. Finally, in 1983, when Tracy was seven and David almost four, the children were adopted by a black couple living in Salt Lake City, Utah, and Tracy knew they finally had a new home.

IT took a while and some convincing by family members and others, but finally Ron came to know that he had lost Tracy and David, just as he had lost Monte. He also knew he had to find some meaningful purpose, or he would lose Jill, too.

Phillip served as a kind of sounding board during those weeks and Bill stood by to help, but it wasn't until one day while Ron was talking to Dennis Nelson that he decided to take one of the few routes readily available to former boxers.

Dennis had been feeling ashamed of his drunken behaviour; in a moment of lucidity, he thought of his Uncle Buck, the career F.B.I. agent who knew some people in Las Vegas and might help Ron get a foothold there. Ron made the call, after which 'Uncle Buck' remembers he made a few phone calls of his own, and within a few days, Ron received an offer for a job as a security guard at a gambling casino. The salary was good, and with nothing else on the horizon, he decided to take it. Asked why he went out of his way to help Ron back then, Robert Nelson says simply: 'Because he's a good guy. He's been there for me, too, all this time. Seven years ago, my daughter was killed in an accident and Ron came to the funeral. He also came when I lost my wife $2^{1}/_{2}$ years ago. He's a good guy, and I was happy to help him.'

In the summer, Ron and Jill moved to Las Vegas and for the next 20 years he would move back and forth between Denver, the city his heart called home, and Vegas, where he could always find work. His first security job, at the medium-sized Ellis Island Casino, set the stage for most of the years he lived in the glitzy gambling town. His responsibilities consisted primarily of walking around, staying alert for troublemakers and quietly moving them off the floor. Because of all the bouts he had fought in Las Vegas, he was often recognised by patrons of the bars and casinos, and for a time, he revelled in his celebrity. Former boxers were hired, not only as formidable deterrents to wrongdoers, but to attract clientele who liked to rub shoulders with athletes.

The first year at Ellis Island was relatively quiet, except for one incident. Ron had been called to a table tucked in a corner by the bar where a guy was standing on a table, hollering drunken obscenities. Ron told him to hush and get off the table. The guy screamed: 'Get away from me, nigger,' and Ron pulled him off the table, then punched him so hard, the manager ended up calling an ambulance. The guy wasn't seriously hurt, and Ron didn't lose his job, but he was directed to be more cautious in his reactions and was probably watched more closely in the months that followed.

Jill settled easily into their upscale condo in what was still a relatively small town. She, like Ron, made friends easily and the mutual devotion of the couple was evident to everyone who knew them in those days, but characteristically, she soon realised she needed something of her own. So, while Ron fell into a comfortable pattern of security work at Ellis Island, the slim, lovely young woman with experience in retail clothing fell naturally into modelling as lucrative part-time work. Jill wasn't tall enough to be a ramp model, but she managed to land some print work for newspaper ads and regular stints as a 'tearoom model.' She also managed a shop in Caesars Palace called Michael Valenti and worked at another shop across the street in the MGM Grand.

In the meantime, Ron gravitated to a downtown centre for boxers called the Ringside Gym, known as Sonny Liston's old hangout and run for years by a crusty old Italian named Johnny Taco. Known for his tough rules - years later he kicked then world champion Mike Tyson out of his gym - he took a liking to Ron Lyle. As Ron gradually and informally started working with some of the young boxers, Taco gave him a key to the gym, unprecedented for the naturally suspicious manager. It wasn't until months later, when Ron took two personal calls on the gym telephone that Johnny took his key back, but he continued to welcome the former heavyweight contender. He also took a liking to Jill and for a time, she was the only woman allowed in.

Whenever Ron and Jill could manage some time off, they would take the 12-hour drive to Denver, usually arriving just in time for dinner with Sharon or Bill or Phillip or the Kresniks. Ron would also try and find time to stop by Doobie Vigil's restaurant, or call Abbie Espinoza, just to touch base. He avoided Dennis Nelson. It was during one of those Denver visits that Ron ran into his old friend Russ Perron who had left a job with the Department of Commerce in Oklahoma to work back home as an environmental engineer. Russ was the only friend left from the old Curtis Park days, and the two men vowed to stay in touch.

On June 11, 1983, Dennis stopped drinking forever. After 13 days in a rehab center, he was determined to earn his way back to brotherhood with Donny and friendship with Ron. It took a few visits, but Ron was finally convinced that Dennis was staying sober and the two old friends started talking about how great it would be to have their own gym in Denver. Dennis had gone back to work with Donny in Phoenix even as his brother's career started to wind down, and he spent time at the Elks Gym, too, picking up some extra money working with a few of the young fighters who had recently turned pro. But it seemed impossible to conjure up the huge investment it would take to get started, and deep down, Ron knew that owning a gym wasn't the dream he was trying to find.

And so it went, back and forth between Las Vegas and Denver. Most of the time, Ron and Jill managed to feel a part of both places, but sometimes they felt the enormity of what was missing.

41

*

ON gradually began to know that losing Tracy and David was far worse than losing to Muhammad Ali. He hadn't fully realised that his children had anchored his life after boxing until they were gone. Jill held the two of them together and managed to adjust to the ebb and flow of Ron's changing directions, but the heart of his family had been his children, and now they had disappeared - just like Monte ten years before.

In her book, *On Boxing*, Joyce Carol Oates writes: 'For the great majority of boxers, life in the ring is nasty, brutish and short.' And she describes life after the ring as 'diminished.'[14] For several years after Tracy and David were taken from him, Ron's life seemed to fit Oates' characterisation of retired boxers.

He continued to move between Las Vegas, taking jobs at different casinos, and Denver, where he sometimes worked and sometimes didn't. Jill accompanied him less and less. She had her own life to lead, her own living to make, and Ron's aimlessness couldn't sustain her.

Off the Ropes

Ron grew more and more restless as he traversed the two cities over the next couple of years. Even when he and Jill were together, a purpose beyond family eluded him. The couple began to argue, more and more strenuously, and Ron wondered if he had once again made a mistake in trying to settle down. In Vegas he had recaptured a faint semblance of that heady world he had inhabited during his professional years - filled with 'chorus girls and party boys and money flowing in all directions.'

Jill and Ron both take responsibility for what followed. Jill knows she was pushing him too hard and he knows he was too rough with her in those days. They strained against the control each was trying to exert over the other, and one night the pent-up frustration came to a head.

They were sitting on the couch in their living room, arguing about something neither can even remember now when Ron announced that he would be leaving her soon. Without thinking, Jill hit him as hard as she could with her straight right hand. They both knew immediately she had broken his nose. He pulled his hand away from his face; it was covered with blood. He laughed. Then he cried. He told her she was the only woman besides his mother that he would never hit back. And somehow they managed to stay together.

A short time later, a distinguished man Jill describes as a dead ringer for Alfred Hitchcock walked into Michael Valenti and struck up a conversation with the young woman modelling furs. His name was Jay Black and he said he was from a firm in India called The House of Lloyd's that manufactured snakeskin products. He also had an interest in commercial film-making. One thing led to another and Jill ended up running out to grab a copy of her résumé which not only included fashion design and sales, but also her membership in the Screen Extras Guild. He offered her a job on the spot and, within weeks, Jill had taken the first of many trips to India. The huge opportunity Black offered would afford Jill the independence she craved. But even then, even as she spent more and more time in India, she and Ron managed to stay together.

Jill says that never in her life has she stopped thinking of Ron. Even during the exciting times when she was living in India and experiencing the drama of that country's historical changes, he was never far from her mind.

She soon became a partner in The House of Lloyd's and a great friend of Jay Black and his wife. Her own specialty was the design of children's fashion for a company called Alice in Wholesaleland. Over the next two years Jill spent more and more time in India, but she always returned to Las Vegas and Ron Lyle. It wasn't until after Prime Minister Indira Ghandi was killed in an uprising and the Sikh rebels set fire to the three buildings in Bangalore owned by the partners, that the venture came to an end and Jill came home for good.

It was in India that Jill began to take her poetry more seriously. Much of her work was centred in Native American spirituality, but her emotions were almost always tied to Ron. The piece she believes best exemplifies her feelings during that time was called 'Red Tide':

> *We are soul mates, you and I*
> *Meant to be together*
> *But out of nowhere comes the rift*
> *Quickly it breaks the tide.*
> *Someone made a dock on our shore*
> *It keeps love from passing*
> *Into the solid ground, holding*
> *Us in limbo....evermore*
> *Trusting nothing and no one*

Off the Ropes

Unconsciously we set
Our souls to certain misery
To deep water we run
By only our love we are bound
We don't want to be found.

The beginning of the end was almost unrecognisable, unaccompanied by the drama that had characterised their relationship. But in 1984, it was over. Jill and Ron both knew that they couldn't stay together, that they caused each other more frustration than joy and that each had to find a new way to live alone.

For her part, Jill continued working in Vegas for a time, then landed a modelling job with J.F. Images in Denver. She had held on to the Bellaire Street house and soon settled there, falling easily into familiar old friendships. She dated now and then, but never seriously considered living with anyone else.

Jill's absence took its toll on Ron, and winter of '84 found him bartending part-time at the Cheerio Lounge in Denver, barely eking out enough to pay rent on a room. He didn't have a car and when friends or family weren't around to drive him, he couldn't manage to get to work. He had abandoned the strong work ethic that had sustained him for a lifetime. In a few months he drifted back to Vegas. Ron remembers how difficult that time was, but today he much prefers talking about the good things that happened in the eighties rather than the losses he suffered and his lack of purpose. One of those good things was meeting Willie Fields.

By then Ron was working part-time at a place called The Village Pub, but it was at the Desert Inn, where Willie was dealing craps, that the two first met. Willie had been a fighter - a middleweight - and he was spending most of his spare time training boxers at the Ringside Gym, the same place Johnny Taco had welcomed Ron four years before. That night Willie immediately recognised Ron Lyle, and before the evening was over, they were talking and laughing together like old friends.

It wasn't long before Ron was not only helping Willie train young boxers at the Ringside, but also dropping over at his house four or five times a week. Knowing Willie felt much like knowing Dennis Nelson, and Ron was grateful for finding another of the few people he could trust, especially coming after his separation from Jill.

Willie remembers one night shortly after he met Ron; he was having dinner at The Village Pub where Ron was on duty. 'A guy walked in and immediately got out of line, harassing the bartender and other people sitting around. Ron started to help the bartender and the guy made the mistake of throwing a punch at Ron, who immediately knocked him out.' Willie recalls that nobody pressed charges.

A few young kids hung out at Ringside, and Ron starting demonstrating a few of the basics to the boys who showed the most interest. Before long, he would watch for a ring to empty so he could put one or two through their paces. He talked to the boys just like he had always talked to kids in youth centres. For a while, time at the gym filled part of the void, but it didn't feel permanent and he migrated back to Denver.

'I always hated to see Ron go,' Willie says. 'We talked about life in the ring - he was still an amateur when I was fighting pro, even though I am four years younger. We talked about how your life is on the line. We both knew we could have been killed. It made us humble.' He remembers the days he worked alongside Ron Lyle as the most gratifying. 'He was then and is now and has always been a decent person.' He pauses, then: 'He's a hero to me.'[15]

Whenever Ron gravitated back to Denver, he inevitably

spent time with the Kresniks and other friends, but he started seeing more of his family as well. It was beginning to feel like Sharon was pulling his brothers and sisters back together. She would have everybody over on some Sundays after church, and every now and then, when they were all together, Ron would look around the room and feel his mother's presence as a comfort, a glimmer of hope for his life.

He started working out again and found himself pushing the limits, just as he always had. One day he showed up at Mary and John's doorstep, his lower back hurting so bad he couldn't stand up straight. Mary helped him put icy hot on it before he lay down on the waterbed in Brad's room. The next morning, a Saturday, he couldn't move.

'John and I came up with a plan,' she says. 'We thought if we could lay him on our old cedar chest that was on rollers, we could get him to the van and drive him to the chiropractor. Well, we tried to move him, but he was so big, it wasn't working. So we called in a bunch of Brad's friends - he was in junior high by then - to jump on the waterbed, and sure enough, Ron bounced up, and we flipped him over onto the cedar chest. We rolled it to the top of the stairs, then slid him down the staircase and basket-carried him to the van.

'The chiropractor worked on him for a few minutes, but said he needed much more work. So he stayed at our house, and the chiropractor would come with a portable treatment table twice a day, during his lunch break and after work. In the meantime, I had my day care kids to worry about, and Ron would just lie on the floor, unable to move for hours at a time.

'He loved being around the kids, but *Mary Poppins* was big then, and they wanted to see the movie over and over. One day I walked into the room and Ron said: 'I don't ever want to hear the name Mary Poppins again.' The next day he pleaded with me to please not let the day care kids watch *Mary Poppins*. I didn't, not while he was there.

'Our cat had kittens while Ron was staying with us, and when they got big enough to climb out of their box in the kitchen, they gravitated toward Ron lying on the floor, running over his body and even his face. They scared him to death. His back finally got better, and he was happy to leave, I know. He had lived with us for two-and-a-half months.'

Frank Barron remembers Ron in Denver about that same time. 'My son Jeremy was 16 then and screwing up in school. One day he told his counsellor at the Alternative School that he knew Ronny Lyle. The counsellor didn't believe him, so he said he'd prove it - have him there the next day. I managed to track Ronny down through Dennis Nelson. Jeremy called him, and the guy dropped everything to go to the school the next day. Ron ended up spending a couple of hours with the kids, and the counsellor was impressed.'

Months later, at a time when Ron was crashing with Dennis Nelson and his girlfriend Mary Bransfield, Frank lived across the street from their apartment complex. He remembers Ron spending a lot of time with Jeremy. 'Ron was always hoping to make a difference in a kid's life. He even spent his 45th birthday with Jeremy, watching old boxing tapes.' Frank raises his voice a notch: 'It's important to remember that Ronny always wanted to be with the kids.'

Mary, like other friends from back then, remembers Ron going through some tough times, but never giving up. One day she looked out the window and saw him next to the complex swimming pool, down on his knees. She went out to see what was wrong and he invited her to pray with him. Ron remembers that his prayers that day were for his own children. He had never stopped missing them and he continually hoped, prayed and tried to have faith that he would see them all again one day.

Ron still lost control of his anger sometimes, especially when somebody hassled him. One February night in 1986, the Denver police got a call of a disturbance on the street in his old neighbourhood. A squad car arrived at the scene and found Ron Lyle sitting in a truck with two guys outside on the street yelling at him. He started to get out of the truck and one of the guys picked up a large stick and ran at him, yelling: 'nigger.' Ron attacked the two men at once. It took both policemen to subdue him, and he was arrested, along with the other men, on charges of third-degree assault and obstructing police. He was released the next day, and eventually the charges were dropped, but that scene added to the chaotic nature of his life.

Ron Lyle has been variously described during that period of his life as an 'angry loner,' and as 'the gentlest of men.' As Mary Kresnik put it: 'He has climbed the mountains and seen the valleys.' One of Ron's oldest friends Russell Perron says that Ron was always a great guy, but: '....when people got in his way, he had to fight back.' Ron himself says he knows he got 'down in the mud' back then, but he also held onto what his mother told him when he was a little boy: 'It's hard to be right all the time, but it's easy to be a gentlemen.'

Twenty years ago, he fit all of these descriptions and more.

42

*

FTER the last incident with the police, Ron lost heart for a while - it felt like a struggle just to hold on. Wherever he turned, he thought he saw somebody either trying to hurt him or take advantage, and he started avoiding everybody, even old friends he could trust. He says now that: '....it had to get bad before it could get better.'

One day in early spring, Mary Kresnik answered her doorbell. 'Ron was standing there, looking awful - ravaged.' For a long time the Kresniks had told Ron their home was his own and that he didn't even need to knock when he came by. That day, he told Mary he didn't think he should just walk in. But he needed a favour. Could he store some of his things in their garage until he could find another place?

Mary had the sudden thought that her dear friend, the man who loved the children in her care, was something of a child himself that day. 'A child in this enormous body.' She asked him where he would go, and he said: 'I'll sleep on a park bench. I've done it before.' Mary told him to wait and went inside to talk to John, who said: 'Tell him to get his head out of his cavity and get in here.' And so the Kresniks came to his rescue once again.

This time John took it upon himself to offer advice to the man he admired. He told Ron there were people who wanted to take advantage of him, that he needed to stay clear of them. At that time in Ron's life, the Kresniks saw him as a follower, not a leader, and they wanted him to take charge of his life. They both had faith that Ronny would eventually find his way, but they didn't foresee that it would take an exasperatingly long time; in the meantime, he had John and Mary. And Mary's parents.

Her mother used to tease him, and he would tease her right back. She would tell him: 'Don't ever cut my pancakes with a knife.' And when they were playing dominoes, he would always try to put one over on her at which point she would always say: 'If you cheat, Ronny, I will put the dominoes away.' He treated Mary's mother with the same respect he always showed his own mother and in time came to call her his grandma.

Shortly after Ron moved in with the Kresniks, Mary's mother and father were in a serious car accident. Her mother had a broken neck and spent most of five-and-a-half months in the hospital's I.C.U. ward. During most of that time, she was allowed only 15 minutes per visitor. The family hired a college kid to watch over her, and one day the boy called Mary's father. 'Mr. Smith, do you have any black relatives?' Mary's father said: 'No,' but smiled. He thought he knew what was coming. 'Well, there's this big black guy who comes in to tell me he wants to see his grandma, and I'm not about to tell him no.'

For the moment, Ron was more comfortable with the Kresniks than with his own family. He couldn't rid himself of the feeling that he had let his sisters and brothers down. They knew what Nellie would have expected of him and he kept thinking he didn't measure up. So, while Sharon was striving to lead the family back to the spiritual foundation that had sustained them, Ron continued to struggle to find meaning. But even at what seemed the bleakest time of his life, Ron would not give in to despair. He was floundering, but he wasn't lost, and Mary Kresnik remembers him during that time as the same delightful man she had always known.

He always showed affection to whatever foster children Mary and John had living with them. That year, a young boy named Darrell became particularly close to Ron. Stricken with the same cerebral palsy that had killed John John five years before, Darrell seemed to sense Ron as the protector he needed to get through the bad days. He would snuggle up next to the big black man on the couch and Ron would put his arm around him, saying: 'There's my little brother.' Whenever any of the other children got into an argument with Darrell, Ron would always tell them: 'Don't mess with my little brother.'

That year he had Thanksgiving dinner with the Kresniks, and Mary recalls Ronny gobbling down the first course, a fresh salad. Usually a fastidious eater, he had dribbled bacon grease and vinegar down his chin. He took a breath to ask her what was in the salad, and when she told him spinach, he replied: 'But I don't like spinach.' Mary still chuckles when she remembers that dinner and how easily Ron fit into the Kresnik family.

As always, Ron eventually returned to Las Vegas, the casinos, Willie Fields and the gym. He was always welcome, usually recognised as the guy who took Ali 11 rounds and the guy who almost knocked out George Foreman. Some boxing fans even remembered that he had hit Earnie Shavers harder than anybody ever had, before or after. Ron still found it hard to distinguish between people who wanted only to know him and people who wanted something from him, but he was learning. And he was learning to survive.

Ron knew he had to halt the slide that had started when Jerry Cooney knocked him out in 1981. He still hadn't replaced his old compelling dream with a new one, but he started thinking that if he couldn't be world champion, maybe he could help someone else to a title. It had already happened once, and maybe it could happen again.

RON had met Lonnie Smith way back in 1972, when Dennis asked him to watch an energetic little ten-year-old boy learning to box at the Albany Hotel gym, the same place where he had met Patty Jordan. Even then Ron thought the kid showed promise.

In 1980, Bobby Lewis had invited Ron to watch a flamboyant young welterweight training at the 20th Street Gym and Recreation Center. The Denver kid had become 'Lightning' Lonnie Smith and was starting to make an impression on local trainers. Ron remembers: 'He was looking real good even back then.'

When Ron got to Las Vegas in 1981, he followed Smith's fights at Caesars Palace. By then, the 19-year-old fighter was being described variously as a 'welterweight Muhammad Ali,' 'dazzlingly arrogant' and 'idiosyncratic.' By '83, Bobby Lewis had talked Ron into sparring with the young boxer at home in Denver, in Las Vegas and even at a camp in the Catskills. Ron remembers his own major contribution was getting Lonnie to broaden his skills. 'He wasn't a puncher until after I worked with him.'

In 1985, Ron Lyle and Bobby Lewis had partnered in earnest, training Lonnie for his big chance at a championship bout with champ Billy Costello. In August 'Lightning' Lonnie Smith won the championship with a technical knockout. In Madison Square Garden, the referee held up Lonnie's arm, signaling his victory and new title, WBC light welterweight champion of the world. Ron knew it wasn't the same as becoming champion himself, but it was nice to know he'd had a part in Lonny's triumph.

IN the late-eighties, Ron didn't know if training another world champion was his destiny or not, but he found himself more often in Las Vegas than at home in Denver. He moved from apartment to apartment, casino to casino, even woman to woman, always restless, always searching but never quite finding. The only constant was continuing to volunteer at gyms around Vegas that drew young people to boxing. 'Being with the kids kept me going in those days,' he remembers. And the kids, just like those in the Denver youth facilities and Mary Kresnik's foster children and the children of friends, were comfortable with the big man, drawn to his straight talk always tempered with smiles.

But Ron's progress during this period was excruciatingly slow. Sometimes he slipped into a kind of despondency that would leave him, once again, feeling helpless. He was in that kind of a state during a sojourn to Denver in 1990 when Jill ran into him again. She was working for the phone company by then, taking the bus to work, or she probably wouldn't have even known he was in town. She found him sleeping in the bus terminal and took him home. They hadn't seen each other for six years.

Ron had again found himself essentially homeless, too proud this time to call on his friends or family, virtually any of whom would have gladly taken him in. He had slept a few nights on the floor of the Carter Gym, even in the City Park. 'The centre of my soul. That's Jill. She saved me more than once.'

The two stayed in Denver for a few weeks, falling in love all over again before they predictably returned to Las Vegas and pretty much the same routine Ron had followed for years - working casino security, helping out at gyms. Then another opportunity arose when, as Ron describes it: 'A guy knew a guy who knew a guy who knew me.' And that was how it came to be that Robert Stack asked him to play Sonny Liston in an episode of *Unsolved Mysteries*, to be filmed at Liston's former home and at the Golden Gloves Gym in Las Vegas.

Ron jumped at the chance, not just for the money, but because he always believed that Sonny was killed by somebody in the fight game. 'He never used drugs,' Ron maintains to this day. 'Sonny was scared to death of needles. He wouldn't even let himself get shot in the butt with B-12. There's no way he O.D.'ed himself. It was somebody else killed him.' And that was the point of view of the television episode which aired in November with Ron getting favourable reviews for his portrayal of Liston. He still finds it frustrating that the case has never been resolved.

Acting in a programme about a boxer served as a kind of catalyst for Ron. He worked hard to get in shape for the boxing scenes and, more importantly, spent time with a man who would soon become a significant influence in his life.

In 1990, Richard Steele was already recognised as one of the greatest referees in boxing. Ron had known him casually through the years, but it wasn't until the two hooked up at the Golden Gloves Gym, where Ron was filming the boxing segment for *Unsolved Mysteries*, that they started talking about a common belief system.

One of the many reasons Ron admires Richard Steele is the respect he has always shown boxers in his ring. In fact, Steele was sometimes criticised for stopping exciting fights too early in order to prevent serious injury to the fighters, most notably a championship bout between junior welterweight champion Julio Chavez and Meldrick Taylor. With only six seconds left, Meldrick went down hard and got up at the eight count. Steele asked him twice if he was okay and Meldrick couldn't answer, at which point the referee called the fight, sparking a furious outcry which lingers in boxing blogs even today.

'Fans lose all sense of fairness,' Steele says. 'Even people who would not hurt anyone get so emotional, they forget everything except the fight. I avoid watching sporting events on television so I can keep the emotion out of it when I referee.' But it was Richard Steele's devotion to young people that cemented Ron's admiration. In1990, Steele was already working on establishing a boxing club for kids, and the more he talked about how boxing can help young people learn to walk away from trouble, the more Ron realised this man was expressing thoughts Ron had held for decades. Here was a highly-respected, consummate professional confirming his belief that the rules and discipline of boxing could be applied in a youth programme, maybe change kids' lives, maybe save them.

That Richard Steele was also a practicing minister only increased Ron's trust and respect, and he began seeking advice from the younger man who not only understood what was important, but was trying to put his beliefs into action. Richard Steele was helping Ron conceive of a goal that would be more than ten years in the making. But the seed had been planted. And Ron's instincts were on target.

For his part, Richard admired Ron Lyle, not only as a 'gentleman,' but as a boxer. 'During his time in the ring, any of the top-ten contenders could have been heavyweight champion,' Steele says. 'That's never been true before or since. Nowadays, maybe one or two have a chance. Ron was up there with the best.'[16]

Things moved slowly in the right direction for Ron and Jill. Together they carved a place for themselves in the world of Vegas boxing, Jill as much as Ron. Always welcome and increasingly popular, she came to know trainers, fighters, promoters, sportscasters and reporters, referees and judges - just about everybody in the game. Because he was always more interested in working with young boxers than in working security, Ron wasn't making much money, but together they managed a modest lifestyle and, starting with Willie Fields and Richard Steele, they were building the kind of genuine friendships in Las Vegas they had in Denver.

It wasn't always smooth going. Neither Ron nor Jill could quite relinquish the desire for control, and some of their arguments rivalled those of their earlier days together.

But for the next few years, they stuck it out, at least most of the time.

43

*

Moving On

VIII

TWO steps forward, one step back. Ron was moving onward during the early-nineties, but often at a snail's pace, frustrating those who knew and loved him. By 1994, he was again on his own back in Denver, Jill having moved on a few months before for what she thought would be the last time. They had long since stopped questioning the intensity of their love for each other, but Jill had again come to the reluctant conclusion that they could not spend the rest of their lives together.

Ron returned to Denver for any number of reasons. Jill was there and he had some vague hope of reconciling with her, he missed his oldest friends, and he also wanted to find out if the kind of boxing club that Richard Steele was working on in Las Vegas could play in Denver. He was starting to envision a safe place for at-risk kids and hoped he could rouse some interest in his hometown where many of his old fans still remembered his glory years.

But it was Ron's family that became the major factor in his decision. His father William, in his late-seventies, had become quite fragile, and Sharon, who had long since reconciled with him, had been trying to convince Ron that the family needed to be together during their father's last years. She finally succeeded. Ron came home, and most thought his worst days were behind him.

He soon fell back on the only life he knew - boxing. He went back to the old Elks Gym and started training some local boxers who looked promising to him. One of those boxers was Dave Kilgour, who says: 'We called him the Professor, you know, like the scientist in *The Sweet Science*.

Kigour emphasises a strength of Ron's that is often overlooked. 'There was no better trainer in the game,' he says. 'And only another boxer can truly understand that. When somebody asked him what it's like in the ring, Ron said: "It can't be told." And it can't. Only a boxer knows that.' He adds: 'And don't forget. Of all the great ones of the greatest era in boxing, Ronny was undoubtedly the best all-around athlete. He could easily have been world champion.'

Training adult boxers whetted his appetite, and for a brief moment in time, Ron tried to link his dream for a youth boxing centre with his desire to try on the gloves once more. He decided to launch what would become a very short comeback in the ring.

Ever Ron's strongest supporter, Dennis Nelson got the word out to former fans. The first guy to climb on board the comeback train was one Tony Wu, a 77-year-old dapper guy around town who had always been a fan and who volunteered, not only to outfit Ron with the equipment he needed, such as the shoes he imported from Mexico through a 'friend's Mexican cousin,' but also to find a place for him to train. Wu set Ron up in the second floor of a friend's factory, which had a makeshift ring and a big bag, all Ron needed to get back in shape.

For months, Tony Wu would pick Ron up every day and

drive him to the factory, and most days, he would come back and take him for a meal at his own Utopia Restaurant.[17]

Typical of Ron's fans, when Tony met Ron briefly in 1985 at a gym where he was doing massage, he was struck with the former boxer's graciousness and generosity. When asked why he spent all that time and money on the boxer ten years later, Tony replied: 'Whatever we can do for Ron, we'll do for him.'[18]

Alan Katz wrote a moving piece for the December 18, 1994 edition of the *Denver Post*:

> Mornings at dawn, a familiar figure jogs along the dirt path that encircles Cheesman Park. A tall, burly man, he runs easily, punctuating his steps with quick flurries of punches. Nearly 20 years ago, his punches knocked George Foreman to the canvas twice and nearly separated Muhammad Ali from the world heavyweight title.
>
> Back in his hometown after a 10-year absence, Ron Lyle is [53] years old and living alone in a modest Congress Park apartment. Since the mid-1980's, he had lived quietly in Las Vegas, Nevada, training unknown fighters while earning a living as a security guard. During those years, Lyle emerged from obscurity only briefly to portray Sonny Liston in an episode of 'Unsolved Mysteries.' Three months ago, the 235-pound ex-pug loaded his furniture into a rented trailer and drove to Denver to be near his ailing father.....He spends most of his time alone.
>
> 'When you're up in the world, you have a lot of people around you,' he says softly, during the two-block walk from the park to his ninth floor apartment. 'Some are sincere and some are hangers-on. When you reach my age, you don't need that. I never did need people, even when I was fighting. When you're in the ring, you're alone, anyway.'

In late October, Lyle watched 45-year-old Foreman regain the heavyweight title from Michael Moorer. The fight brought back memories of the classic 1976 Lyle-Foreman slugfest that ring fans still speak about with awe....

'....I should have relaxed when I had him in trouble, but I got tense and then I got tired,' Lyle says. 'I would love to fight him again. My skills haven't slipped that much. I'm in good shape. I fought at 220 pounds and I'm 235 now. I run five miles a day. If I had a few fights first, I think there would be some interest. In fact, I've been talking to some influential people in New York and I should know something in a few months.'

On a sunny day, with nothing much to do, Lyle invites a visitor to view a videotape of his two most famous bouts.

'If I didn't get a sincere vibe off of you, you wouldn't be up here,' he says with a hard stare. Popping the tape into his VCR, he settled down on his brown velveteen sofa as crowd noise filled the small living room.

'Lyle's story has been well-chronicled,' barks Howard Cosell on the 1976 'Wide World of Sports' broadcast. 'He learned to box in a Colorado prison, where he spent $7^1/_2$ years for second-degree murder.'

The fighter is expressionless as he hears this. On the tape, he glares at Foreman, their faces an inch apart, as the referee gives them instructions. Then, as the late afternoon sun filters into the apartment, the bell rings a thousand miles and many years away.

ALMOST a year later, a *Denver Post* article by Bill Briggs begins with the identical setting - Ron pounding through Cheesman Park at 'the eye-burning' hour of 4:00 a.m. Still recalling the Foreman fight, still thinking of a rematch, but now 54 years old and talking about a nobler purpose: 'He's fighting these days, he says, for the kids of Denver, especially for those in the Curtis Park area where he grew up. His goal is to start a neighbourhood gym where young folks can learn how to box and how to live right.'

People continued to believe in Ron Lyle. Even though it would be years before the dream of a youth programme was fulfilled, many old friends and fans had faith in Ron's own aspirations, whether he wanted to make a comeback or to provide a community service.

Another Denver sportswriter described it this way: 'A gladiator's heart still seeks expression.' There was no question that Ron Lyle was sincere in his desire to start a youth boxing programme, but he also wanted to get back in the ring - to once again prove something, if only to himself. And he wanted one last crack at George Foreman.

Foreman, who had successfully launched his own short-lived comeback (after refusing to defend his title, the WBA took it away), declined to consider fighting Lyle again. In a December 28, 1994 *Philadelphia Daily News* piece, Foreman recalled his '76 meeting with Ron Lyle. 'It's the fight I remember most of all....When I was down and the count got to five or six, I was thinking: "Do you really want this? Do you really want to get up?" I never had to ask myself those questions before.' Whether Foreman was afraid to meet Ron in the ring, or more likely, had nothing to prove, he left no doubt that a rematch was out of the question.

But Ron may have been seeking something else in entering the ring again. A year earlier, Alan Katz had reported a rare moment of nostalgia:

> When Lyle talks about boxing, his voice is filled with longing. He misses the competition, the intensity, the adrenaline, the atmosphere, the crowds, the violence.

'I loved it. I loved it. I loved luring a guy into throwing a punch, then landing my own right hand and hurting him and dropping him. I loved it. It was the only way I was ever able to express myself.

'I loved the fight crowd. They're the most exciting crowd I know - the high rollers. The night life. The politicians and movie stars. Business people. Street people. Ladies of the night. And they all come for one reason - to see you knocked down and pull yourself up. They want to see you put it on the line. And when you do, that's like you telling them, "This is what I have to give you tonight."'

Dennis Nelson served as Ron's trainer and Frank Barron as his bucket man, two of the people he had long trusted, and both were proud of his courage and determination. 'He needed to do that at the time,' Dennis says, and Frank remembers: 'I was happy to help him.'

USA TODAY covered his first comeback fight after the fact. With no fanfare, Ron had quietly set up a bout in a small nightclub called Peel's Palace in Erlanger, Kentucky. The Kentucky Athletic Commission chairman was quoted as saying the fight was not publicised at Lyle's insistence and was attended by about 300 people. They had recorded Ron's age as 47, possibly to support his eligibility. Ron was testing both his wings and the wind. He knocked out a 28-year-old boxer by the name of Bruce Johnson, who had lost 13 fights in a row, in the fourth round.

Ron would fight three more times in 1995, once again in Kentucky, a state known for its laxity in approving professional fights, and in Denver. He beat all three fighters by knockouts in the second round, but none of the three were worthy contenders, not even for a 54-year-old heavyweight who had been retired for 15 years. For the record, Tim Pollard's life performance was six wins, nine losses and two draws; he was 25 when he met Lyle. Dave Slaughter, who was 37, had a career of five wins, 29 losses and one draw.[19]

Not a glorious year for Ron Lyle, but he finally got the comeback out of his system, and managed to put away a few dollars toward the still hoped-for youth gym, even though it would take five more years and a huge boost from an old friend to make it happen.

Then, out of nowhere, Ron's 25-year-old son Monte came to see him. It had been several years since Nadine had told Monte who his father was, but he didn't seek Ron out until he was married and thinking of starting a family of his own.

Tongue-tied, unable to stop staring at the boy he hadn't seen since he was four years old, Ron let Monte take charge of the reunion. A professional chef and married to a girl in the Army, the young man presented himself as mature, easygoing - a man who had overcome early obstacles to achieve a comfortable place in life. In his current state Ron felt humbled by the boy he had loved and nurtured but who barely remembered him. And then, almost as soon as he appeared, he was gone.

It would be another five years before Ron saw Monte again, but in the meantime, his daughter came back into his life.

44

*

TRACY had been determined to find her birth parents
ever since she turned 18 and adoption laws were
relaxed, allowing her access to such details. But she
waited until she was 21 to begin looking, first for Patty,
locating her in Colorado Springs after only a few phone
calls. Within weeks she had talked her brother David into
flying there for a reunion with their birth mother, even
though David had no memory of his earliest years.

That visit in 1996 brought some closure and answered
some questions and so was enough for a while. But Patty
had not been particularly forthcoming about Ron during the
visit and had planted the suspicion in David that his
biological father had been somebody else.

Tracy could not stop thinking of the times she had been
with the man she called 'daddy,' and a year later she knew
she had to discover more of who she was. She set about
finding her birth father.

Ron was on another migration to Las Vegas by that time,
but finding members of her extended birth family turned

out to be as simple as calling Denver information and discovering her grandfather William Lyle and Uncle Bill Lyle. Bill's wife Margie immediately invited Tracy to stay with them and to bring David along. The two flew again to Colorado Springs after Patty promised to drive them to Denver to be with the other side of the family.

The gathering at Bill's house with Patty present was comfortable enough, but Tracy was eager to get on with finding her father. Margie gave her Jill Sellers's telephone number, and, after putting it off for a day, she took a deep breath and called the woman who had served as the children's surrogate mother so many years before.

Jill remembers every second of that phone call - hearing the shaky voice on the other end asking if she was the woman who had lived with Ron Lyle, realising immediately who was calling, and starting to cry. In a conversation that lasted almost an hour, Jill related many of Ron's and her experiences over almost two decades. And just before they hung up, she promised Tracy she would find her daddy and bring him home. After allowing herself a few minutes to absorb the earth-shattering experience of talking to the child she had once cared for, Jill set about finding Ron.

It didn't take long. She knew everybody and every haunt Ron knew in Vegas, and it only took a few calls to find him in his latest temporary dwelling. Jill tried to prepare him for the experience of talking to his daughter, but he couldn't know what it would be like to hear the voice of the child he still loved.

Tracy called her birth father that evening before dinner, introduced herself and calmly asked if he could come to Denver the next day. After hearing her voice, Ron couldn't wait a single day to see her, so he drove all night to get there, a feat that required intense concentration from a man with impaired driving skills.

'My heart bubbled over when she talked to me,' Ron says. 'All I could do was listen to her. And I had to see her.' He wouldn't get to see David though, who would be gone before he got to Denver, partly because he was playing football and had to get back to practice. In all probability, David had no desire to see a man whom he believed at the time was not his father, a man he didn't remember.

Ron drove directly to Jill's house where Tracy was waiting, and when she came to the door, as he had done with Monte, he stood still, silent, taking in the sight and sound of his daughter. At that moment he thought he would never be able to get enough of this beautiful, poised 22-year-old young woman who had been the light of his life so many years before.

Ron learned a lot that day. He learned that his two young children had gone through two very difficult years in foster homes and he was moved to tears when Tracy spoke of how she had always kept her word not to let anyone separate her from David. Even today his voice holds wonder as he describes what she did, adding: 'She is the strongest, most amazing person.'

He learned that a year after being adopted by the Bowens, their adoptive father had died of a heart attack, and that their mother Yvonne had moved the family back to her hometown of Detroit where she still had family. She had later met and married Frank Williams and the couple turned out to be 'awesome' parents. He also learned that Tracy had played basketball at Michigan State University and that David was playing football at the University of Michigan; an excellent defensive player as a freshman, he had 'exploded' in '96 with a school record 12 sacks.

Ron and Tracy ended up staying at Jill's house for four days, and they never stopped talking, trying to catch up on the lost 17 years. Dozens of photographs were taken and Jill and Ron pulled up every memory they had of the children when they were young. Being in Jill's house reminded Tracy of so much more, and she continually amazed Ron with her ability to remember things that had happened to her when she was four and barely five years old, including details about the little girl who had lived across the street. Every day all three would end up laughing through their tears, as one would start a story, 'remember when....' and the other two would chime in with other details.

'It was okay, the reunion with my birth mother, but later, when I saw my daddy, it was more like picking up where we left off,' Tracy remembers of that day.

Ron yearned to see David, but accepted that he couldn't be there because of his football schedule. Later, he would wonder why David hadn't been as eager to see him as Tracy had. He convinced himself it was because David had been too young to remember him. It would be ten years before he knew the real reason.

IN spite of the stable, happy home life he had known after being adopted, and his belief that Ron Lyle was not his father, David Bowens had often felt something was missing. In 2000 he gave an interview during which he talked about the emotional impact of not knowing who his father was.

'For four or five years after my adoptive father died of a heart attack, I didn't have a male figure,' Bowens said. 'I [had been told] that somewhere in this world my father was a professional boxer, and I would try to be like him even though he wasn't there. I wanted to box and my adoptive mother wouldn't let me, because of my asthma. I didn't have anybody to identify with. I was seeing a psychotherapist. I just lost it. I couldn't find myself. I've always been on an honour roll of some kind, but I gave up on school.'

Maybe because of the less-than-conclusive visits to

Colorado, David experienced another lapse of confidence when he was at the University of Michigan and he dropped out. But eventually, he managed to find the strength to do what his father had always done - move on. He made up credits he had missed and enrolled at Western Illinois, where his 14 sacks in '98 led to a fifth-round selection by the Denver Broncos in 1999. He would be acquired by Green Bay in 2000 and move on the next year to the Miami Dolphins as a starting defensive end.

SEEING Tracy changed something in Ron. After she left, he found himself finally ready to take on the next part of his life. It was as though he had to know that all three of his children were all right before he could dedicate the rest of his time to other young people. But it would be almost a year before he would get the opportunity to accept that kind of serious responsibility.

In 1998 Ron was on one of his umpteenth rotations from Denver back to Las Vegas; still marking time, he again found work as a security guard, this time at the Tropicana, so he could spend almost all of his daylight hours in one gym or another, with Willie Fields or Richard Steele.

One day he ran into Bob Cox, who was staying across the street at the MGM, and the two quickly renewed their old friendship, forged far back in the days when Greg Cox had idolised the heavyweight contender and solidified after Greg's tragic death in 1981. Bob was especially happy to see Ron at that time because it brought back such happy memories of Greg just when he and his family were working on ideas for a memorial to his son.

Bob had greatly expanded his equipment business, now known as Cox and Associates, and had started spending a significant amount of time in construction-friendly Las Vegas. For a few months he would see Ron regularly in his treks across the street, where he spent some time at the Tropicana Sports Club. It was there he picked up the inside scoop about an incident that got Ron fired from a security position. The *Las Vegas Review-Journal* reported: 'Another security guard was giving Ron Lyle a hard time, really getting in his face. Finally, after several minutes of taunting, Ron opened a "can of whupp-ass" on the guy. The fight was over in one punch.'

Bob learned that a newly-hired guard had immediately set out to torment Ron whenever and wherever he could. The first night he was on the job, he scoffed at the notion that Ron had ever been a professional boxer. 'The wonder is that Ron held off as long as he did,' Cox says. The taunting went on constantly, inside and outside the casino. One night, the new guard asked Ron: 'What do you think of Nelson Mandela?' Ron replied: 'I admire him very much.'

'He's nothing but a fucking communist,' was the comeback. Ron was quiet for a few minutes, then said: 'It doesn't matter what I used to be, but if I come to work tomorrow and you pop off one more time, you're going to wish you hadn't.' And, of course, that was it. The next day Ron put the guy out with one blow and had to be let go, reluctantly, it seems, by the head of Tropicana security. Bob wasn't really surprised. He believes that Ron was generally able to channel his anger, but sometimes not having the ring as an outlet or the right woman to steady him, he boiled over.

Bob knew his old friend needed a stabilising force in his life. And he remembered that Ron had told him how much he wanted to start a youth boxing centre. He had the feeling at the time that Ron was starting to think that dream was as elusive as his dream of being heavyweight champion. One day after he and Ron had spent time talking about the past and their respective hopes for the future, it happened that Bob had his moment of revelation, and he put it all together - a youth boxing centre as a memorial to Greg. The seed

Richard Steele had planted in Ron was replanted in Bob Cox. But it still had to take root.

By 1999 Bob had established a home in San Diego, but he returned to Las Vegas frequently and always made it a point to look up Ron, encouraging him to hang on to the idea of a youth gym. At the time, Ron was unable to find security work and found himself helping Richard Steele train young boxers for the highest salary Steele could afford - a little over $500 a month.

Bob didn't tell Ron right away, but he had heard about a youth gym in National City, south of San Diego, and had driven by the place, a modest converted garage, started by a former boxer from Mexico and dedicated to serving young people in the mostly Latino neighbourhood. He had driven by the facility, grandly named the Community Youth Athletic Center and was struck by the logos on the building - UPS, Holiday Inn, National Latino Police Officers and the Barona Tribe. This could work.

He kept driving by the place, hoping to talk to someone about how they had managed to get corporate sponsorship. He finally got an appointment with Victor Nunez, vice-president of the board, who told him support for youth south of San Diego was crystallised in boxing, a very popular sport in the Latino community. Nunez said significant contributions, especially from the Barona Tribe and UPS, would result in building a new facility within a couple of years, which, in fact, came to pass.

Bob Cox had just taken the first step to turning Ron Lyle's dream into reality.

45

*

The Twelfth Round

IN the beginning, Bob Cox thought the logical home for a community centre based on the one he saw in National City would be Las Vegas, where boxing was ever popular. But after weeks of testing the water and talking it over with Ron, he changed his mind. The kind of youth centre they both envisioned belonged in Denver. Ron Lyle was still a well-known name there, meaning more likelihood of sponsorship than in Las Vegas, home to any number of retired boxers. Bob's daughter, Susan Carlin, made the final convincing argument - Colorado had always been home to her brother Greg.

Early in 2000, Bob and Ron took the first of many trips to Denver, where they began the search for funding. Bob called upon representatives of the same corporations that had sponsored the National City centre - Holiday Inn and UPS - but came away empty-handed. So they began to solicit donations, person to person. Bob composed a letter for mailing and posting on his website which included information about Greg and Ron, ending with: 'Greg had no opportunity to make his mark in the world. Greg's sister Susan and I have decided to help Ron realise his dream and create a memorial to Greg by establishing The Cox/Lyle Community Youth Center, a place to get kids off the streets and into a healthy environment.'

In the next letter, Bob reported that site selection for the centre was 'under consideration' and asked for donations to the Memorial Youth Center fund. Phil Spano, a community leader and Ron Lyle fan whose own son had been killed in a helicopter accident, immediately contributed $10,000 and Bob thought they were on their way. Six months later, the fund totalled only $13,750.

With the youth centre temporarily stalled, Ron was given the rare opportunity to reconcile with an old adversary. Out of nowhere, he received an invitation to an autograph and sports memorabilia show in Edison, New Jersey. It seems Muhammad Ali had specifically asked if Ron Lyle was coming and, because the former champ had fewer and fewer moments of lucidity and asked for little, his friends made a special pitch for Ron to attend. Even though he was hard pressed to come up with travel expenses, Ron decided to find the time and money to see the man he so admired.

Ring magazine reported on the reunion:

> ....[Ali's] tired eyes and mask-like expression flickered with recognition. Ron Lyle walked to Ali and hugged him. Ali held Lyle for a few moments and whispered, "Still think you can take me? Still think you can knock me out?"
>
> "Oh no," insisted Lyle. "You're still the champ. You'll always be the champ."

In the same *Ring* magazine report:

> Ron Lyle ate dinner that night at a local restaurant and didn't have to wait for a table, despite the dozens of others ahead of him hoping for a seat. When the

[maître d'] saw Lyle enter, he immediately cleared an area and escorted Lyle and his party to their seats.... He looks younger than his 59 years and his physique is still powerful. Yet the face that once featured a menacing goatee and stare is now relaxed, and his calm manner speaks of serenity and sincerity. Boxing did not beat Ron Lyle. But it did not leave him either.

And, indeed, it has not.

While Bob Cox continued the struggle for donations, Ron returned to Las Vegas where he and Willie Fields began working with a young fighter named Farid Shahide, the first boxer Ron had trained since 'Lightning' Lonnie Smith who he thought had a real chance at being a contender. But even as he moved from one city to the other and back again, he was no longer in limbo. Ron had found the purpose he had been seeking for 20 years and, with the same kind of faith he had during his years of boxing, he knew that it would only be a matter of time before he would open his youth centre.

Bob brought Ron to Denver frequently to participate in small gatherings designed as low-key fundraisers. He was picking up all the expenses by this time, including Ron's transportation and housing in Denver and found himself neglecting his own business at substantial additional cost. But once the project was in motion, Cox never considered quitting, even in the midst of frequent disappointments. At one point he thought he had nailed a high six-figure pledge from a potential contributor he had been working on for months, only to lose the entire donation to the Catholic Church, the donor expressing concern about the cost of the emerging Church paedophile scandal.

Ron diverted his attention from the setback by continuing to work every day with Shahide and other young boxers in Vegas, but his days in that city were numbered. He was beginning to picture himself living in Denver more and more, not least because of Jill.

After the reunion with Tracy and David, Jill stayed on the fringes of Ron's life. He would see her nearly every time he returned to Denver and she made a couple of trips to Las Vegas. They told themselves that they saw each other simply because of their long history, and so it seemed as one or the other moved into and out of other romantic entanglements, including a period when Ron lived with another woman.

Because they had tagged what they had as 'friendship,' both Ron and Jill were more comfortable with each other during this time than they had been in the years when they were an 'item'. But in the back of Jill's mind was the thought that they had never been apart longer than six years. She couldn't help but wonder if the time would come when they would reconcile yet again.

In the meantime, the transition back to Denver became even more compelling as Ron's brothers and sisters gathered round. They were all giving support to their ailing father and those left in Denver had begun spending more and more time together. Whenever he was there, Ron slipped back into his role of favourite brother as though he had never been away.

He was finally able to laugh comfortably with Russ Perron about the old days in the projects, and with Doobie Vigil about the years in Canon City. He spent time with Dennis Nelson nearly every time he returned home. The friendship that started the year Ron was released from prison had continued unbroken, through success and hardship, for over 30 years. And he always managed to call or visit the Kresniks. He didn't know it yet, but Ron was already back home in Denver. He would make it official right after he experienced one of the most gratifying events of his life.

46

*

IN June of 2001, three people were invited for the first time to attend the Boxing Hall of Fame Induction weekend in Canastota, New York - Ernie Terrell, Ruben 'Hurricane' Carter and Ron Lyle. And for the first time Ron knew, really knew, that he belonged with the greats.

From *Boxing World*:

> .....the banquet included a touching moment, as Ron Lyle thanked everyone for remembering him and told how he wished his preacher father could have been there. At that point he got a little choked up, and there wasn't a dry eye in the house. Ron will be returning for sure, now that he has seen the love that abounds at Canastota.

Stephen Brunt interviewed Ron Lyle for his book *Facing Ali* that weekend in Canastota, and a moving portrait of the heavyweight emerged:

The trip to the Hall of Fame has given Lyle a rare opportunity, to mingle with boxing fans and to acknowledge his career though, unlike some of the other old fighters, he doesn't seem inclined to milk that semi-celebrity.

The organizers have to track him down and ask him to speak. He is called to the microphone to say a few words to the crowd and does so reluctantly, shyly. One on one, he is passionate about making his point. Now, though, the ferocity disappears and Lyle seems vulnerable, his words poignant.

"Thank you for inviting me to your community," he begins. "You have to be a champion to get into the Boxing Hall of Fame. I was never a champion. But if I get in before I die, if I can ever see my name in the Boxing Hall of Fame then I can say that it's been worthwhile."

The ovation that follows is loud and warm and genuine.[20]

Dennis Nelson believes that was a defining moment for Ron. 'He didn't know how important he was until he went to Canastota. It was all about being accepted by his peers.' And Ron recalls: 'I cried at Canastota. My mother was standing there, saying: 'What did I tell you?' She was always right, and I know it now. My life does have great meaning.'

THE time had come to go home, to begin that other important part of his life. But first Ron and his protégé junior middleweight, Farid Shahide, gave one last Las Vegas interview to radio announcer Ron Gerrard on a programme called *Straight Jab*. Shadhide talked about beginning his professional career with Ron Lyle in his corner: 'I opened my mind and let him in,' a prelude to what dozens of young people would do with Ron Lyle in the years to come.

Today Farid says: 'Ron treated me as his son, but he was also a great trainer. He was a technician, teaching me to "pick any lock in the ring", an old expression used by Chickie Ferrara. Also, Ron and Willie taught me how to breathe, how to relax after a hit. And talk about training. I used run up the River Mountain Trail near Boulder City - 6,000 feet up and three miles of switchback. But I learned to channel my own strength.'

During the 2001 broadcast, Ron was already thinking ahead to his new life. He told Ron Gerrard: 'God blessed me for a reason. I owe it back. If I can help someone, it's my duty to do that. I owe that. Someone pointed me in the right direction and now it's my turn.'

And so Ron Lyle finally went home to Denver for good where a plan for a new youth centre was waiting for him.

BOB COX had been trying to obtain a space at a public park when his daughter Susan came up with a better idea - why not ask the very organisation she had passionately believed in and supported for years? The Salvation Army had long established the Red Shield Community Center in the Five Points-Curtis Park area and was always on the lookout for programmes that would appeal to the youth in the neighbourhood.

The second that Susan mentioned the Salvation Army, Bob knew it was a natural - the answer. He immediately got in touch with Bob Leino, a member of the Salvation Army's Board of Directors, and Ron McKinney, the Associate City Co-ordinator of the Salvation Army Denver Red Shield Corps and Community Center. The three men met together for lunch and dinner a number of times before they had an absolute meeting of minds, the condition necessary for selling the idea to the rest of the Salvation Army Board.

Ron McKinney, as a former Marine Drill Sergeant,

reflected a no-nonsense approach to getting the programme underway and keeping it viable. He had a good-sized room at Red Shield that could accommodate a boxing ring and workout bags. He found himself once again going over the demographics of the neighbourhood and came to the conclusion that a boxing gym would be a real draw for the Latino community.[21]

Bob needed somebody to carry out promotion for the project and he found that person in Jan Williams, who had started the very successful Inner City Health non-profit in Five Points. After a short interview, he immediately offered her a fee, and she enthusiastically agreed to join the team. Bob had finally pulled together the right people at the right time in the right place - it was time to launch the Red Shield Cox-Lyle boxing programme. And Ron Lyle came home.

Bob Cox and Ron Lyle became the single entity Cox-Lyle, and agreed on virtually every aspect of the programme. Their first major decision was to bring Richard Steele into the early planning and as an honorary member of the Cox-Lyle Boxing Programme Board. Richard's advice on setting up the ring and purchasing of boxing equipment was invaluable in the early days, but his greatest contribution was the creed he used in his own programme, one which expressed the philosophy Ron had begun to formulate as early as the old Epworth Center days: '.....a place where young folks can learn how to box and how to live right.' Even then, Ron had known that self-discipline would be the most important thing he could ever teach kids.

Richard Steele's 'Seven Qualities' fully characterised that philosophy and were adopted across the board for the Denver Programme: Positive Thinking, Integrity, Adaptation, Focus, Selflessness, Courage and Persistence. And every kid who has ever been in the programme knows what those characteristics mean, in the ring and in their lives.

Ron's friends and family remember so much of Ron's own life that illustrates each of the 'seven qualities.' They remember that Ron has always tried to put a positive spin on even the worst that has happened to him; that he has overcome his distrust of people and developed a passionate desire to be part of an orderly system of rules; that he has become flexible in adjusting to whatever springs up in life; that he continues to concentrate on his own personal performance as both an athlete and a teacher; that he is the least selfish, least self-serving person they know. They remember his courage in overcoming one hardship after another and that he has never given up. 'That's not being sentimental,' says Sharon. 'It's just true.'

The beauty of the plan conceived by Bob Cox, Ron Lyle, Richard Steele, Ron McKinney and Bob Leino was the concept of an ideal alliance. The existing Red Shield programme would reinforce the qualities Ron would teach, and the boxing programme would reinforce the moral values of the Salvation Army. The wording in the brochure reflected the team's enthusiasm:

> The Cox-Lyle Boxing Program will be an attraction to the other services provided by the agency and the classes provided by the agency will strengthen and fulfill the purpose of the boxing programme. This is a wonderful example of a 'win-win' situation with two great programmes collaborating to strengthen the outreach to the young people in the community.

The outreach to the community from the mantle of the Salvation Army and the celebrity of Ron Lyle was wildly successful, even beyond Bob's expectations. Donations for equipment and expenses came rolling in from large fundraisers and small. Parents who had lost children supported the Greg Cox Memorial. Patrons of the Salvation Army supported the programme designed to help Latino and other inner-city youth. Ron Lyle fans supported his personal quest.

One of the most gratifying contributions came from the Bill Daniels Foundation, set up before the entrepreneur's death to support educational goals. Bob Cox likes to think Bill Daniels would have approved.

And so at 4:00 p.m. on November 15, 2002, the Red Shield Cox-Lyle Boxing Center officially opened its doors.

47

*

EVERYONE involved with the Cox-Lyle programme agreed it was meant to be the way it turned out. Richard Steele, who had lent his considerable stature to the undertaking, expressed gratitude to Ron and others for furthering his own dream. Bob Cox knew the memorial was the finest he could have conceived for his son, Greg.

The programme was a godsend for Ron. At an age when most people are retired or thinking about it, he began receiving a monthly salary with a generous bonus at Christmas and full medical, dental and vision benefits. John Kresnik remembers telling him: 'What you have here is a new chance. Don't screw it up.' But Ron didn't need the advice. He knew his work at Red Shield would give him the security he had needed and, more importantly, that what he did there would mean something important.

Dennis Nelson immediately volunteered to help out and he knew, from the very first day the kids appeared at the centre, that Ron would apply the same tenacity in the gym that had seen him through his life. It soon became apparent, though, that paperwork and record-keeping would not be Ron's strong suit; rather, he would see to it that the rags were damp, the buckets clean and the workout equipment in good condition.

That first day set the standard for every day since. Ron arrived early to stock the gym and double-check the supply room. As kids began to drift in, he started each one on the basics and then rotated through the group, moving them to a higher level until they reached the ring. There, his gentle guidance through a series of tough exercises dazzled the kids, and they returned the next day and the next, day after day, Saturdays and after school.

Early on, Ron started using the Salvation Army Red Shield as a symbol for self-defence, telling his young charges: 'Just like in fencing, you parry with your shield and jab with your left. You protect yourself until it's automatic. Then, if you get hit, it's your own fault.'

Even as the kids' boxing skills improved, Ron soon realised there was something more important he could do for them. He recently described what has become his main purpose at the centre: 'Young people find it difficult to swallow their pride. I have to somehow let them know it's okay to show a weakness. So I let them see my weakness, then it's okay for them, too. I tell them boxing is the proving ground of a man's worth, and they learn that when they have the courage to get in that ring, they are worthy.'

Word about the new center got around, and people in Denver who had always pulled for Ron Lyle, the boxer, let him know they still cared. One day, shortly after the gym opened, a guy Ron remembered only as 'Ralph' from the prison board that originally refused his parole, walked into the gym and over to Ron, holding out his hand.

'Congratulations,' he said. 'You made it.'

In order to highlight the kids' achievement and to

maintain interest from contributors, Bob and Ron started setting up boxing matches with other clubs who were members of the USA Amateur Boxing Association. More familiar faces appeared with every event.

As the matches piled up, it wasn't long before the Cox-Lyle Red Shield programme started getting attention from an even broader community. Press releases attracted new patrons, impressed with what the programme had achieved:

> ....Last week the Denver Red Shield received 'Official Notice' from USA Boxing that Jairo [Delgado] has been invited to the Western Regional Boxoff in Bakersfield, Calif., in February to compete for a spot on the U.S. Olympic Team as a Bantam Weight.
>
> In addition to pursuing his dream, Jairo has raised his GPA to 3.1, he has left his gang involvement behind, he has given his life over to the Lord, and with Ron Lyle's tutoring and help he has developed into a very promising young boxer....[22]

Other fundraisers followed, sometimes fancy black-tie affairs for the boxing fan elite, others auctioning off memorabilia from boxers who were happy to donate to Ron's cause. Often Ron asked Jill to accompany him to the events, and before long they were attending other community functions as well. Jill saved a photo taken on the balcony of Brooks Towers during one of those functions. Ron is on his knees proposing to Jill, whose back is to the camera. 'I had never seen Ron so mellowed out,' Jill remembers. 'We were happy just being together, but it wasn't the right time to make a commitment.'

As the Cox-Lyle boxing programme grew, so did the stories about Ron and his kids. Mary Bransfield told about seeing a little kid crying outside the ring at a fundraiser. 'Ron stopped the match, climbed out of the ring, consoled the kid and waited for his tears to dry before he started the match again.'

Frank Barron repeated a story about a time he saw a kid shadow-boxing without shoes on. 'Ron asked: "Where's your shoes?" The kid looked like he wanted to cry, said he didn't have any and started to climb out of the ring. Ron stopped him and told him he didn't need shoes. "Just stay in there today, and I'll make sure you get shoes." And, of course, he did.'

Dennis Nelson has seen Ron's relationships with the kids develop. 'They call him Papa and hug him and tell him about their lives. He's like a father to them. And he never lectures the kids. He treats them with the same respect he showed to kids in detention centres and youth camps. He mostly listens, but almost every kid has improved, not just in boxing, but in school grades.' When one of the young boxers was asked recently if he gets special attention from Mr. Lyle, the boy replied: 'He gives special attention to everyone.'

Ron's life outside the gym reinforced the feeling that he was finally where he belonged - there to share the good times and the not-so-good with his family and friends. When Dennis lost his mother a few months after the gym opened, Ron was his greatest consolation, just as he had been when Dennis lost his father 33 years before. 'He's always been there for me. That's true friendship,' Dennis says quietly.

Ron was in Michael Kresnik's wedding party. 'He walked me down the aisle,' Mary says. 'And I think he was proud to do that.' The year before, Mary had been diagnosed with leukaemia. 'He was there for me from the beginning,' she says. 'He even gave me the jacket he had used when he was training for the Olympics. I framed that jacket.' When the Kresniks won a community Citizens of the

Year award, the first person they invited to the ceremony was Ron Lyle, and Jill went with him.

When Joe Garcia - the coach who was there from the first year of the Denver Rocks team - died that year, most of his protégés from over 40 years attended the memorial service, including Dennis and Donny Nelson, Jimmy Farrell and Ron Lyle. The old boxers were still tightly bound together.

In 2003, the youngest Lyle son, Gerald Mathew, long diagnosed as an AIDS victim, began to fail rapidly. Again, Ron overcame his own devastation to help care for his brother. 'The family is the most important thing in life,' he says. 'We help each other. That's what we're here to do.'

Shortly after Gerald died, it became clear that William Lyle couldn't hang on much longer, and his church paid tribute to him with an appointment as Bishop, the highest honour in the Holiness Church. Ron honoured his father in his own way, requesting that he bless the Cox-Lyle Youth Center. In a wheelchair, barely able to move, William Lyle said he would be proud to be a part of this good thing his son had started and old demons were put to rest. He died a few weeks later.

In 2004, the entire Lyle family came together for the funeral of their father. Along with the brothers and sisters who had stayed in Colorado - Bill, who had recently lost his own beloved wife, Ron, Kenneth, Sharon, Phillip, Marilyn, Norman and Karen - Edward came from Middleton, Ohio; Joyce flew in from Germany; Donna from California; Mark from Cheyenne; and Robert and James came from Washington D.C.

They mourned together and celebrated the lives, not only of William and Gerald, but of the oldest, Barbara, who had died before most of them were born; Michael, who had died almost 40 years before in Vietnam; Gerald, who had died of AIDS just a few months before; John John, who lost his battle with cerebral palsy in 1981; and, of course, their beloved mother. And they prayed for their brother Raymond, still hospitalised with schizophrenia. The family had survived.

Patty Jordan came to William's funeral, her two adopted children in tow, and Ron welcomed her as an old friend. Hundreds of old friends and members of churches the family had known also came to pay their respects. 'It was fitting,' Ron says. 'My father got the respect he deserved.'

And finally, Jill, the centre of Ron's soul, came back to him too.

48

*

AT age 65 Ron Lyle still gets up well before dawn, even in cold Colorado winter months. He runs 5½ miles through a graceful old Denver neighbourhood and is back home in less than 40 minutes to the three-bedroom brick house he shares with Jill Sellers, the one on Bellaire Street. They live barely three miles from the Cox-Lyle Center in Curtis Park.

Having never wholly given up the extraordinary workout regimen he developed in prison more than 40 years ago, he cools down with sets of 100 push-ups before he finally sits down with Jill to devour a huge breakfast.

Jill laughs when she relates how in the old days she used to help with the run. 'We used to get up at 4:00 a.m. I'd drive the car and he would run for five miles. He would shadow-box and run backward, and there I was, smoking a cigarette and blowing it out the window. He never complained.'

'She was my road woman,' Ron injects.

Ron has lost some of the people who earned his trust over the years. Clifford Maddox is gone; so are Bill Daniels and Doobie Vigil. Two great rocks in his life, Abby Espinoza and Frank Barron, have passed away, both of cancer, and both too young. But other parts of his life remain intact. He is still keenly interested in rehabilitating prisoners and visits the penitentiary in Canon City periodically.

In April 2005, he wrote a statement supporting the Congressional resolution calling for a Presidential pardon of Jack Johnson, the first African American world heavyweight champion who was the victim of racially-motivated trumped-up charges. Ron stated that it was time for the pardon so that Johnson can 'receive the respect he is long past due.' The history of Jack Johnson holds a special poignancy for Ron, and he knows the power of a pardon, the only action that can wipe the slate clean.

People from Ron's past come around now and then. Ron considers attorney Walter Gerash a good friend, and Barney O'Grady, the man who has always and continues to clip press articles about Ron, is still around. A chiropractor, he recently pledged volunteer time for kids at the gym who could use his services.

Sister Sharon and brother Bill are both pastors in the Holiness Apostolic Church. Sharon describes Ron as having strayed, but not departed, from the Church. She counsels him on occasion, welcoming him to her Church whenever he is moved to come.

Kenneth and Phillip and Marilyn and Karen and others further away still take great pride in their brother Ron. The special friendship Ron and Phillip forged in the late-seventies remains intact, and whenever members of the family gather, the joy they derive from being together is palpable.

Ron still misses his own children and was overjoyed when his younger son called not long ago. After so many years, David finally decided that it was past time to discover that part of him he had always missed, even through his success and the joy he feels with his daughter Cyan. He told his girlfriend Katrini Young of the void that never went away, and she set about working towards the reunion.

Although Ron always had faith he would eventually be reconciled with his youngest son, he wasn't prepared for the emotional impact of hearing David's voice describe his own life in terms that sounded so familiar. Ron listened, then finally found his own voice and blurted out: 'How does it feel to be a superstar?'

David Bowens still plays professional football. He has been recognised as a person who 'enjoys working with kids' and has donated his time to a number of causes, including a foster home for abused and neglected children. In 2005, he created The David Bowens Foundation to help kids who suffer from asthma and cystic fibrosis. Katrina had compared old photos of Ron with David and concluded that not only do the two share athletic prowess and character traits, they look alike - their physiques are identical. And that's not all. On a three-hour conference call, Tracy couldn't differentiate her father's voice from her brother's.

The family has talked about getting a DNA paternity test, and maybe that will happen, but Tracy and Jill and Katrina all believe Ron is David's father. Jill: 'It's not just their physical characteristics. It's the passion and the competitive nature and giving to others. It's all of it.' David hopes Ron is his father; *Ron knows he is.*

Tracy has graduated from Beauty School and lives in Atlanta. Whenever she talks about how much she loves her two-year-old son Malik, Ron remembers how she took care of her little brother David at the same age so many years ago. Ron takes pride in all his children's accomplishments, even though he knows he cannot take credit for who they have become. The pain of losing Monte and Tracy and David lingers, and he makes no excuses, but he does allow himself a measure of comfort in knowing that he has made the difference in the lives of other children throughout the years. Film-maker Peter Townsend recently completed a documentary based on Stephen Brunt's *Facing Ali*, in which he interviews ten of Ali's greatest rivals. He describes Ron's appearance: 'Ron is magnificent in the film. Of the boxers, his voice is the first we hear and the last we hear; he's charming, insightful, intense, funny, many memorable lines, and he looks great too.'

Ron still doesn't trust everybody, but he knows who he can trust and that is enough. People who know him well tend to offer unsolicited, heartfelt expressions of admiration for the person he has always been. The tributes abound, maybe best summed up by Jimmy Farrell: 'Ron is a good human being, and he seems finally to be at peace with himself.'

Ron is invariably surprised and touched by the regard of those who have been in his life for so long and by those he never knew. Voice cracking, he says: 'I didn't know. I didn't know they felt that way.'

Even the Denver crowds still reflect the love of that city for their favourite boxer. At a recent exhibition fight at the Regency Inn with some of the local greats, including 'Lightning' Lonny Anderson, the chanting didn't begin until Ron Lyle was introduced: 'Go, big Ron, Go big Ron.....'

The chant went on and on.

*

Epilogue

THE boys, ranging from 12 to 19, are working out on
the bags or jogging in place, awaiting their turns. The
majority are Latino; some are black, some white. The
neighbourhood kids are where they always are on Saturday
morning and most days after school, at the Cox-Lyle Red
Shield Youth Center gym, trying their best to do what Mr.
Lyle keeps telling them they can do - conquer their fears.

Ron beckons to a young man named Jacob. Of the 60 or
so young boxers enrolled in the programme, only this boy
comes to the gym every single day. The high point of his
Saturday morning is climbing into the ring with Lyle who
holds up his gloves and shouts out, '*three*.' Jacob punches his
trainer's gloves, right, left, right, fast and hard. The sound
slapping gloves make is startlingly loud. Then Lyle shouts,
'*four*,' followed by right, left, right, left, even faster and
harder. The ante is raised after every few punches, '*five*,' then
'*six*.' Jacob can hardly lift his arms when he climbs down out
of the ring, but he beams at Lyle.

'Did you listen to the sounds, Jacob?'

'Yeah. I got my own internal rhythm, just like when I run. I got my own beat.'

'Good. You know it's yours. Remember, each person is different. The most important thing is to believe in yourself.'

Jacob nods.

Asked why he comes to the centre every day, Jacob says: 'Mostly, I want to be a boxer. That's different from a puncher or a brawler. You know? A boxer is like a chess player, figuring out all the moves. A puncher hits hard, but lets you come in. And a brawler just swings. He lets the boxer make him mad. The best would be a boxer-puncher like him.' He looks at Lyle. 'Tough and smart, but keep my cool.'

It's almost one o'clock and the kids fall into place along the side of the ring. Ron says: 'You all did great today.' He takes a few steps toward one of the younger kids and lowers his voice. 'You left your hands down too much. Remember, the name of the game is defence. Boxing is the art of self-defence. You gotta protect yourself until it's automatic. Then, if you get hit, it's your own fault. It's about survival.'

The youngster nods and Lyle gives him a high five, then moves on to the rest of the kids, touching shoulders and fists. They linger for a while, until one boy and then the others begin filing out of the gym. Another Saturday morning.

FIGHTERS may always be a mystery to those of us who never entered a ring, but Ron Lyle seems to hold a key to that mystery. He tells his kids at Cox-Lyle: 'It's not a disgrace to get knocked down. It's a disgrace not to get back up.'

He insists boxing is not a brutal sport, that it is rather a proving ground of a man's worth. He believes that boxing is the highest level of competition, even though, as others have maintained, it is also the most primitive. He says: 'There are no easy fights - the ones you think are easy are the ones you lose.'

And the lessons of his life are the same lessons he learned in boxing: 'You prepare for the unexpected, you never look back, and you're always true to the game. You pick yourself up in the ring, just like you pick yourself up in life. You learn from your mistakes; if you don't, the game is over.'

And, finally, knowing all lives have twists and turns, and most have moments of almost unbearable sadness, Ron says: 'All you can do is keep trying. Then you can look back and say that your accomplishment in life was to give it everything you got....to do your best. That's all anybody can do.'

Ron Lyle is at peace with himself. And every day, he is somebody's idol.

Afterword

*

Ron Lyle

NOBODY can predict what will be around the next turn in the road. Since this book was written, the Red Shields Cox-Lyle Center reached an important goal when Denver hosted the USA Boxing National Championships. My main purpose in life - working with young people at the gym - is still the most satisfying.

At any given time, we have 60 to 80 kids in the programme, many of whom have competed and won fights. When other kids see those successes, they believe that with self-discipline and dedication, they can make it happen for themselves. Jacob Domingues has been with me from the beginning; he went pro a while back and is still undefeated. Elan Simon is the 132lb National champion and Malik Elliston is the National Junior champion. My heavyweight, Terrence Perro, has come a long way from being on probation to becoming the Regional Silver Gloves champion.

I am lucky to have friends who are always there for me, and I talk to my children often. Tracy is still the light of my life, and just a few weeks ago David was named Cleveland

Browns defensive captain. Thank God they are both doing well.

People from the old days still get in touch from time to time and tell me I was an inspiration in their lives. Not too long ago, Candace received an email message from a man named Tim Borrego, who described himself years ago as '....a goofy-looking Latino kid from North Denver,' and wrote that I instilled in him a discipline that is still important in his life.

I am happy to be remembered in a good way by Tim. If I have been decent to people, it was because of my mother's lesson in life - she called it Love of Heart. She taught me to understand people of all colour and not to let the negative rub off on me. She told me we were all in the same boat and that I needed to grab a paddle and help out, not let the boat sink.

I am still paddling for all I'm worth.

Ronald D Lyle

Ron Lyle
January 2010

Footnotes

1 Alan Prendergast, 'Safely Behind Bars', *Westword*, July 3, 1997

2 Brunt, Stephen, *Facing Ali*, The Lyons Press 2002, page 234

3 Oates, Joyce Carol, *On Boxing*, Harper Collins 2002, page 167

4 In addition to the WBA, *Boxing Illustrated* magazine, *Ring* magazine and the World Boxing Council rate boxers.

5 It took decades and the system isn't perfect, but at least today the champion is required to fight a leading contender within six months of his last fight or lose his title.

6 Brunt, Stephen, *Facing Ali*, The Lyons Press 2002, page 237

7 Oates, Joyce Carol, *On Boxing*, Harper Collins 2002, page 179

8 As in many other newspaper and magazine articles through the years, the *News* was off by one year. Ron Lyle would be 33 in February 1974. Though he denies it, Ron has been accused by some of fudging his birthdate to alleviate speculation about his being 'too old' to compete.

9 Jimmy Ellis had become world champion after the World Boxing Association stripped Ali of his title when he refused induction into the U.S. Army. Immediately, an elimination tournament had been ordered with eight heavyweight challengers entered, including Jerry Quarry, Oscar Bonavena and George Chuvalo; Jimmy Ellis emerged as champion. He successfully defended his title against Floyd Patterson, but Joe Frazier challenged Ellis in 1970 and knocked him out in the fifth round to gain general acceptance of the championship by all the governing bodies. After losing to his former sparring partner Muhammad Ali two years before, Ellis had won ten of his last 13 fights to move up to seventh among contenders - a genuine comeback.

10 Brunt, Stephen, *Facing Ali*, The Lyons Press 2002, page 238-239

11 Jimmy Young never did get any closer to the championship, even after beating Foreman in '77, and most boxing historians believed he fought for too many years, sustaining heavy blows that resulted in what is called, 'pugilistic dementia'. He died in 2005 at the age of 56, another victim of what has been called the 'cruellest sport'.

12 Larry Holmes went on to win the heavyweight title in June, defeating Ken Norton in 15 rounds. Holmes would successfully defend his title 20 times.

13 Walter Gerash recalls that for several years the Lyle jury held annual reunions, perhaps celebrating their verdict.

14 Oates, Joyce Carol, *On Boxing*, Harper Collins 2002, page 186

15 Willie Fields worked the casinos and the gym for 30 years. He didn't retire until the Desert Inn closed in 2000, but he still works with young boxers, spending most of his time at the Las Vegas Boxing gym.

16 Richard Steele was Honoured ten years later by Nelson Mandela for

refusing to referee fights in South Africa while it was under the apartheid regime. In 2000, he was inducted into the Boxing Hall of Fame.

[17] By 1994, it was clear that, even though he continued to drive, Ron was a 'menace' on the road. To this day, the devotion of Ron's friends and family is often manifested in their willingness to transport him.

[18] Later, Tony Wu garnered some attention when he was found to be the first person in Denver to teach women's boxing. Retired now at 87, Tony still goes to Bally's Gym every day to do aerobics and volunteer massage therapy for athletes training there.

[19] The record of a guy named Strickland is unknown.

[20] Brunt, Stephen, *Facing Ali*, The Lyons Press 2002, page 243

[21] In another of those twists of fate that characterise the Ron Lyle story, the fingerprint expert who had testified for the defence in Ron's 1978 murder trial, James W. Blake, eventually became a member of the Salvation Army Red Shield Board of Directors that supported the Cox-Lyle Youth Center.

[22] *Off the Ropes: The Ron Lyle Story* From a February 5, 2004 Salvation Army press release. Jairo Delgado has since won four Golden Gloves championships.